Grace upon Grace

A History of the Diocese of Monterey in California

Geoffrey W.M.P. Lopes da Silva

ÉDITIONS DU SIGNE

This book is humbly dedicated to

Our Lady of Bethlehem,

Patroness of the Diocese of Monterey in California.

Publisher
Editions du Signe

1, rue Alfred Kastler
CS 10094 Eckbolsheim
67038 Strasbourg Cedex 2 - France
Tel (++33) 3 88 78 91 91
Fax (++33) 3 88 78 91 90

Director of Publication: Christian Riehl
Production Manager: Marc de Jong

Author: Geoffrey W.M.P. Lopes da Silva

Layout: Sylvie Tusinski
Photographer: John Glover

Printed in China

Ref: 110058
ISBN 978-2-7468-3314-2

"Historians will record a narrative of

'grace upon grace' in this diocese

for future generations."

THE MOST REV. RICHARD J. GARCIA, D.D.

4th Bishop of Monterey in California

2007; cf. *John* 1:16

Table of Contents

Part II
The Parishes of the Diocese

We as the people of God, with trust in our merciful and loving Father, embrace this Year of Mercy as we celebrate our fiftieth anniversary as a diocese. Our history is truly grace-filled and that is why I chose the title, "Grace upon Grace" for this book recounting the rich history of both the geographical area as well as the current Diocese of Monterey.

Each year, during the Christmas season, I read and reread the beautiful and consoling message of Jesus spoken in the first chapter of the Gospel of St. John. In this passage, I listen closely to and internalize these words, "From his fullness we have all received, grace upon grace" (*John* 1:16). What a powerful and loving message from our all-merciful God. As St. Elizabeth of Schönau († 1164) wrote:

> *Rich is the mercy of our God,*
> *and abundantly does He bestow grace upon grace*
> *on those who love Him.* *

I would like to point out some of the very special graces bestowed on us by God over the past history of the Monterey area as well as the current Diocese of Monterey. Through this lens, I look toward a future full of hope, with ever such great gratitude to our loving God, who bestows those graces:

1. God's wondrous creation and the beauty of our coastal area.

2. The seven historic Missions of the chain of Missions founded by St. Junípero Serra and his companions.

3. Our multi-cultural families with their rich customs who teach us so much.

4. Our very dedicated priests, consecrated men and women, our permanent deacons, their wives and families, our incredible lay leaders and ministers who serve in such a united and valuable way, and our extremely dedicated diocesan pastoral staff who have served the People of God through these past fifty years.

Bishop Garcia in the Our Lady of Guadalupe Chapel of Old Mission San Juan Bautista, originally constructed around 1799 and restored in 1997.
Photo courtesy of Juan Mendoza, October 31, 2010.

5. Our rich agricultural area, the people who own and work in the agricultural industry and those who pick our many crops.

6. All the fishermen and women and all individuals in our large fishing industry.

7. Our forty-six parishes and mission stations, where our faithful people come together to celebrate the Sacraments.

8. Our youth, who are a true blessing to us and deserve our attention and protection.

9. Our Native American Peoples, who have taught us and continue to teach us so much about God's creation and the need for us all to protect and respect our land and our people.

---

* *Elisabeth of Schönau: The Complete Works,* translated by Anne L. Clark and published by Paulist Press, 2000.

10. Our families who are at the very heart of our communities and continue to ask us for support, guidance and hope.

11. Our Catholic Schools, our young boys, girls and teens who attend the schools, their teachers, principals and staff who guide and instruct them about God and prepare them for their future.

12. Our Catechetical and religious education programs, with thousands of children and youth involved, as well as those at our Newman Centers.

13. My wonderful and dedicated predecessors, who shepherded our people for years, Bishops Harry Clinch, Thaddeus Shubsda, and Sylvester Ryan.

14. Our Catholic Charities, who at their six centers now serve thousands each year with family support, assistance with mental health problems, immigration, and tattoo removal.

15. And all of you, our faithful people of God and all of your ancestors who helped to build and to maintain all we have as the Diocese of Monterey.

In this memorial to commemorate these past fifty years of graces upon graces, I will close my introduction with the dream and vision I offered as I became the bishop of this remarkable diocese.

I dream of a diocesan Church, where we:

1. Can pray together

2. Can celebrate together

3. Can open doors to new hopes and dreams

4. Can accept new immigrants as God accepts us all

5. Can reach out to the troubled, lonely, marginalized, or lost in themselves

6. Can tear down barriers or walls that may separate us

7. Can see each child as a gift of God and put an end to all abortion

8. Can truly respect life at all stages, and not take the life of others

9. Can respect and affirm the gifts that are unique to each of us

10. Can respect the earth, and its beauty, that God has lent to us for our enjoyment and care

11. Can touch the hearts of those men and women and youth in our correctional facilities with our prayers and visits

12. Can build on the strong foundations of my predecessors Bishop Clinch, Bishop Shubsda and Bishop Ryan

13. Can reach out and love the victimized, those hurt by our Church or its ministers in any way

14. Can instill in our youth purpose and direction, recognizing their importance and the gifts they bring to our Church at this time

15. Can nurture religious and priestly vocations

16. Can together grope for God and find God

17. Can live together and move and have our being in Him, and Him alone

18. Can truly trust and believe that God is never far from any one of us

Lastly, I am so indebted to Mr. Geoffrey Lopes da Silva, *Éditions du Signe,* and all who assisted them with this project. I ask our loving God to bless us all and all who follow us in this Diocese of Monterey. For it is in Christ that "we live and move and have our being" (Acts of the Apostles 17:28).

Let us thank God for the graces still to come, for those graces for which we dream and those graces to be treasured; may God bless our future.

✠ *The Most Rev. Richard J. Garcia, D.D.*
Bishop of Monterey in California

On Divine Mercy Sunday, April 27, 2014, just prior to the Mass of Thanksgiving for the Canonization of Saints John XXIII and John Paul II at my parish of Carmel Mission Basilica, His Excellency the Most Rev. Richard J. Garcia, 4th Bishop of Monterey in California, first told to me his intentions for a book chronicling the history of the diocese and each of its 46 parishes. He hoped to publish this book for the occasion of the 50th anniversary of the establishment of the Diocese of Monterey in California.

The history of the Church is rich, varied, and exciting. Our Holy Mother Church takes pride and joy in both the victories and defeats of her children; in her saints and sinners. She has warriors and peacemakers, martyrs and confessors, virgins and widows, mystics and heretics, scientists and visionaries. Her children have contributed much to the world of art, music, architecture, and culture; from great cathedrals to humble missions, from frescos to sculptures, from polyphony to hymns.

The theme that runs throughout the 2,000 year history of the Church is obedience to our Blessed Lord's *missionale mandatum*: "Go therefore and make disciples of all nations, baptizing them in the name of the Father and of the Son and of the Holy Spirit, teaching them to observe all that I have commanded you" (*St Matthew* 28:19-20). It was in obedience to this "missionary mandate" that Franciscan friars, led by Saint Junípero Serra, set out under the banner of the Blessed Virgin Mary as *La Conquistadora* to bring the Gospel of Jesus Christ to what we now call California over 200 years ago.

Blessed John Henry Cardinal Newman, an Anglican priest who converted to the Roman Catholic faith in 1845, credited the study of history as playing a part in his conversion. It is my hope that all who read this book will come to appreciate the rich history of the Church in Monterey, and that it will help to increase their faith in the "one, holy, catholic and apostolic Church" of Jesus Christ.

Geoffrey W.M.P. Lopes da Silva

The author would like to expresses his gratitude to the following for their gracious assistance in the creation of this book:

The staff of the Diocese of Monterey in California, especially the Rev. Carl M.D. Faria, manager of the diocesan archives, Sr. Patricia Murtagh, IM, Chancellor of the Diocese, Susan Mayer, general counsel and director of human resources for the diocese, as well as Leticia Flores-McPherson and Bernardine Johnson.

I am most grateful to the late Mr. Roger R. Hilleary († 2011), who as a volunteer at the diocesan archives prepared thumbnail histories of each parish in the diocese that formed the foundation of part II of this book.

My thanks must also go to Mr. Juan Mendoza and to Mrs. Jonabel O. Perez (who I always refer to as "the unofficial diocesan photographer") for sharing their personal collection of photographs.

My loving thanks to Agnieszka A. Klasa, for her help with last-minute photographs and support.

Gratitude must also go to Mr. John M. Haidich, editor of *A Special Day in Monterey: The Historic Visit of Pope John Paul II*, Mr. Patrick T. Kraft, KM, KHS, for information regarding the Sovereign Military Order of Malta, Mr. Matthew D. Herrera of the Byzantine Catholic parish of Saint Anne in San Luis Obispo, Sr. Louise Smith, archivist for the Sisters of St. Mary of Namur, the Rev. Steve Porter and Mrs. Dolores Real Robertson Kaelin of the Catholic Daughters of the Americas, Danalynn Hays, administrative assistant for the California State Council of the Knights of Columbus, Anita Grohs, Grand Secretary of the Young Ladies' Grand Institute, Charlene Kramer, administrative assistant for the Italian Catholic Federation, and Barrie McCleary of the Monterey Curia of the Legion of Mary.

Grateful mention must also be made of the work of the Carmel Mission Docent Association and the California Room of the Monterey Public Library, for the wealth of information that is available to researchers.

A special thanks to *Libreria Editrice Vaticana*, for permission to include excerpts from the writings of Pope St. John Paul II, Pope Benedict XVI, and Pope Francis.

Texts from Sacred Scripture in the English language are taken from the *Second Catholic Edition of the Revised Standard Version of the Bible* (2006), copyright 1965, 1966, by the Division of Christian Education of the National Council of the Churches of Christ in the United States of America. Used by permission. All rights reserved.

On behalf of the Diocese of Monterey in California, I wish to thank the entire team at *Éditions du Signe*, for designing and publishing this book.

The author of this book has attempted to give proper credit to all sources used in the text, illustrations, and graphics. Any miscredit or lack of credit is unintended. *Mea culpa!*

It has been a tremendous honor to work on this project, and my thanks and gratitude for that must go to His Excellency the Most Rev. Richard J. Garcia, 4th Bishop of Monterey in California. May he serve as our shepherd for many more years to come. *Ad multos annos!*

Acknowledgements

The Diocese of Monterey in California was officially established by Pope Blessed Paul VI on October 6, 1967 and is the ecclesiastical territory of the Roman Rite of the Catholic Church in the Central Coast region of the State of California in the United States.

Although the present diocese is only 50 years old, the origins of the Church in Monterey can be traced to the original Diocese of Monterey of the mid-1800s, and even before that, to the mission era of the 1700s. *Grace upon Grace: A History of the Diocese of Monterey in California* is an attempt to briefly chronicle the rich history of the Catholic faith in these lands. This book is divided into two parts: "The History of the Diocese" and "The Parishes of the Diocese."

The first part, "The History of the Diocese," chronicles the history of the Church in Monterey beginning with Saint Junípero Serra and the Mission Period (1769-1833) and concluding with the canonization of Saint Junípero Serra on the eve of the 50th anniversary of the official establishment of the Diocese of Monterey in California. Also included is a history of religious life, associations of the lay faithful, schools, cemeteries, and other institutions. The use of ecclesiastical heraldry in the diocese is also detailed.

The second part, "The Parishes of the Diocese," consists of the histories of all 46 parish communities currently located in the Diocese of Monterey in California. A parish (Latin: *parœcia, parochia*; Greek: *paroikia*) is "a certain community of the Christian faithful stably constituted in a particular church, whose pastoral care is entrusted to a pastor (*parochus*) as its proper pastor under the authority of the diocesan bishop."[1]

The parishes in the Diocese of Monterey in California are territorial. Some dioceses also have personal parishes, meaning that they are "established determined by reason of the rite, language, or nationality of the Christian faithful of some territory,

or even for some other reason."[2] All parish churches have a "titular", which may be "the Blessed Trinity; our Lord Jesus Christ invoked according to a mystery of his life or a title already accepted in the liturgy; the Holy Spirit; the Blessed Virgin Mary, likewise invoked according to some appellation already accepted in the liturgy; one of the angels; or, finally, a saint inscribed in *The Roman Martyrology*."[3]

A church is dedicated or set apart for divine worship by way of a *simple blessing* or a *solemn consecration*. The walls of a church that has been consecrated are decorated with twelve small consecration crosses with a bracket and candle set before each one. These mark the places where the walls were anointed with sacred chrism by a bishop during a solemn dedication or consecration. In such churches, the anniversary of dedication is celebrated as a solemnity.

There are 46 parishes in the Diocese of Monterey in California, some of which have a *mission station*— a community of the faithful that is "dependent on some parish church."[4] The term *chief station* is generally used for a mission station that has at least one resident missionary and the term *sub-station* is generally used for a mission station where the sacred liturgy is celebrated periodically by a non-resident missionary.[5]

Following the cathedral, pro-cathedrals, and basilica, all parishes are listed in alphabetical order. Parish chapels and mission stations are listed under their respective "mother" parishes.

Also highlighted in "The Parishes of the Diocese" is the community of Catholic faithful dedicated to the Extraordinary Form of the Roman Rite as well as the Byzantine Catholic parish in San Luis Obispo.

Various terms and phrases appear in the Latin language, which is the official language of the Catholic Church.

> 1 *Code of Canon Law,* can. 515 §1.
> 2 *Ibid.,* can. 518.
> 3 *The Roman Pontifical: Dedication of a Church and an Altar* (1977), chapter II, n. 4.
> 4 Auguste Boudinhon and William Fanning, *The Catholic Encyclopedia* (1911), vol. 11.
> 5 cf. Thomas Kennedy, *The Catholic Encyclopedia* (1911), vol. 10.

Part I

The History of the Diocese

The Mission Period

1769-1833

The Missionary Mandate
Missionale mandatum

"And Jesus came and said to them, 'All authority in heaven and on earth has been given to Me. Go therefore and make disciples of all nations, baptizing them in the name of the Father and of the Son and of the Holy Spirit, teaching them to observe all that I have commanded you; and behold, I am with you always, to the close of the age.'"

St Matthew 28:19-20

"Having been divinely sent to the nations that she might be 'the universal sacrament of salvation', the Church, in obedience to the command of her founder and because it is demanded by her own essential universality, strives to preach the Gospel to all men.

"Although in ways known to Himself God can lead those who, through no fault of their own, are ignorant of the Gospel, to that faith without which it is impossible to please Him, the Church still has the obligation and also the sacred right to evangelize all men."

Second Vatican Council
Decree on the Missionary Activity
of the Church Ad Gentes, 1, 7

It was in December of 1602 when the faith of the one "Holy Catholic Apostolic Roman Church"[6] first reached what is now known as the Diocese of Monterey in California. Don Sebastián Viscaíno († 1624) had been sent by the Viceroy of New Spain, Gaspar de Zúñiga Acevedo y Fonseca († 1606), 5th Count of Monterrey, by order of King Philip III of Spain († 1621), on a "voyage of search in three small vessels." Viscaíno "visited various points on the coast, among them San Diego."[7] On December 16, 1602, Viscaíno's expedition reached a bay that he would name *Monterey,* "in honor of Count Monterey."[8] The first European to set foot on what is now California was actually João Rodrigues Cabrilho (Spanish: Juan Rodríguez Cabrillo) († 1543), the Portuguese-born navigator and explorer who 60 years earlier explored the west coast of North America on behalf of the Spanish Empire.

On December 17, the Viscaíno expedition anchored near the site of what is now the City of Monterey. The Rev. Antonio de la Ascensión (born between 1573 and 1574), a Discalced Carmelite Friar, celebrated the Holy Sacrifice of the Mass "under a large oak by the sea-side."[9] The expedition left Monterey Bay on January 3, 1603. No record would make mention of the region again for more than 160 years.

The Founding Painting by Léon Trousset (1877)
depicts Saint Junípero Serra's first Mass at Monterey.
The 53" x 72" oil on canvas resides at Carmel Mission Basilica.

It was as early as 1697 that Spanish priests of the Society of Jesus (Jesuits) had established missions in what is now known as the State of Arizona and Baja (Lower) or "Old" California. In 1767, all Jesuits were expelled from the Kingdom of Spain and its dominions, including Baja California. The care of the existing missions was then entrusted to Spanish priests of the Order of Friars Minor (Franciscans).

In 1768, Saint Junípero Serra († 1784), "a Franciscan Friar of great zeal and learning, and whose labors and life are interwoven into the history of the California missions, was appointed missionary president of the Californias."[10] Saint Junípero Serra began his ministry with determination and spirit. Not satisfied with the work accomplished by his predecessors in Baja California, he was determined to evangelize the natives of Alta (Upper) California as well.

> 6 *"Sancta Catholica Apostolica Romana Ecclesia"* (First Vatican Council (1869–1870), Dogmatic Constitution on the Faith *Dei Filius* (24 April 1870), chapter 1: *Acta Sanctæ Sedis,* vol. 5 (1869-1870), p. 484).

> 7 Elliott & Moore, *History of Monterey County, California, With Illustrations* (1881); reprinted by Valley Publishers, 1979, p. 13.

> 8 Ibid., p. 11.

> 9 Ibid., p. 13.
> 10 Ibid., p. 141.

Portolá's Cross

Pious Portolá, journeying by land,
Reared high a cross upon the heathen strand,
    Then far away
Dragged his slow caravan to Monterey.
The mountains whispered to the valleys, "Good!"
The sun, slow sinking in the western flood,
    Baptized in blood
The holy standard of the Brotherhood.
The timid fog crept in across the sea,
Drew near, embraced it, and streamed far and free,
    Saying: "O, ye
Gentiles and Heathen, this is truly He!"
All this the Heathen saw; and when once more
The holy Fathers touched the lonely shore—
    Then covered o'er
With shells and gifts—the cross their witness bore.

F. Bret Harte
1836 – 1902

The flag of the Viceroyalty of New Spain (*Virreinato de Nueva España*) which existed from 1522 until 1821.

The *Visitador* or Inspector-General in New Spain, José de Gálvez y Gallardo († 1787), Marquis of Sonora, received the following orders: "Occupy and fortify San Diego and Monterey for God and the King of Spain." King Carlos III of Spain († 1788) wished to establish a strong Spanish presence in order to forestall the Russian Empire from expanding into Alta California by way of Alaska.

The Marquis of Sonora established a naval base at *San Blas* (Saint Blaise, † c. 316 AD) on the Pacific coast of Mexico and on November 6, 1768, he proclaimed Saint Joseph to be the patron of the "sacred expedition" to Alta California which would set out in 1769. Under the command of Captain Gaspar de Portolà de Rovira († 1786), the expedition also included a group of Franciscan missionaries, led by Saint Junípero Serra.

On July 16, 1769, Saint Junípero Serra founded the first of the missions of Alta California, giving it the name Mission *San Diego de Alcalá*. The *presidio* of San Diego was also founded. Saint Junípero Serra wrote that all of the natives "want my habit which they tug at by the sleeve. If I had given the habit to all who wanted it, there would be by this time a pretty large community of gentile friars. What I would like to imprint deep in their hearts is this: *Induímini Dóminum Iesum Christum* [Put on the Lord Jesus Christ]."[11]

The Portolà expedition continued north to explore the Alta California coast and re-establish the Port of Monterey that had been visited in 1602 by Don Sebastián Viscaiño and the Rev. Antonio de la Ascensión, OCD. In early November, the Portolá expedition discovered the San Francisco Bay and then returned to San Diego, sailing past and missing Monterey Bay.

As 1769 progressed at the Presidio-Mission of San Diego de Alcalá, "scurvy killed many of the Spanish soldiers and sailors, provisions ran perilously low, and the first scheduled supply ship did not return from Mexico with replenishments. The dire situation forced a decision to abandon San Diego if the ship did not soon arrive."[12] March 20, 1770 was designated as the deadline, one day after the feast of Saint Joseph.

> 11 Saint Junípero Serra (1713-1784): Antonine Tibesar, ed., *Writings of Junípero Serra* (1955-1966), vol. I, p. 113: Martin J. Morgado, *Junípero Serra: A Pictorial Biography* (1991), p. 29; cf. Romans 13:14).
> 12 Martin J. Morgado, *Junípero Serra: A Pictorial Biography* (1991), p. 41.

"Realizing how close was the feast of the most holy Patriarch Saint Joseph," Saint Junípero Serra proposed that a novena to Saint Joseph be observed.

"This was agreed upon, and all the men attended. The novena prayers were held after the daily recitation of the Rosary. Saint Joseph's day arrived, and the feast of this great saint was celebrated with a High Mass and sermon. Everything belonging to the expeditionary force had already been prepared for departure... But on that very afternoon [at 3pm] God willed to satisfy the ardent longings of His servant [Junípero] through the intercession of Saint Joseph, and to bring comfort to all by allowing them to see clearly and distinctly a ship [on the southern horizon]. The men attributed it to a miracle, through the intercession of the holy Patriarch that on his very feast day, the day the expedition had set as its term of stay, the ship was descried."[13]

Saint Junípero Serra "ceaselessly thanked God, as well as the blessed Saint, consoler of the afflicted, Saint Joseph, whom he openly acknowledged as the bestower of so special a favor. Showing his gratitude to the Saint, he sang a High Mass in his honor with the greatest solemnity... This holy devotion he continued [on the nineteenth of each month] up to the very last month of his life."[14]

"With replenished supplies and a restored sense of purpose, the expedition decided not to abandon San Diego,"[15] but continue north in the hopes of finally locating Viscaíno's Monterey Bay. The expedition entered Monterey Bay aboard the *San Antonio* on May 31, 1770, with Saint Junípero Serra first setting foot on shore on the first day of June.

Saint Junípero Serra described the day in these words:

"Our arrival was greeted by the joyful sound of the bells suspended from the branches of the oak tree. Everything being in readiness, and having put on alb and stole, and kneeling down with all the men before the altar, I intoned the hymn *Veni, Creator Spiritus* at the conclusion of which, after invoking the help of the Holy Spirit on everything we were about to perform, I blessed the salt and water. Then we all made our way to a gigantic cross which was all in readiness and lying on the ground. With everyone lending a hand we set it in an upright position. I sang the prayers for its blessing. We set it in the ground and then, with all the tenderness of our hearts, we venerated it. I sprinkled with holy water all the fields around. And thus, after raising aloft the standard of the King of Heaven, we unfurled the flag of Our Catholic Monarch likewise. As we raised each one of them, we shouted at the top of our voices: 'Long live the Faith! Long live the King!' All the time the bells were ringing, and our rifles were being fired, and from the boat came the thunder of the big guns... I began the High Mass, [and] a sermon after the Gospel; and, as long as the Mass lasted, it was accompanied with many salvos of cannon... As a conclusion to the liturgical celebration, standing up I intoned the *Te Deum laudamus* [Thee, O God, we praise]; we sang it slowly, and solemnly, right to the end... While I was making my thanksgiving after the Mass of the day, the officers proceeded to the act of formal possession of that country in the name of His Catholic Majesty, unfurling and waving once more the royal flag, pulling grass, moving stones and other formalities according to law, all accompanied with cheers, ringing of bells, cannonades, etc. In addition, there was a banquet served afterwards to all of us gathered on the beach; later a walk at sunset along the ocean concluded the celebration."[16]

> 13 Maynard Geiger, *Palóu's Life of Fray Junípero Serra* (1955), p. 87: Martin J. Morgado, *Junípero Serra: A Pictorial Biography* (1991), p. 41.
> 14 Ibid.
> 15 Martin J. Morgado, *Junípero Serra: A Pictorial Biography* (1991), p. 42

> 16 Saint Junípero Serra (1713-1784): Antonine Tibesar, ed., *Writings of Junípero Serra* (1955-1966), vol. I, pp. 168-169, 171: Martin J. Morgado, *Junípero Serra: A Pictorial Biography* (1991), p. 42.

The Apostle of California would go on to found a total of nine missions before his death in 1784. His successor as Father-President of the Alta California Mission system was Fray Fermín de Francisco Lasuén de Arasqueta († 1803). Sometimes known as the "forgotten friar," Fray Fermín Lasuén founded nine additional missions in California between 1786 and 1798. The last three missions were established by other Franciscan missionaries between 1804 and 1823. Seven missions are located in what is now the Diocese of Monterey in California.

El Camino Real, Spanish for "The Royal Road" or "The King's Highway," refers to the historic 600-mile (966-kilometer) California Mission Trail, connecting the former Alta California's 21 missions (along with a number of sub-missions), four presidios, and three pueblos, stretching from Mission San Diego de Alcalá in San Diego in the south to Mission San Francisco Solano in Sonoma in the north. Plans to establish a twenty-second mission in Santa Rosa in 1827 never came to fruition. At the peak of its development in 1832, the mission system controlled an area equal to approximately one-sixth of Alta California.

21. San Francisco de Solano

SACRAMENTO

20. San Rafael Arcángel

SAN FRANCISCO

6. San Francisco de Asís "Dolores"

8. Santa Clara de Asís

14. San José de Guadalupe

15. San Juan Bautista

12. Santa Cruz

MONTEREY

2. San Carlos Borroméo de Carmelo

13. Nuestra Señora de la Soledad

3. San Antonio de Padua

16. San Miguel Arcángel

5. San Luis Obispo de Tolosa

11. La Purísima Concepción

19. Santa Inés

10. Santa Barbara

PACIFIC OCEAN

SANTA BARBARA

9. San Buenaventura

17. San Fernando Rey de España

4. San Gabriel Arcángel

LOS ANGELES

7. San Juan Capistrano

18. San Luis Rey de Francia

1. San Diego de Alcalá

SAN DIEGO

Mission Daily Life

The daily routine at all the missions was very much alike, and was about as follows: They rose at sunrise and proceeded to the church, to attend morning prayers. Breakfast followed. Then the day's work. Towards noon they returned to the mission and passed the time till two o'clock in the afternoon, between dinner and repose. After that hour they resumed work and continued it till about sunset. Then all betook themselves to the church for evening devotions, and then to supper. After supper came amusements till the hour for retiring. Their diet consisted of beef and mutton with vegetables in the season. Wheaten cakes and puddings or porridge, called *atole* and *pinole*, formed a portion of the repast. The dress was for the males, linen shirt, trousers, and a blanket. The women had each two undergarments a year, a gown and a blanket. What a dreamy secluded life it must have been, with communication with the outer world only at intervals.

ELLIOTT & MOORE,

History of Monterey County, California, With Illustrations (1881); reprinted by Valley Publishers, 1979, p. 18

18

The Father-Presidents of the *Alta California* Mission System

The "Father-*Presidente*" was the head of the missions in Alta and Baja California, appointed by the College of San Fernando de Mexico until 1812, when the position became known as the "Commissary Prefect" who was appointed by the Commissary General of the Indies (a Franciscan residing in Spain). Beginning in 1831, separate individuals were elected to oversee Upper and Lower California.

1. Saint Junípero Serra (1769 – 1784)
2. Fray Francisco Palóu (*presidente pro tempore*, 1784 – 1785)
3. Fray Fermín Francisco de Lasuén (1785 – 1803)
4. Fray Pedro Estévan Tápis (1803 – 1812)
5. Fray José Francisco de Paula Señan (1812 – 1815)
6. Fray Mariano Payéras (1815 – 1820)
7. Fray José Francisco de Paula Señan (1820 – 1823)
8. Fray Vicente Francisco de Sarría (1823 – 1824)
9. Fray Narciso Durán (1824 – 1827)
10. Fray José Bernardo Sánchez (1827 – 1831)
11. Fray Narciso Durán (1831 – 1838)
12. Fray José Joaquin Jimeno (1838 – 1844)
13. Fray Narciso Durán (1844 – 1846)

The Missions of California

Missiones Californiæ

Founded by St. Junípero Serra, OFM:
1. Mission (Basilica) San Diego de Alcalá (July 16, 1769)
2. Mission (Basilica) San Carlos Borromeo de Carmelo (June 3, 1770)*
3. Mission San Antonio de Padua (July 14, 1771)*
4. Mission San Gabriel Arcángel (September 8, 1771)
5. Mission San Luis Obispo de Tolosa (September 1, 1772)*
6. Mission (Basilica) San Francisco de Asís or Mission Dolores (October 9, 1776)
7. Mission (Basilica) San Juan Capistrano (November 1, 1776)
8. Mission Santa Clara de Asís (January 12, 1777)
9. Mission San Buenaventura (March 31, 1782)

Founded by Fr. Fermín de Lasuén, OFM:
10. Mission Santa Barbara (December 4, 1786)
11. Mission La Purísima Concepción (December 8, 1787)
12. Mission Santa Cruz (August 28, 1791)*
13. Mission Nuestra Señora de la Soledad (October 8, 1791)*
14. Mission San José (June 11, 1797)
15. Mission San Juan Bautista (June 24, 1797)*
16. Mission San Miguel Arcángel (July 25, 1797)*
17. Mission San Fernando Rey de España (September 8, 1797)
18. Mission San Luis Rey de Francia (June 13, 1798)

Founded by Fr. Estévan Tapís, OFM:
19. Mission Santa Inés (September 17, 1804)

Founded by Fr. Vicente Francisco de Sarría:
20. Mission San Rafael Arcángel (December 14, 1817)

Founded by Fr. José Altimira:
21. Mission San Francisco Solano (Sonoma) (July 4, 1823)

* Located in the Diocese of Monterey in California.

Saint Junípero Serra • The Apostle of California

"Siempre adelante, nunca atrás — Always forward, never back."

Saint Junípero Serra was born Miquel Josep Serra i Ferrer at Petra on the Spanish island of Majorca on November 24, 1713. He entered the Order of Friars Minor (Franciscans) on September 14, 1730, taking the religious name Junípero in honor of the Servant of God "Brother" Juniper († 1258), one of the original followers of Saint Francis of Assisi.

For his proficiency in his studies, St. Junípero Serra was appointed lector of philosophy before his ordination to the priesthood. Later he received the degree of Doctor of Theology from the Lullian University at Palma, where he also occupied the Duns Scotus chair of philosophy until joining the missionary college of San Fernando in Mexico in 1749.

In 2008, the parish community of Carmel Mission Basilica commissioned a contemporary-style icon of Saint Junípero Serra. The icon was "written" by Brother Claude Lane, OSB, of the Mount Angel Abbey in Oregon, supported by the prayers of parishioners. "Written is the term used for preparing to create an icon by initially discerning the nature of the subject matter. A preliminary drawing is then made and from that, the final icon" (*Art of the Carmel Mission* (2011), p. 40). This image is based on a portrait of Saint Junípero Serra that was painted by Andres Caymari in 1790. The icon rested above his final resting place in the sanctuary of his favorite mission church until May 2015.

While traveling on foot from Vera Cruz to the capital, St. Junípero Serra injured his leg in such a way that he suffered from it throughout his life, though he continued to make his journeys on foot whenever possible. At his own request he was assigned to the Sierra Gorda Indian Missions some 30 leagues (90 miles) north of Querétaro. He served there for nine years, part of the time as superior, learned the language of the Pame Indians (*Xi'úi*), and translated the catechism into their language. After being recalled to Mexico, he became famous as a fervent and effective preacher. His zeal frequently led him to employ "extraordinary means" in order to move the faithful to penance.

In 1767, St. Junípero was appointed the superior of fifteen Franciscans for the Indian Missions of Baja (Lower) California. Early in 1769, he accompanied Portolá's land expedition to Alta (Upper) California. On the way, he established Mission San Fernando de Velicatá in Baja California on May 14. He arrived at San Diego on July 1, and on July 16 he there founded the first of the twenty-one California missions, which accomplished the conversions of all the natives on the coast as far as Sonoma in the north.

In 1773, difficulties with Pere Fages († 1794), the second Lieutenant Governor of the Province of *Las Californias* in New Spain, caused St. Junípero Serra to bring the issue before the Viceroy of New Spain, Fra Antonio María de Bucareli y Ursúa († 1779), Marquis of Vallehermoso

and a Knight of Justice of the Order of Malta. At the capital of Mexico, by order of the Viceroy, he drew up his "*Representación*" in thirty-two articles. Everything except for two minor points was decided in his favor. In late 1774, St. Junípero returned to California.

In 1778, St. Junípero Serra received the faculty to administer the Sacrament of Confirmation. After he had exercised his privilege for a year, Felipe de Neve († 1784), the fourth governor of the Spanish Province of the Californias (*Provincia de las Californias*), directed St. Junípero to suspend administering the sacrament until he could present the papal Brief. For nearly two years St. Junípero Serra refrained, and then Viceroy Majorga gave instructions to the effect that Saint Junípero Serra was within his rights. St. Junípero Serra would spend the remaining three years of his life travelling 600 miles, celebrating the sacrament of Confirmation at each mission. He suffered intensely from his crippled leg and from his chest, but he would use no treatments.

In 1784, St. Junípero Serra felt that he was "breaking up in health" and prepared for death. On May 26, he completed his last trip, celebrating the sacrament of Confirmation for the northern missions. After returning to Mission *San Carlos Borromeo del Río Carmelo*, he celebrated the sacraments for the last time: the marriage of Conrado José and Carola María, both local Christian Indians, on June 14; the Confirmation of 10-year-old Mustíola María on July 6; and a *Requiem* Mass for Roque Juan Cordero, an Indian and "father of various Christians," on July 30. Before dying, St Junípero Serra administered to him the "last sacraments" (Confession, Holy Communion as Viaticum, and Extreme Unction). On August 2, he baptized an 8-day-old Indian girl named Estefana Francisca. The date of Saint Junípero Serra's last Mass is unknown.

St. Junípero Serra died at Mission *San Carlos Borroméo del río Carmelo* in Alta California on August 28, 1784 and buried next to Fray Juan Crespi in the sanctuary of what is now more commonly known as Carmel Mission Basilica.

> So ended Junípero's life at age 70 years, 9 months and 4 days. He had been a Franciscan for almost 54 years, a priest for 45 and an apostolic missionary for 35. In California alone he had baptized over 6,000 Indians and confirmed 5,308.[17]

Besides extraordinary fortitude, St. Junípero Serra's most conspicuous virtues were insatiable zeal, love of mortification, self-denial, and absolute confidence in God. His executive abilities have been especially noted by non-Catholic writers. The esteem in which his memory was held by various people in California may be gathered from the fact that Mrs. Jane L. Stanford, a non-Catholic, had a granite statue erected to him in Monterey in 1890. A bronze statue of heroic size represents him as the "Apostle of California" in Golden Gate Park, San Francisco.

In 1882, the graves of St. Junípero Serra and his companions were opened for the first time. The remains were verified and the graves re-sealed. In 1884 the California legislature passed a resolution making August 29 of that year, the centennial of St. Junípero Serra's burial, a legal holiday. Of his writings, many letters and other documentation have survived. The principal ones are his *Diario* of the journey from Loreto to San Diego, which was published in *Out West* magazine in 1902, and the *Representación*.

The cause of beatification and canonization was officially opened in 1934, giving him the posthumous title of "Servant of God." In 1943, the remains of St. Junípero were exhumed for the second time, this time as part of the beatification and canonization process. On May 9, 1985, he was declared "Venerable" (cf. *AAS* 77 [1985] 1003-1008). In July of 1987, the remains of St. Junípero were exhumed for the third time and relics were extracted.

St. Junípero Serra was beatified by Pope St. John Paul II in Rome on September 25, 1988 and canonized by Pope Francis in Washington, DC on September 23, 2015. Although his *dies natalis* is August 28, his liturgical feast day is observed on July 1, the day that the Portolá expedition arrived in San Diego. St. Junípero Serra is considered the patron of vocations.

---

17 Martin J. Morgado, *Junípero Serra: A Pictorial Biography* (1991), p. 51.

The Secularization of the Missions
1833-1840

The 21 California missions founded by the Franciscan missionaries were originally intended to evolve into parishes, with the Franciscan priests giving way to the "secular" priests of a diocese, hence the use of the word "secularization." Instead, non-Indian landholders ended up taking possession of the mission lands (*ranchos*) and the mission Indians were dispersed as laborers on these *ranchos*.

The missions deteriorated from 1836 to 1846, at which time the government of Pío de Jesús Pico († 1894), the 27th and last governor of Alta California, confiscated what remained of their lands and buildings and sold them at auction, an illegal act under Mexican law. The original intention of converting the missions into parishes was thus thwarted.[18]

---

18 *The Role of the Central Coast in the History of the Catholic Faith in California*, published by the Diocese of Monterey in California in 2007.

THE DIOCESE OF CALIFORNIA
1840-1849

On April 27, 1840, Pope Gregory XVI († 1846) promulgated the papal bull *Apostolicam sollicitudinem*, creating the new Diocese of California (*Dioecesis Californiensis*), taking territory from the Diocese of Sonora, which had been erected in 1779.[19] A diocese (Latin: *dioecesis*; Greek: *dioikesis*) is the territory or churches subject to the jurisdiction of a bishop. After the eleventh century, the creation and modification (*innovatio*) of dioceses has been reserved exclusively to His Holiness the Pope as the Supreme Pontiff of the Universal Church.[20]

The Rt. Rev. Francisco José Vicente Garcia Diego y Moreno, OFM († 1846) was appointed the first bishop of California on April 27, 1840. Also known as the Diocese of the Two or Both Californias, the new diocese was a suffragan diocese of the Archdiocese of México (*Archidioecesis Mexicanus*). The boundaries included Alta California, which corresponds to the present-day American states of California, Nevada, Arizona, Utah, western Colorado, and southwestern Wyoming, as well as Baja California, which corresponds to the modern Mexican states of Baja California and Baja California Sur. The bishop's *cathedra* was designated at San Diego and Mission Santa Barbara served as his residence and pro-cathedral. Bishop Garcia Diego died on April 30, 1846, and is buried in Mission Santa Barbara in the Archdiocese of Los Angeles.

In 1846, during the Mexican-American War (1846-1848), the United States occupied Alta California. After the war, Alta California was ceded to the United States in 1848. The government of Mexico objected to a bishop based in the United States having jurisdiction over Mexican parishes in Baja California, resulting with the Holy See dividing the Diocese of California into two administrative sections: American and Mexican.

Pope Gregory XVI, born Bartolomeo Alberto Cappellar in 1765, was elected the 254th Bishop of Rome in 1831. He was a member of the Camaldolese Order and the last non-bishop to be elected to the papacy. In 1839, he issued the encyclical letter *In Supremo Apostolatus*, which condemned the Atlantic slave trade. He died in 1846.

The Rt. Rev. Francisco José Vicente Garcia Diego y Moreno, OFM 1st Bishop of California

Nota bene: This painting is kept at Mission *San Fernando Rey de España* in the Archdiocese of Los Angeles.

> 19 The complete Latin text of *Apostolicam sollicitudinem*, along with an English translation, can be found in the *Report of Jackson H. Ralston, Agent of the United States and of Counsel* (pp. 439-446), which was printed in *Appendix II: Foreign Relations of the United States, 1902* and published in 1903 by the Government Printing Office, Washington.

> 20 ALPHONSE VAN HOVE, *The Catholic Encyclopedia*, vol. 5 (1909).

THE DIOCESE OF MONTEREY
1849-1859

On November 20, 1849, the Diocese of California was renamed the Diocese of Monterey (*Dioecesis Montereyensis*) by Pope Blessed Pius IX († 1878). The Rt. Rev. Joseph Sadoc Alemany y Conill was appointed the first Bishop of Monterey on May 31, 1850. Born in Vich, Spain on July 13, 1814, Bishop Alemany was ordained a priest of the Order of Preachers (Dominicans) on March 11, 1837. Upon his episcopal appointment, he was consecrated bishop on June 30, 1850. Baja California was not withdrawn from Bishop Alemany's jurisdiction until December 21, 1851—one year after California officially became the thirty-first state admitted to the United States.

In May of 1852, the First Plenary Council of Baltimore was held, which was a national meeting of bishops in the United States. "The Bishop of Monterey, California, was also present, although his diocese, lately separated from Mexico, had not yet been incorporated with any American province... In the acts of this council is found a statement of the Bishop of Monterey concerning the California Missions. He informed the Fathers that a large sum of money had formerly been placed in the hands of the Mexican Government to be used under the sanction of Spanish law for the support of the Californian missionaries. For years they had received none of this money and the late revolutions made any hope of reparation unlikely. However, as it is reported that the civil power in California intends to demand this money from the Mexican treasury for public purposes, he desired to know what effort the American bishops thought it desirable to make in the premises. The outcome of the whole discussion was the sending of a letter on the subject to the Archbishop of Mexico. The money was later recovered and employed for the Church in California."[21]

On July 29, 1853, Pope Blessed Pius IX promulgated *Ad animarum regimen*, creating the new Archdiocese of San Francisco (*Archidioecesis Sancti Francisci*) and establishing new boundaries for the Diocese of Monterey, which then became a suffragan diocese of the new Ecclesiastical Province of San Francisco.[22]

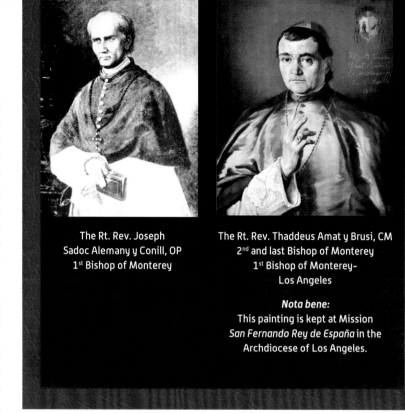

The Rt. Rev. Joseph
Sadoc Alemany y Conill, OP
1st Bishop of Monterey

The Rt. Rev. Thaddeus Amat y Brusi, CM
2nd and last Bishop of Monterey
1st Bishop of Monterey-
Los Angeles

Nota bene:
This painting is kept at Mission
San Fernando Rey de España in the
Archdiocese of Los Angeles.

Bishop Alemany was appointed the first Archbishop of San Francisco and the Rt. Rev. Thaddeus Amat y Brusi († 1878), CM, was appointed the second Bishop of Monterey, with his official residence designated at Santa Barbara. Born at Barcelona, Spain on December 31, 1810, Bishop Amat was ordained a priest of the Congregation of the Mission (*Congregatio Missionis*) on December 23, 1837. After his appointment as Bishop of Monterey, he was consecrated bishop on March 12, 1854.

Both Archbishop Alemany and Bishop Amat were among the bishops of the world who attended the First Vatican Council as council fathers between 1869 and 1870. The First Vatican Council was the twentieth ecumenical or general council of the Church, and only the first such assembly since the Council of Trent (1545-1563). The Council's goal was to "place Catholic doctrine in opposition to the errors of the day." The First Vatican Council is probably best known for solemnly defining the doctrine of papal infallibility.[23]

> 21 WILLIAM FANNING, *The Catholic Encyclopedia*, vol. 2 (1907).

> 22 The complete Latin text of *Ad animarum regimen*, along with an English translation, can be found in the *Report of Jackson H. Ralston, Agent of the United States and of Counsel* (pp. 446-447), which was printed in *Appendix II: Foreign Relations of the United*

States, 1902 and published in 1903 by the Government Printing Office, Washington.

> 23 HEINRICH J.D. DENZINGER and PETER HÜNERMANN, *Enchiridion symbolorum, definitionum et declarationum de rebus fidei et morum* [*Compendium of Creeds, Definitions, and Declarations on Matters of Faith and Morals*], 43rd edition (2012), p. 600.

THE DIOCESE OF MONTEREY - LOS ANGELES
1859-1922

On July 7, 1859, Pope Blessed Pius IX changed the name of the diocese from Monterey to Monterey-Los Angeles (*Dioecesis Montereyensis-Angelorum*). On July 9, 1859, Blessed Pius IX permitted Bishop Amat to "remove his residence to Los Angeles, but with instructions to retain the old title" of Bishop of Monterey.[24] On July 29, 1873, the name of the diocese was altered and Bishop Amat became the first bishop of Monterey-Los Angeles. The Diocese of Monterey-Los Angeles consisted of 80,000 square miles and included the counties of Fresno, Inyo, Imperial, Kern, Los Angeles, Monterey, Riverside, San Benito, San Bernardino, Orange, San Diego, San Luis Obispo, Santa Barbara, Ventura, and Tulare, plus parts of the counties of Santa Cruz, Santa Clara, and Merced.

On May 20, 1873, the Rev. Francisco Mora y Borrell († 1905) was appointed Coadjutor Bishop of Monterey-Los Angeles. A coadjutor bishop is a titular bishop "appointed to assist an ordinary bishop in the administration of the diocese... He possesses some powers of jurisdiction determined by the letters Apostolic appointing him. Often also, notably in missionary countries, the coadjutor bishop is named *cum iure successionis*, i.e. with the right of succession; on the death of the diocesan bishop he enters on the ordinary administration of the diocese."[25]

On May 12, 1878, Bishop Amat died at the age of 67 and he is buried at the Cathedral of Our Lady of the Angels in the Archdiocese of Los Angeles. Bishop Francisco Mora y Borrell succeeded

Pope Bl. Pius IX, born Count Giovanni Maria Mastai-Ferretti, was elected the 255th Bishop of Rome in 1846. He opened the First Vatican Council, lost the Papal States of the Church to the new Kingdom of Italy, and defined *ex cathedra* the dogma of the Immaculate Conception. He was the longest reigning Supreme Pontiff in history. He was beatified by St. John Paul II in 2000; his feast day is February 7.

him as the second Bishop of Monterey-Los Angeles. Born at Gurb in Spain on November 25, 1827, Bishop Mora was ordained a priest of the Diocese of Monterey on March 19, 1856. After his appointment as Coadjutor Bishop of Monterey-Los Angeles, he was appointed Titular Bishop of Mosynopolis and consecrated bishop on August 3, 1873.

On January 26, 1894, George T. Montgomery († 1907) was appointed Coadjutor Bishop of Monterey-Los Angeles. On March 13, 1896, Bishop Mora resigned and was appointed Titular Archbishop of Hierapolis in Syria on May 6, 1896. Bishop Montgomery succeeded him as the third Bishop of Monterey-Los Angeles and he was solemnly installed on June 20, 1896. Archbishop Mora died on August 3, 1905, at the age of 77.

Bishop Montgomery was born in Saint Lawrence, Kentucky on December 30, 1847 and ordained a priest of the Archdiocese of San Francisco on December 20, 1879. Upon his 1894 appointment as Coadjutor Bishop of Monterey-Los Angeles, he was appointed Titular Bishop of Thmuis and consecrated bishop on April 8, 1894.

On September 17, 1902, Bishop Montgomery was appointed Coadjutor Archbishop of San Francisco and on March 27, 1903, Thomas J. Conaty († 1915) was appointed the fourth Bishop of Monterey-Los Angeles. Born in Kilnaleck, Ireland on August 1, 1847, Bishop Conaty was ordained a priest on December 21, 1872. On October 5, 1901, he was appointed Titular Bishop of Samos and consecrated bishop on November 24, 1901.

> 24 Zephyrin Engelhardt, *The Catholic Encyclopedia*, vol. 10 (1911).
> 25 Alphonse van Hove, *The Catholic Encyclopedia*, vol. 2 (1907).

The Rt. Rev.
Francisco Mora y Borrell
2nd Bishop of Monterey-Los Angeles

Photo courtesy of the diocesan archives

The Rt. Rev. George Thomas Montgomery
3rd Bishop of Monterey-Los Angeles

Photo courtesy of the diocesan archives

The Rt. Rev.
Thomas James Conaty
4th Bishop of Monterey-Los Angeles

Photo courtesy of the diocesan archives

The Great San Francisco Earthquake

On Wednesday, April 18, 1906, at 5:12am, an earthquake struck the City of San Francisco and the coast of Northern California. Devastating fires broke out in the city that lasted for several days. As a result of the quake and fires, about 3,000 people died and over 80% of the City of San Francisco was destroyed. The earthquake and resulting fire are remembered as one of the worst natural disasters in the history of the United States. The death toll from the earthquake and resulting fire remains the greatest loss of life from a natural disaster in California's history. In Monterey County, the earthquake permanently shifted the course of the Salinas River. Where the river had originally emptied into the Monterey Bay between Moss Landing and Watsonville, the earthquake had diverted it six miles south to a new channel just north of Marina. Several churches in the Diocese of Monterey-Los Angeles suffered damage, including Holy Cross in Santa Cruz, Mission San Juan Bautista, and Saint Patrick in Watsonville.

Bishop Conaty died on September 18, 1915 and he is buried at the Cathedral of Our Lady of the Angels in the Archdiocese of Los Angeles. On March 22, 1917, the Rt. Rev. Peter J. Muldoon († 1927), 1st Bishop of Rockford (Illinois), was appointed Bishop of Monterey-Los Angeles. However, Bishop Muldoon's appointment never took effect "due to strong appeals of both clergy and laity of Rockford"[26] and he remained the Bishop of Rockford until his death in 1927.

On September 21, 1917, John J. Cantwell was appointed the fifth Bishop of Monterey-Los Angeles. Born at Limerick in Ireland on December 1, 1874, Bishop Cantwell was ordained a priest of Monterey-Los Angeles on June 18, 1899. Upon his appointment he was consecrated bishop on December 5, 1917.

The Rt. Rev.
John Joseph Cantwell
5th and last Bishop of
Monterey-Los Angeles
1st Bishop of
Los Angeles-San Diego
1st Archbishop of
Los Angeles

*Photo courtesy
of the diocesan archives*

> 26 Archdiocese of Chicago Archives & Records Center.

THE DIOCESE OF MONTEREY - FRESNO
1922-1967

O n June 1, 1922, Pope Pius XI promulgated the Apostolic Constitution *Montereyensis Angelorum aliarum*,[27] dividing the Diocese of Monterey-Los Angeles into the new Diocese of Monterey-Fresno (*Dioecesis Montereyensis-Fresnensis*) and the new Diocese of Los Angeles-San Diego (*Dioecesis Angelorum-Sancti Didaci*). The Diocese of Monterey-Fresno was created with a northern boundary which placed all of Santa Cruz County, including Boulder Creek, in the new diocese; all of Santa Clara County, including Gilroy, became part of the Archdiocese of San Francisco. Both the new Diocese of Monterey-Fresno and the new Diocese of Los Angeles-San Diego remained suffragan dioceses of the metropolitan Archdiocese of San Francisco (*Archidioecesis Sancti Francisci*).

Pope Pius XI, born Achille Ambrogio Damiano Ratti, was elected the 259th Bishop of Rome in 1922. In 1929, he signed the Lateran Treaty with the Kingdom of Italy, establishing the State of the Vatican City as a sovereign state. He inaugurated Vatican Radio and established the feast of Christ the King. He also re-organized the Vatican archives and was a well-known mountain climber.

The First Bishop of Monterey-Fresno

On June 1, 1922, Bishop Cantwell was appointed the first Bishop of Los Angeles-San Diego and the Rt. Rev. John B. MacGinley († 1969), 28th Bishop of Nueva Cáceres in the Philippines, was appointed the first Bishop of Monterey-Fresno on March 24, 1924.

Born at Croagh in Ireland on August 19, 1871, Bishop MacGinley was ordained a priest in Rome on June 8, 1895. He was appointed Bishop of Nueva Cáceres on April 2, 1910 and consecrated bishop on May 10, 1910.

> 27 *Acta Apostolicæ Sedis*, vol. 14 (1922), pp. 539-541.

The Most Rev.
John Bernard MacGinley
1st Bishop of
Monterey-Fresno

*Photo courtesy
of the diocesan archives*

This picture taken in June of 1911 in Camalig, Albay, shows Bishop MacGinley when he was the Bishop of Nueva Cáceres in the Philippines.

*Photo courtesy
of the diocesan archives*

The Second Bishop of Monterey-Fresno

Due to age and poor health, Bishop MacGinley resigned as the ordinary of the diocese on September 26, 1932. He was subsequently appointed Titular Bishop of Croae and "returned to his family home in County Donegal where he was cared for by the Medical Missionaries of Mary."[28] On April 28, 1933, Philip G. Scher († 1953) was appointed the second Bishop of Monterey-Fresno.

On December 12, 1946, Aloysius J. Willinger, 2nd Bishop of Ponce in Puerto Rico and a member of the Congregation of the Most Holy Redeemer (C.Ss.R.), was appointed Coadjutor Bishop and Apostolic Administrator of the Diocese of Monterey-Fresno and Titular Bishop of Bida. Born at Baltimore in Maryland on April 19, 1886, Bishop Willinger had become a professed member of the Congregation of the Most Holy Redeemer at the age of 20 on August 2, 1906 and he was ordained to the priesthood on July 2, 1911. On March 8, 1929, he was appointed Bishop of Ponce in Puerto Rico and consecrated bishop on October 28, 1929. Bishop Willinger authored *The Eucharist and Christian Life: Theological Studies and Supernatural Psychology Concerning the Blessed Sacrament*. It was published in 1949 by Saint Anthony Guild Press of Paterson, New Jersey.

The Third Bishop of Monterey-Fresno

On January 3, 1953, Bishop Scher died and was buried at Holy Cross Cemetery in what is now the Diocese of Fresno. Bishop Willinger succeeded him as the third Bishop of Monterey-Fresno. On December 5, 1956, the Rev. Monsignor Harry A. Clinch was appointed Auxiliary Bishop of Monterey-Fresno by Pope Venerable Pius XII. He was appointed pastor of Carmel Mission in 1958 by Bishop Willinger.

The Most Rev.
Philip George Scher
2nd Bishop of Monterey-Fresno

*Photo courtesy
of the diocesan archives*

The Most Rev.
Aloysius Joseph Willinger, C.Ss.R.
3rd and last Bishop
of Monterey-Fresno

*Photo courtesy
of the diocesan archives*

The coat of arms of the Most Rev. Harry A. Clinch, auxiliary bishop of the Diocese of Monterey-Fresno and Titular Bishop of Badiae.

SALUS ANIMARUM SUPREMA LEX

> 28 *The Observer*, October 23, 1969, vol. 1, no. 30.

The Second Vatican Council

Both Bishop Willinger and Bishop Clinch were among the over 2,600 bishops of the world who attended the Second Vatican Council. Bishop Willinger attended the first session in 1962, while Bishop Clinch attended the second, third, and fourth sessions between 1963 and 1965. Vatican II was the twenty-first ecumenical or general council of the Church, and only the second such assembly since the Council of Trent (1545-1563). The Council's goal was to address "the growth of the Catholic faith, the restoration of sound morals among the Christian flock, and appropriate adaptation of Church discipline to the needs and conditions of our times."[29]

The greatest concern of the Ecumenical Council is this: that the sacred deposit of Christian doctrine should be guarded and taught more efficaciously. That doctrine embraces the whole of man, composed as he is of body and soul. And, since he is a pilgrim on this earth, it commands him to tend always toward heaven.[30]

The Second Vatican Council was a pastoral council that wished to lead to an *aggiornamento* or "renewal" of the life of the Church; it did not define any new dogma in matters of faith or morals. However, its documents do have a dogmatic character. This can be seen not only with the dogmatic constitutions *Lumen gentium* and *Dei verbum*, but also with some parts of the remaining documents. It would fall to Bishop Clinch to implement many of the reforms that followed the Council as the first Bishop of Monterey in California.[31]

The bishops of the Church gathered in the Papal Basilica of Saint Peter in the Vatican for the twenty-first ecumenical or general council.

> 29 SAINT JOHN XXIII, encyclical letter *Ad Petri cathedram* (29 June 1959), n. 61: *Acta Apostolicae Sedis*, vol. 51 (1959), pp. 497–531; English translation: *The Pope Speaks*, 5 (autumn, 1959), pp. 359–383.

> 30 SAINT JOHN XXIII, *allocutio in sollemni SS. Concilii inauguratione* (11 October 1962): *Acta Apostolicæ Sedis*, vol. 54 (1962), p. 790).
> 31 *Monterey Peninsula Herald*, January 19, 1982, p. 1.

THE DIOCESE OF MONTEREY IN CALIFORNIA

1967

On October 6, 1967, Pope Blessed Paul VI promulgated the Apostolic Constitution *Montereyensis-Fresnensis,* creating the new Diocese of Monterey in California (*Dioecesis Montereyensis in California*):

> We, of Our supreme authority and in accordance with the thinking of Our venerable brothers, the Cardinals of Holy Roman Church who preside over the Sacred Congregation of the Consistory, have reached the following decisions. From the Diocese of Monterey-Fresno We separate the 'counties' bearing the name of Santa Cruz, Monterey, San Benito, and San Luis Obispo, that are enclosed by the unbroken mountain chain popularly called Coastal Range and by the Pacific Ocean, and constitute the region called Coastal Area, so as to establish a new diocese to be named *Monterey in California* and to be coterminous with the territory of the counties named above.[32]

The same document also designates the parish church of San Carlos Borromeo or "Royal Presidio Chapel" in the City of Monterey as the cathedral or mother church of the new diocese.

The Diocese of Monterey in California measures 8,475 square miles (21,916 square kilometers), which is equivalent to the Kingdom of Belgium and the Kingdom of the Netherlands combined.

The diocese does not have its own seminary and instead utilizes the major seminaries of the Archdiocese of Los Angeles and the Archdiocese of San Francisco, as well as the minor and major seminary of the Archdiocese of Portland in Oregon, and in the Archdiocese of San Antonio, Texas. [33]

Pope Bl. Paul VI, born Giovanni Battista Enrico Antonio Maria Montini, was elected the 262nd Bishop of Rome in 1963. He was the last pope to be crowned with the papal tiara and the first pope since 1809 to travel outside Italy. He was the first pope to travel to the United States and Australia. He closed the Second Vatican Council and implemented most of its reforms. He promulgated the prophetic encyclical letter *Humanæ Vitæ* in 1968. He was beatified by Pope Francis in 2014.

The Diocese of Monterey in California is a suffragan diocese of the Metropolitan Archdiocese of Los Angeles in California (*Archidioecesis Angelorum in California*). A suffragan diocese is one of the dioceses that are grouped together to form an ecclesiastical province under the jurisdiction of a metropolitan archdiocese. The Ecclesiastical Province of Los Angeles also includes the suffragan dioceses of Fresno, Orange, San Bernardino, and San Diego.

Although a suffragan diocese is governed by its own bishop, the metropolitan archbishop has certain rights and duties of oversight. He has no power of governance within a suffragan diocese, but does have some limited rights and duties of intervention in cases of neglect by the authorities of the suffragan diocese itself.

Ecclesiastical Province of Los Angeles

- Los Angeles
- Monterey
- San Diego
- Fresno
- Orange
- San Bernardino
- Province of San Francisco

> 32 Official Latin text: « *De suprema Nostra potestate deque sententia venerabilium Fratrum Nostrorum S.R.E. Cardinalium qui Sacrae Congregationi Consistoriali praesunt, sequentia decernimus. A dioecesi Montereyensi-Fresnensi Comitatus, quos dicunt disiungimus, quibus appellatio Santa Cruz, Monterey, San Benito et San Luis Obispo, qui, continuis montibus vulgo Coast Range et Oceano Pacifico circumscripti regionem Area Coast nuncupatam* constituunt; *iisque novam dioecesim condimus, Montereyensem in California appellandam iisdemque finibus terminandam ac Comitatus, quos diximus* » (Beatus Paulus VI, constitutio apostolica *Montereyensis-Fresnensis* (6 octobris 1967): *Acta Apostolicæ Sedis,* vol. 60 (1968), p. 186.

> 33 Cf. *Quinquennial Report* 2003-2011, p. V-3.

The First Bishop of Monterey in California
The Most Rev. Harry A. Clinch

"I always wanted to be a priest.
I know that I never wanted to be anything else." [34]

Ten days after the new diocese was established, Bishop Willinger resigned as the third and last Bishop of Monterey-Fresno and was appointed Titular Bishop of Tiguala. Pope Blessed Paul VI appointed the Most Rev. Harry A. Clinch, Auxiliary Bishop of Monterey-Fresno and pastor of Carmel Mission Basilica, the first bishop of the newly-created Diocese of Monterey in California. He was solemnly installed as the first bishop of the new diocese on December 14, 1967.

Harry Anselm Clinch was born in San Anselmo on October 27, 1908. He was the first child to be baptized at the parish of Saint Anselm. Entering the seminary in 1925, he studied for the priesthood at Saint Benedict's Seminary in Kansas, Saint Joseph's College in Mountain View, and Saint Patrick's Seminary in Menlo Park. He was ordained a priest of the Diocese of Monterey-Fresno on June 6, 1936 in Saint John's Cathedral in Fresno by the Most Rev. Philip G. Scher, 2nd Bishop of Monterey-Fresno.

He was named the diocesan director of the Propagation of the Faith and the Holy Childhood Association, founded the Catholic Association of Youth Organization in the diocese, and the first director of Camp Teresita for boys. In 1942, he was appointed chaplain at Saint Agnes Hospital in Fresno until 1946 when he was appointed pastor of Our Lady of Perpetual Help in Clovis. In 1947, he was appointed the diocesan director of the Legion of Decency, established the new parish of Sacred Heart in Fresno, and served as the editor of the *Central California Register*. He was later appointed to the parish of Saint Mary in Taft. In October of 1952, he was made a Domestic Prelate of His Holiness (monsignor) by Venerable Pius XII. On December 5, 1956, Monsignor

Clinch was appointed Auxiliary Bishop of Monterey-Fresno and Titular Bishop of Badiae. He was consecrated bishop on February 27, 1957. The principal consecrator was the Most Rev. Aloysius J. Willinger, C.Ss.R., 3rd Bishop of Monterey-Fresno. The principal co-consecrators were Bishop Timothy Manning († 1989), an auxiliary bishop of Los Angeles, and Bishop Merlin J. Guilfoyle († 1981), an auxiliary bishop of San Francisco. Bishop Clinch was the thirteenth native Californian to become a Catholic bishop and his episcopal lineage includes John Carroll, SJ († 1815), the first Archbishop of Baltimore and cousin of Charles Carroll († 1832), the only Catholic signer of the Declaration of Independence.

In 1958, Bishop Clinch was appointed pastor of Carmel Mission in Carmel-by-the-Sea until he was appointed the first Bishop of Monterey in California in 1967.

**The Most Reverend Monsignor
Harry Anselm Clinch
1st Bishop of Monterey in California**

> 34 *The Observer*, April 14, 1982, vol. 14, no. 2, p. 3.

The Patrons of the Diocese

On August 28, 1968, Pope Blessed Paul VI promulgated the Apostolic Letter *Evangelii præconum* ("Heralds of the Gospel"), designating the Blessed Virgin Mary, under the title of Our Lady of Bethlehem, and Saint Charles Borromeo as the principal patrons of the Diocese of Monterey in California. In the same document, Saint Patrick and Saint Thérèse of the Child Jesus were designated as the secondary patrons of the diocese.[35]

Devotion to **Our Lady of Bethlehem** (Latin: *Domina nostra de Bethlehemensis*; Spanish: *Nuestra Señora de Belén*; Portuguese: *Nossa Senhora de Belém*) began in 15th century Portugal with Dom Henrique de Avis (1394-1460), Infante of Portugal, 1st Duke of Viseu, and Grand Master of the Order of Christ. Better known in the English language as "Prince Henry the Navigator," Dom Henrique had a small chapel dedicated to *Santa Maria de Belém* constructed at Belém near Lisbon so that Portuguese sailors could seek the intercession of the Blessed Virgin before every voyage, and offer prayers of thanksgiving upon each safe return. During the so-called "Iberian Union" (1580-1640), when the Portuguese Empire was politically united with the Spanish Empire under the Habsburg kings of Spain, Spanish sailors learned of the devotion to Our Lady of Bethlehem and began to seek her intercession as well.

The Statue of *"La Conquistadora"*
Francisco Antonio de Lorenzaña y Butrón, 23rd Archbishop of Mexico († 1771), gave a Mexican-made statue of Our Lady of Bethlehem to Jose de Gálvez, the Inspector General of New Spain, who then gave the statue to Gaspar de Portolá for the "sacred expedition" to San Diego and Monterey. Our Lady of Bethlehem was to be the patron of the conquest of this new land, and for this reason was called *"La Conquistadora."*[36]

The statue resided at Mission San Diego until it was taken aboard the *San Antonio* to Monterey in 1770. Saint Junípero Serra placed the statue on the temporary altar under the "Vizcaino Oak" for the celebration of Mass, followed by the solemn chanting of the *Salve, Regina*.

Saint Junípero Serra, believing the statue to be on loan from Gálvez, sent it back to Mexico aboard the *San Antonio*. However, Gálvez had it immediately sent back to Mission San Carlos Borromeo de Monterey. When the mission was moved to Carmel, the statue was also moved and placed above the high altar. As Mission San Carlos Borromeo grew and prospered, the statue of Our Lady of Bethlehem continued to be held in esteem and veneration. The image of *"La Conquistadora"* is the oldest religious statue in the State of California and resides in a chapel of its own at Carmel Mission Basilica.

The liturgical feast of Our Lady of Bethlehem is December 30, the sixth day within the Octave of the Nativity of the Lord (Christmas).

Photo courtesy of Agnieszka A. Klasa, June 7, 2015.

> 35 *Acta Apostolicæ Sedis*, vol. 60 (1968), pp. 708-709.

> 36 *Art from the Carmel Mission* (2011), p. 64.

Prayer to Our Lady of Bethlehem

Dear Lady of Bethlehem, Virgin most pure, Mother of Our Saviour, may the memory of the cold on the night Thy Divine Child was born bring Thy powerful intercession to bear upon the world's coldness towards the Babe of Bethlehem. Send down into the hearts of all men some warmth of the flames of love that Thy Immaculate Heart gives forth.

Do Thou who suffered such great loneliness when Thy Son was taken from Thee, look with pity upon the void in the hearts of those who know and love Him not. Bring Him to them and with Him His Angels and Saints that they too may be our intimate friends. Do Thou who journeyed wearily to Bethlehem look down with mercy upon mankind trudging along the way of evil, lost and confused. Do Thou guide us to the path of Thy Son and the habitation He had prepared for us.

Look down with compassion upon us as we commend to Thy maternal care the needs of Holy Mother Church, our beloved country, our families. We all place all at Thy blessed feet. Through Thy powerful intercession may God grant to us and to the whole frightened world the grace of mutual understanding and the sacred Peace of Bethlehem.

Our Lady of Bethlehem, pray for us now, pray for us in every need, and be Thou with us at the hour of our death. Amen.

Nihil Obstat:
J. Cullerton
Censor Librorum

Imprimatur:
+ A.J. Willinger
Bishop of Monterey-Fresno
Fresno, California
March 5, 1954

From San Carlos Cathedral in Monterey.
Photo courtesy of Agnieszka A. Klasa, 2016.

Saint Charles Borromeo (Latin: *Sanctus Carolus Borromeus*; Italian: *San Carlo Borromeo*; Spanish: *San Carlos Borromeo*), Bishop and Confessor, "was born at Arona, in Lombardy, in the year 1538. After having taken honors in both civil and canon law, he was made cardinal and bishop of Milan by his uncle, Pope Pius IV. As a true pastor of his flock he tirelessly promoted Christian life by the reform of his diocese, the convocation of synods, and the promulgation of regulations intended to foster the Church's mission. He died on November 3, 1584" (*The Liturgy of the Hours*, 4 November). He was canonized on November 1, 1610, by Pope Paul V "for the holiness of his life and for his renown for miracles" (*The Roman Martyrology*, 3 November). His liturgical feast on November 4 was added to the General Roman Calendar three years later.

In addition to being a principal patron of the diocese, St. Charles Borromeo is the titular patron of both San Carlos Cathedral in the City of Monterey and Carmel Mission Basilica in the City of Carmel-by-the-Sea.

Saint Thérèse of the Child Jesus and the Holy Face (Latin: *Sancta Teresia ab Infante Iesu et Sancto Vulto*; French: *Sainte Thérèse de l'Enfant-Jésus et de la Sainte-Face*; Spanish: *Santa Teresa del Niño Jesús y de la Santa Faz*), Virgin and Doctor of the Church, "was born at Alençon, in France, in 1873. While still a young girl, she entered the Carmelite monastery at Lisieux. There she lived a life of humility, evangelical simplicity, and trust in God. By word and example she taught these virtues to the novices of the community. Offering her life for the salvation of souls and the growth of the Church, she died on September 30, 1897" (*The Liturgy of the Hours*, 1 October).

"Seeing her to be most wonderful for her innocence of life and simplicity," she was canonized in 1925 by Pope Pius XI, who also "appointed her as special patron before God of all missions" (*The Roman Martyrology*, 30 September). Her feast day was added to the General Roman Calendar in 1927. In 1997, Pope St. John Paul II declared her the 33rd Doctor of the Church, one of only four women so honored. Her liturgical feast day is October 1; October 3 in the extraordinary form of the Roman Rite.

In addition to being a secondary patron of the diocese, St. Thérèse is the patron of the Carmelite Monastery in Carmel. During the Great Jubilee of 2000, the relics of Saint Thérèse of Lisieux visited the diocese, being venerated by the faithful at Saint Francis Xavier in Seaside, Carmel Mission Basilica, and the Carmelite Monastery.

From the parish of St. Patrick in Watsonville.
Photo courtesy of John Glover, 2015.

Saint Patrick (Latin: *Sanctus Patricius*; Irish: *Naomh Pádraig*; Spanish: *San Patricio*), Bishop and Confessor and "Apostle of Ireland," "was born in Great Britain about the year 385. As a young man he was captured and sold as a slave in Ireland, where he had to tend sheep. Having escaped from slavery, he chose to enter the priesthood and later, as a bishop, he tirelessly preached the Gospel to the people of Ireland where he converted many to the faith and established the Church. He died at Down in 461" (*The Liturgy of the Hours*, 17 March). His liturgical feast is March 17, where in the dioceses of Ireland it is both a solemnity and a holy day of obligation.

In addition to being a secondary patron of the diocese, St. Patrick is also the titular patron of the parish churches in Arroyo Grande and Watsonville, as well as the seminary and university in Menlo Park (Archdiocese of San Francisco).

The Firsts of the New Diocese [37]

- The first pastoral appointment to be made in the new diocese was on March 9, 1968, when the Rev. Silvano Girolami was assigned to the parish of Saint Joseph in Nipomo.

- The Sacrament of Confirmation was celebrated for the first time on March 10, 1968, at the parish of the Immaculate Conception in *Tres Piños*; 45 young people were confirmed.

- The Sacrament of Holy Orders was celebrated for the first time in the new diocese on May 24, 1968, when the Rev. Michael Adams was ordained to the priesthood at San Carlos Cathedral in Monterey.

The Sun is risen early in the morning.
All is a new Creation.
The rains are over and the winter is past
for He has risen as He said.

The Observer

The first issue of *The Observer*, "the official newspaper of the Diocese of Monterey in California," was published on April 3, 1969, under the editorship of the Rev. James Fallon. The weekly newspaper was priced at 15 cents per copy, with the annual subscription priced at $6.

The editorial offices were first located in the Pastoral Office in Monterey, where local copy, photographs, and national and international copy from news services were processed and made ready for publication. Tentative logs were made up for the pages and then the copy was sent by special delivery airmail to the printers in San Francisco, where it was set on a linofilm machine in the correct column widths, preparatory to putting it on pages. Monday at noon was the deadline.

On Tuesday mornings, Fr. Fallon would drive to San Francisco to proof-read the copy and begin creating the page layouts. The final making up of the pages at the printers in San Francisco was completed late on Wednesday, with Fr. Fallon standing by in case of emergency. The paper was then printed on Wednesday night and in the mail on Thursday morning. On Thursday afternoon, the procedure began all over again in the Monterey office, getting ready for the following week's issue. [38]

> 37 *The Observer*, July 1993, p. 9.
> 38 *Ibid.*, April 24, 1969, vol. I, no. 4, p. 9.

The Death of the First Bishop of Monterey-Fresno

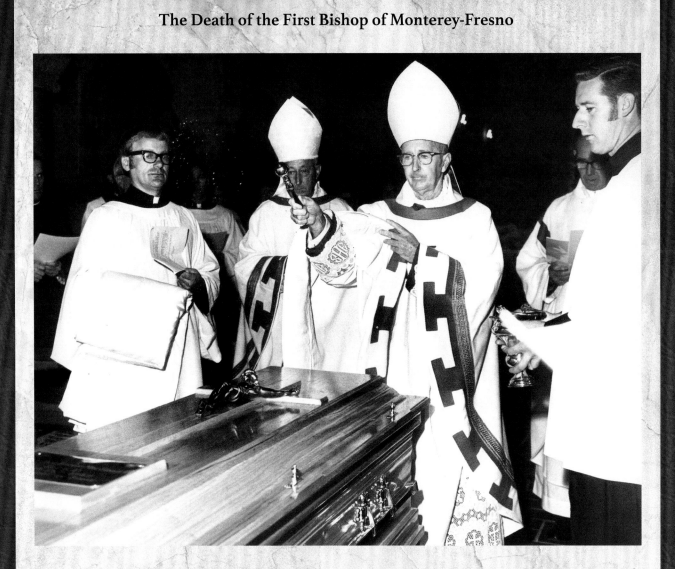

On October 18, 1969, the Most Rev. John B. MacGinley, the first bishop of the Diocese of Monterey-Fresno, died at Killebegs in Ireland. At the age of 98, he was "the oldest Roman Catholic bishop in the world" (*The Observer*, October 23, 1969, vol. 1, no. 30). The funeral Mass took place at the Carmelite Monastery in Carmel-by-the-Sea, where Bishop MacGinley had desired to be entombed. Among the concelebrants were Bishop Clinch (pictured above, sprinkling the coffin with holy water) and the Most Rev. Hugh A. Donohoe, 2nd Bishop of Fresno. The funeral Mass of Bishop MacGinley marked the very first time that the new *Order of Christian Funerals* was officially used in the diocese (cf. *The Observer*, October 30, 1969, vol. 1, no. 31).

Photo by Patricia Rowedder and courtesy of the diocesan archives.

The Portolá – Crespi Cross

On December 9, 1969, a 20 foot cross was erected on the beach at the spot where the Portolá expedition had an overlook of the natural harbor in Monterey Bay exactly 200 years earlier on December 9, 1769. The cross was hand-hewn by Harry Downie out of local redwood. An explanatory plaque was also erected: "In the winter of 1769, the Spanish expedition in search of Monterey Bay, under the command of Don Gaspar de Portola and Father Juan Crespi, erected a cross on or near this site and left the following message: 'The land expedition is returning to San Diego for lack of provisions today, December 9, 1769'. This monument was dedicated December 9, 1969, by the citizens of Monterey in honor of our 200th birthday."

Photo courtesy of The Monterey County Herald.

THE 1970S

The Mass of Paul VI

On Sunday, February 15, 1970, all parishes in the diocese "began instructional preparation for the liturgical changes in the Mass" which were to go into effect for the entire Church in the United States on March 22. This preparation consisted of six bulletin inserts and homilies that explained the new Order of Mass of Blessed Paul VI, which was replacing the over 400-year-old Mass of Saint Pius V as the *Missa normativa* or Ordinary Form of the Roman Rite. The liturgical changes were introduced gradually during the first six Sundays of Lent, so that the new Mass texts could be used beginning on March 22.[39]

Anticipated Masses

That same year, Bishop Clinch decreed that beginning on February 28, any parish church in the diocese may schedule up to two Masses between 4pm and 8pm on Saturday or on the vigil of a Holy Day of Obligation, with attendance at one of these Masses fulfilling the obligation. "As reasons for the extension of this privilege, already processed by the Diocese but used only sparingly in mission and resort areas, Bishop Clinch cited the heavy schedules of crowded churches on Sunday, convenience for Sunday workers, more opportunity for those careless in Mass attendance, scarcity of priests, and the lessening of legitimate excuses for missing the great graces of weekly Mass."[40]

The Death of the Last Bishop of Monterey-Fresno

On July 25, 1973, the Most Rev. Aloysius J. Willinger, C.Ss.R., Bishop Emeritus of Monterey-Fresno, died. His funeral Mass was celebrated on Monday, July 30, at Saint John's Cathedral in Fresno. The Most Rev. Joseph T. McGucken, 5th Archbishop of San Francisco, was the principal celebrant, and Bishop Clinch was the homilist.[41] Bishop Willinger was buried at Saint Peter's Cemetery in the Diocese of Fresno. He was a priest for 62 years and a bishop for 43.

The Permanente Diaconate

Three years after Pope Blessed Paul VI had reformed the diaconate in 1967, the first "permanent" deacon in the diocese was ordained by Bishop Clinch at San Carlos Cathedral on June 12, 1970. During his ordination Mass, Deacon Earl J. Currivan distributed Holy Communion to his wife Margaret and was later "assigned to the apostolate of the sick," working "principally in the convalescent hospitals and rest homes of the Monterey Peninsula" (*Monterey Peninsula Herald*, June 11, 1970). Deacon Currivan died four years later died in 1974, at the age of 70.

Photos courtesy of The Observer, *June 17, 1970, vol. 2, no. 11, p. 3 and January 30, 1974, vol. 5, no. 42, p. 1.*

> 39 *The Observer*, February 18, 1970, vol. 1, n. 46, p. 2.
> 40 *Ibid.*, p. 1.
> 41 *Ibid.*, vol. 5, no. 17, August 1, 1973, p. 2.

THE 1980s

After suffering a heart attack in 1969 and a minor stroke in 1978, doctors at Northwestern University Hospital in Chicago told Bishop Clinch "to avoid pressure and stress."[42] He procrastinated for four years until January 19, 1982, when Bishop Clinch resigned as the ordinary of the diocese.

His Holiness, Pope John Paul II, graciously taking into consideration my state of health, has granted my petition to resign as the bishop of Monterey in California and to seek retirement... Though mandatory retirement would ordinarily take place next year at age 75, this decision to anticipate it was not made hurriedly, but after prayerful consideration.

On April 17, 1982, Bishop Clinch commemorated the silver jubilee of his episcopal consecration (ordination), with a Mass celebrated at the parish church of Saint Francis Xavier in Seaside. Timothy Cardinal Manning, 3rd Archbishop of Los Angeles, was the principle celebrant and homilist. Cardinal Manning described Bishop Clinch as having "been a very important part of the weaving of the garment of the Church in California,"[43] and Pope St. John Paul II himself sent a personal testimonial.

"You have been equal to the task". The truth of that statement is clear from your apostolic zeal, the source of the strength you have brought to the faithful discharge of your work in the Diocese of Monterey. Your labors there have been the more difficult inasmuch as in that extensive diocese there are fewer Catholics than non-Catholics. But you initiated there movements you perceived as appropriate for strengthening Gospel values; furthermore you took into account the traditions of your people dedicated to living in inviolate freedom. Finally, there is your personal integrity, manifest to the eyes of all...

POPE ST. JOHN PAUL II
4 February 1982
The Observer, April 14, 1982, vol. 14, no. 2;
cf. *The Sunday Peninsula Herald*, April 18, 1982, p. 4A

> 42 *Monterey Peninsula Herald*, January 20, 1982, p. 23.
> 43 *The Sunday Peninsula Herald*, April 18, 1982, p. 4A.

The Second Bishop of Monterey in California
The Most Rev. Thaddeus A. Shubsda

"I... ask that you continue to pray so that all of us may follow God's words, eternal words, and the Word that He gave to us, and that all of us may pray and be people of prayer."[44]

On May 26, 1982, Pope St. John Paul II appointed the Most Rev. Thaddeus A. Shubsda as the second Bishop of Monterey in California. Bishop Shubsda was solemnly installed on July 1, 1982 at Carmel Mission Basilica. 16 bishops concelebrated, including Timothy Cardinal Manning, 3rd Archbishop of Los Angeles, the Most Rev. John R. Quinn, 6th Archbishop of San Francisco, and the Most Rev. Roger M. Mahoney, 3rd Bishop of Stockton, and the Most Rev. Harry A. Clinch, Bishop Emeritus of Monterey. A total of 440 people were in attendance. In his homily, Cardinal Manning noted "that the installation date was the exact date in 1769 that Junípero Serra first set foot on California soil" some 213 years earlier.[45]

Thaddeus Anthony Shubsda was born in Los Angeles on April 2, 1925. The son of Polish immigrants, "he attended public schools in Los Angeles before entering Los Angeles College Junior Seminary in 1939, and Saint John's Major Seminary in Camarillo in 1944" (*Monterey Peninsula Herald*, June 1, 1982, p. 1).

He was ordained a priest of the Archdiocese of Los Angeles on April 26, 1950 in Saint Vibiana's Cathedral in Los Angeles by the Most Rev. James F.A. McIntyre, 2nd Archbishop of Los Angeles († 1979). He was appointed associate pastor of San Antonio de Padua church in Los Angeles and remained there until 1955, when he was appointed pastor of Saint Vibiana's Cathedral, where he remained until 1964.

In 1952, he was appointed a notary of the Matrimonial Tribunal. In 1964, he was appointed tribunal secretary. In 1970, he was appointed defender of the bond.

He was also the associate director of the Society for the Propagation of the Faith and treasurer of the Los Angeles Senate of Priests and the spiritual director of the Catholic Labor Institute, as well as a member of the board of directors of *The Tidings,* the newspaper of the Archdiocese of Los Angeles.

He was appointed an auxiliary bishop of Los Angeles and Titular Bishop of Tragurium on December 20, 1976 and ordained (consecrated) bishop on February 19, 1977. The principal consecrator was Timothy Cardinal Manning, 3rd Archbishop of Los Angeles († 1989); the principal co-consecrators were Bishop John J. Ward († 2011) and Bishop Juan A. Arzube († 2007), both auxiliary bishop of the archdiocese. The episcopal lineage of Bishop Shubsda includes Pope Clement XIII († 1769), Pope Benedict XIV († 1758), and the Servant of God Pope Benedict XIII († 1730).

> 44 *The Observer,* July 7, 1982, vol. 14, no. 14, p. 17.
> 45 *Ibid.,* p. 1.

Imple Superna Gratia

Your Holiness:

Your visit is historic and unique. How grateful we are that you have accepted the invitation to come to the Monterey Peninsula in order that we may join you in offering the Eucharistic Sacrifice for the greater honor and glory of God and for the salvation of souls.

May your coming among us be a great grace in our lives and may it be an opportunity for us to rededicate ourselves to the living of the Christian life.

Sincerely yours in Christ,

THE MOST REV. THADDEUS A. SHUBSDA, D.D
2nd Bishop of Monterey in California

The Apostolic Visit of Saint John Paul II

In 1987, Pope St. John Paul II made his 36th apostolic journey or pastoral visit outside Italy from September 10-21. During his fourth visit to the United States, "the Pilgrim Pope" visited the cities of Miami in Florida, Columbia in South Carolina, New Orleans in Louisiana, San Antonio in Texas, Phoenix in Arizona, Detroit in Michigan, and San Francisco, Los Angeles, Monterey, and Carmel-by-the-Sea in California.

St. John Paul II arrived at the Monterey Peninsula Airport from Los Angeles at 9:30am on Thursday, September 17. He was officially welcomed by Bishop Shubsda, who accompanied the Holy Father during his entire visit. St. John Paul also greeted 16 representatives of federal, state, and municipal governments, including "Clint Eastwood, who was the mayor of Carmel at the time."[46] St. John Paul II then boarded the *Marine Corps One* helicopter that took him to Laguna Seca Raceway, where the faithful had been gathering since 2am.

Laguna Seca Regional Park was covered in very heavy fog, causing the faithful to fear that they would not be able to see St. John Paul II celebrate Mass. Moments before Mass began, just as St. John Paul II was vesting in a motorhome that served as a makeshift sacristy, the fog lifted. "Miraculously, many believed."[47] [**Nota bene:** Bishop Ryan would later relay this story during his first meeting with Pope St. John Paul II in 1992. The Holy Father responded: "Some miracle!"]

Pope St. John Paul II prepares to incense the altar.

Photo courtesy of the diocesan archives.

> 46 *The Monterey County Herald,* 3 April 2005.
> 47 *Ibid.,* 5 April 2005, p. A10.

Presentation of the Gifts
Photo courtesy of the diocesan archives.

**The faithful preparing to receive
Holy Communion from Pope St. John Paul II.**
Photo courtesy of the diocesan archives.

Pope St. John Paul II greats "the multitude."
Photo courtesy of the diocesan archives.

Pope St. John Paul II arrives.
Photo courtesy of the diocesan archives.

Pope St. John Paul II, with Msgr. Piero Marini, Master of
Pontifical Liturgical Celebrations from 1987 to 2007.

Photo courtesy of the diocesan archives.

Pope St. John Paul II in prayer next to
the official logo for the papal visit, based
on the window of Carmel Mission Basilica.

Photo courtesy of the diocesan archives.

Homily of Saint John Paul II

Mass for the Rural Workers at Laguna Seca in Monterey
Thursday, 17 September 1987

"Be careful not to forget the Lord, your God" (*Deuteronomy* 8:11).

Dear Brothers and Sisters of the Monterey Peninsula,
Brothers and Sisters of California and other areas of the United States,

1. Originally these words were addressed by Moses to the Israelite people as they were on the point of entering the promised land—a land with streams of water, with springs and fountains welling up in the hills and valleys, a land producing an abundance of every fruit and food, a land where the people would lack nothing (cfr. *ibid.* 8:7-9). Today these words are addressed to the People of God here in Monterey, in the State of California, against the background of an extraordinary beauty of land and sea, of snow-capped mountains and deep lakes, oak groves and forests of fir and pine and mighty redwoods, a land among the richest and most fruitful of the earth. Yes, today, these words are addressed to all of us gathered here: "*Be careful not to forget the Lord, your God.*"

2. These words, pronounced thousands of years ago, have still today a special meaning and relevance. Moses, the great teacher of his people, was concerned that in their future prosperity they might abandon God—the God who brought them out of the land of slavery and guided them through the desert with its parched ground, feeding them with manna along the way (cfr. *Deuteronomy* 8:15-16). Moses knew the tendency of the human heart to cry out to the Lord in time of need, but easily "to neglect His commandments and decrees and statutes" (cfr. *ibid.* 8:11) in the time of well-being and prosperity. He knew that *God is easily forgotten.*

   In our own day are we not perhaps witnesses of the fact that often in rich societies where there is an abundance of material well-being, permissiveness and moral relativism find easy acceptance? And where the moral order is undermined, God is forgotten and questions of ultimate responsibility are set aside. *In such situations a practical atheism pervades private and public living.*

From the moment of *original sin*, man has been inclined to see himself in the place of God. He often thinks, just as Moses warned he might: "It is my own power and the strength of my own hand that has obtained for me this wealth" (*ibid.* 8:17). He acts as if the one who is the source of all life and goodness were just not there. He ignores a fundamental truth about himself: *the fact that he is a creature,* that he has been created and owes everything to his Creator, who is also his Redeemer.

In these closing years of the twentieth century, on the eve of the third millennium of the Christian era, a part of the human family—the most economically and technically developed part—is being specially tempted, perhaps as never before, to imitate the ancient model of all sin—the original rebellion that expressed itself saying: "I will not serve." *The temptation today is to try to build a world for oneself,* forgetting the Creator and his design and. But sooner or later we must come to grips with this: that *to forget God, to feign the death of God, is to promote the death of man* and of all civilization. It is to threaten the existence of individuals, communities and all society.

3. Today's readings from the New Testament are in contrast to such a position. They speak of *God's presence which permeates the human heart and the whole of created reality.* Jesus teaches that the Reign of God is like the growth of the seed that a man scatters on the ground (cfr. *Mark* 4:26-29). Certainly, human activity is essential. Man "goes to bed and gets up every day…" He plants. And "when the crop is ready he wields the sickle." Even the rich valleys of California would produce nothing without human ingenuity and toil. But the word of God says that "*the soil produces of itself* first the blade, then the ear, finally the ripe wheat in the ear" (*ibid.* 4:28). As if to say: the growth of the wheat and its maturing, which greatly depends on the fertility of the soil, comes from the nature and vitality of creation itself. Consequently there is *another source of growth*: the one who is *above nature and above the man who cultivates the earth.*

In a sense, the Creator "*hides Himself*" in this life-giving process of nature. It is the human person, with the help of intellect and faith, who is called to "discover" and "unveil" the presence of God and His action in all of creation: "*So may Your way be known upon earth; among all nations, Your salvation*" (*Ps.* 67 [66]:3).

If the parable of the seed indicates the growth of the Kingdom of God *in the world*, the words of Saint Paul in the second reading speak of how God's generous giving aims at drawing "good works" *from the human heart*: "God can multiply His favours among you… for good works." The whole of human activity must be finalized in works of justice, peace and love. All human work—including, in a very direct way, the noble work of agriculture in which many of you are engaged—is to be carried out at the service of man and for the glory of God.

4. *The land is God's gift.* From the beginning, God has entrusted it to the whole human race as a means of sustaining the life of all those whom He creates in His own image and likeness. We must use the land to sustain every human being in life and dignity. Against the background of the immense beauty of this region and the fertility of its soil, let us proclaim together our gratitude for this gift, with the words of the responsorial psalm: "*The earth has yielded its fruit, the Lord our God has blessed us*" [*Ps.* 67 [66]:7].

As we read in Genesis, human beings earn their bread by the sweat of their brows (*Gen.* 3:17). We toil long hours and grow weary at our tasks. Yet *work is good for us*. "Through work man not only transforms nature, adapting it to his own needs, but he also achieves fulfilment as a human being and indeed in a sense becomes 'more a human being'" (Ioannis Pauli PP. II, *Laborem Exercens*, 9).

The value of work does not end with *the individual*. The full meaning of work can only be understood in relation to *the family* and *society* as well. Work supports and gives stability to the family. Within the family, moreover, children first learn the human and positive meaning of work and responsibility In each community and in the nation as a whole, work has a fundamental social meaning. It can, moreover, either join people in the solidarity of a shared commitment, or set them at odds through exaggerated competition, exploitation and social conflict. *Work is a key to the whole social question*, when that "question" is understood to be concerned with *making life more human* (cfr. *ibid.* 3).

5. Agricultural work exemplifies all these principles—the potential of work for the fulfilment of the human person, the "family" dimension of work, and social solidarity. *Agricultural work is*—as Pope John XXIII described it—*a vocation, a God-given mission, a noble task and a contribution to civilization* [cfr. John XXIII, *Mater et Magistra*, 149). God has blessed the United States with some of the richest *farm land* in the world. The productivity of American agriculture is a major success story. Clearly, it is a history of hard and wearying work, of courage and enterprise, and it involves the interaction of many people: growers, workers, processors, distributors and finally consumers.

I know too that recently thousands of *American farmers* have been introduced to poverty and indebtedness. Many have lost their homes and their way of life. Your bishops and the whole Church in your country are deeply concerned; and they are listening to the voices of so many farmers and farmworkers as they express their anxieties over the costs and the risks of farming, the difficult working conditions, the need for a just wage and decent housing and the question of a fair price for products. On an even wider scale is heard *the voice of the poor*, who are bewildered in a land of plenty and still experience the pangs of hunger.

6. All agree that the situation of the farming community in the United States and in other parts of the world is highly complex, and that simple remedies are not at hand. The Church, on her part, while she can offer no specific technical solutions, does present a social teaching based on the primacy of the human person in every economic and social activity. At every level of the agricultural process, *the dignity, rights and well-being of people must be the central issue*. No one person in this process—grower, worker, packer, shipper, retailer or consumer—is greater than the other in the eyes of God.

Giving voice therefore to the sufferings of many, I appeal to all involved to work together to find appropriate solutions to all farm questions. This can only be done in a community marked by a sincere and effective *solidarity*—and, where still necessary, *reconciliation*—among all parties to the agricultural productive process.

And what of our responsibility to futures generations? The earth will not continue to offer its harvest, except with *faithful stewardship*. We cannot say we love the land and then take steps to destroy it for use by future generations. I urge you to

43

be sensitive to the many issues affecting the land and the whole environment and to unite with each other to seek the best solutions to these pressing problems.

7. *Each one of us is called to fulfil his or her respective duties before God and before society.* Since the Church is constrained by her very nature to focus her attention most strongly on those least able to defend their own legitimate interests, I appeal to landowners, growers and others in positions of power to respect the just claims of their brothers and sisters who work the land. These claims include the right to share in decisions concerning their services and the right to free association with a view to social, cultural and economic advancement [Ioannis Pauli PP. II, *Laborem Exercens,* 21]. I also appeal to all workers to be mindful of their own obligations of justice and to make every effort to fulfil a worthy service to mankind.

New legislation in your country has made it possible for many people, especially migrant farmworkers, *to become citizens* rather than remain strangers among you. Many of these people have worked here with the same dream that your ancestors had when they first came. I ask you to welcome these new citizens into your society and to respect the human dignity of every man, woman and child.

Two hundred years after the Constitution confirmed the United States as a land of opportunity and freedom, it is right to hope that there may be a general and renewed *commitment to those policies needed to ensure that within these borders equity and justice will be preserved and fostered.* This is an ever present requirement of America's historical destiny.

It is also important for America at this time *to look beyond herself* and all her own needs *to see the even greater needs of the poorer nations of the world.* Even as local communities mobilize to work ever more effectively for the integral human advancement of their own members, they must not forget their brothers and sisters elsewhere. We must be careful not to forget the Lord, but we must be careful also not to forget those whom He loves.

8. The hidden attributes of the Creator are reflected in the beauty of his creation. The beauty of the Monterey Peninsula attracts a great number of visitors; as a result so many of you are involved in *the tourist industry.* I greet you and encourage you to see your specific work as a form of service and of solidarity with your fellow human beings.

Work—as we have seen—is an essential aspect of our human existence, but so also is the necessary rest and recreation which permits us to recover our energies and strengthen our spirit for the tasks of life. Many worthwhile values are involved in tourism: relaxation, the widening of one's culture and the possibility of using leisure time for spiritual pursuits. These include prayer and contemplation, and pilgrimages, which have always been a part of our Catholic heritage; they also include fostering human relationships within the family and among friends. Like other human activities, tourism con be a source of good or evil, a place of grace or sin. I invite all of you who are involved in tourism *to uphold the dignity of your work* and to be always willing *to bear joyful witness to your Christian faith.*

9. Dear brothers and sisters: it is *in the Eucharist* that the fruits of our work—and all that is noble in human affairs—become an offering of the greatest value in union with the Sacrifice of Jesus Christ, our Lord and Saviour. In fostering what is authentically human through our work and through deeds of justice and love, we set upon the altar of the Lord those elements which will be transformed into Christ: "Blessed are You Lord, God, of all creation. Through Your goodness we have this bread to offer, which earth has given and human hands have made. *It will become for us the bread of life.*"

I ask you to join with me *in praising the Most Holy Trinity* for the abundance of life and goodness with which you have been gifted: "The earth has yielded its fruit. God, our God, has blessed us" [*Ps.* 67 [66]:7]. But may your abundance never lead you to forget the Lord or cease to acknowledge him as the source of your peace and well-being. Your prayer for yourselves and for all your brothers and sisters must always be an echo of the psalm: "May God have pity on us and bless us; may He let His face shine on us" [*ibid.* 2].

For years to come may the Lord's face shine on this land, on the Church in Monterey, and on all America: "From sea to shining sea." Amen.

St. John Paul II personally distributed Holy Communion to 100 communicants that were seated near the foot of the cross while 500 clergy and extraordinary ministers of Holy Communion distributed to the 70,000 faithful present for the Mass. Music for the Mass was provided by a 500-voice choir, composed of parishioners from throughout the diocese, and the diocesan orchestra. After the Mass, St. John Paul II took the "pope-mobile" to the waiting helicopter and departed for Carmel Mission Basilica.

The *Marine Corps One* helicopter landed in the baseball field at Junípero Serra School below Carmel Mission Basilica at 1pm. St. John Paul II boarded an armored sedan that took him up to the entrance of the basilica, escorted by a Secret Service motorcade. As St. John Paul II entered the basilica, Mr. Ed Soberanes, the parish organist, played James Ployhar's *March Triumphant*. After praying before the grave of St. Junípero Serra, St. John Paul II delivered his address from the side of the altar to the over 400 faithful gathered inside. The 3,000 persons who held tickets for the papal visit to the basilica had begun gathering at 9am.

Pope St. John Paul II enters Carmel Mission Basilica.
Photo courtesy of the diocesan archives.

Pope St. John Paul II greets sisters from the local Carmelite Monastery.
Photo courtesy of the diocesan archives.

Pope St. John Paul II arrives at Carmel Mission Basilica.
Photo courtesy of the diocesan archives.

45

The History of the Diocese

Pope St. John Paul II greets members of other faith communities.

Photo courtesy of the diocesan archives.

Pope St. John Paul II prays before the image of Our Lady of Bethlehem, Patroness of the Diocese of Monterey in California.

Photo courtesy of the diocesan archives.

Pope St. John Paul II prays before the Blessed Sacrament and the grave of St. Junípero Serra, with Bishop Shubsda.

Photo courtesy of the diocesan archives.

Pope St. John Paul II lays
a wreath at the grave
of St. Junípero Serra.

*Photo courtesy
of the diocesan archives.*

Pope St. John Paul II addresses the faithful gathered in the large courtyard of Carmel Mission Basilica.

Photo courtesy of the diocesan archives.

48

Pope St. John Paul II exits the Chapel of Our Lady of Bethlehem, accompanied by Bishop Shubsda. Also pictured is the Holy Father's personal secretary, the Rev. Stanisław Dziwisz, who served the saintly pontiff for almost 40 years. Pope Benedict XVI would appoint him Archbishop of Kraków in 2005 and a cardinal in 2006.

Photo courtesy of the diocesan archives.

Pope St. John Paull II greeting members of the U.S. Armed Forces.

Photo courtesy of the diocesan archives.

Pope St. John Paul II greets the sick.
Photo courtesy of the diocesan archives.

Pope St. John Paul II proceeds to the rectory, accompanied by Bishop Shubsda.
Photo courtesy of the diocesan archives.

Pope St. John Paul II addresses the faithful gathered in the large courtyard of Carmel Mission Basilica.
Photo courtesy of the diocesan archives.

Address of Saint John Paul II

To the faithful gathered in the Basilica of the Mission of San Carlos in Carmel
Thursday, 17 September 1987

Dear Bishop Shubsda,
Dear Brothers and Sisters,

1. I come today as a pilgrim to this Mission of San Carlos, which so powerfully evokes the heroic spirit and heroic deeds of Fray Junípero Serra and which enshrines his mortal remains. This serene and beautiful place is truly *the historical and spiritual heart of California*. All the missions of *El Camino Real* bear witness to the challenges and heroism of an earlier time, but not a time forgotten or without significance for the California of today and the Church of today.

These buildings and the men who gave them life, especially their spiritual father, Junípero Serra, are reminders of an age of discovery and exploration. The missions are the result of a conscious moral decision made by people of faith in a situation that presented many human possibilities, both good and bad, with respect to the future of this land and its native peoples. It was a decision rooted in a love of God and neighbour. It was *a decision to proclaim the Gospel* of Jesus Christ at the dawn of a new age, which was extremely important for both the European settlers and the Native Americans.

2. Very often, at crucial moments in human affairs, God raises up men and women whom He thrusts into roles of decisive importance for the future development of both society and the Church. Although their story unfolds within the ordinary circumstances of daily life, they become larger than life within the perspective of history. We rejoice all the more when their achievement is coupled with a holiness of life that can truly be called heroic. So it is with Junípero Serra, who in the providence of God was destined to be *the Apostle of California*, and to have a permanent influence over the spiritual patrimony of this land and its people, whatever their religion might be. This apostolic awareness is captured in the words ascribed to him: "In California is my life and there, God willing, I hope to die." Through Christ's Paschal Mystery, that death has become a seed in the soil of this state

that continues to bear fruit "thirty—or sixty—or a hundred-fold" (*Matthew* 13:9).

Father Serra was a man *convinced of the Church's mission*, conferred upon her by Christ himself, to evangelize the world, to "make disciples of all the nations, baptizing them in the name of the Father and of the Son and of the Holy Spirit" (*ibid.* 28:19). The way in which he fulfilled that mission corresponds faithfully to the Church's vision today of what evangelization means: "...the Church evangelizes when she seeks to convert, solely through the divine power of the message she proclaims, both the personal and collective consciences of people, the activities in which they engage, and the lives and concrete milieu which are theirs" (PAUL VI, *Evangelii Nuntiandi*, n. 18).

He not only brought the Gospel to the Native Americans, but as one who lived the Gospel he also became their *defender and champion*. At the age of sixty he journeyed from Carmel to Mexico City to intervene with the Viceroy on their behalf—a journey which twice brought him close to death—and presented his now famous *Representación* with its "bill of rights," which had as their aim the betterment of every phase of missionary activity in California, particularly the spiritual and physical well-being of its Native Americans.

3. Father Serra and his fellow missionaries shared the conviction found everywhere in the New Testament that the Gospel is a matter of life and salvation. They believed that in offering to people Jesus Christ, they were doing *something of immense value*, importance and dignity. What other explanation can there be for the hardships that they freely and gladly endured, like Saint Paul and all the other great missionaries before them: difficult and dangerous travel, illness and isolation, an ascetical life-style, arduous labour, and also, like Saint Paul, that "concern for all the churches" (*2 Corinthians* 11:28) which Junípero Serra, in particular, experienced as *Presidente* of the California missions in the face of every vicissitude, disappointment and opposition.

Dear brothers and sisters: like Father Serra and his Franciscan brethren, we too are *called to be evangelizers*, to share actively in the Church's mission of making disciples of all people. The way in which we fulfil that mission will be different from theirs. But their lives speak to us still because of their sure faith that the Gospel is true, and because of their passionate belief in the value of bringing that saving truth to others at great personal cost. Much to be envied are those who can give their lives for something greater than themselves in loving service to others. This, more than words or deeds alone, is what draws people to Christ.

This *single-mindedness* is not reserved for great missionaries in exotic places. It must be at the heart of each priest's ministry and the evangelical witness of every religious. It is the key to their personal sense of well-being, happiness and fulfilment in what they are and what they do. This single-mindedness is also essential to the Christian witness of the Catholic laity. The covenant of love between two people in marriage and the successful sharing of faith with children require the effort of a lifetime. If couples cease believing in their marriage as a sacrament before God, or treat religion as anything less than a matter of salvation, then the Christian witness they might have given to the world is lost. Those who are unmarried must also be steadfast in fulfilling their duties in life if they are to bring Christ to the world in which they live.

"In Him who is the source of my strength I have strength for everything" (*Philippians* 4:13). These words of the great missionary, Saint Paul, remind us that *our strength is not our own*. Even in the martyrs and saints, as the liturgy reminds us, it is "(God's) power shining through our human weakness" (*Praefatio Martyrum*). It is the strength that inspired Father Serra's motto: "always forward, never back." It is the strength that one senses in this place of prayer so filled with his presence. It is the strength that can make each one of us, dear brothers and sisters, missionaries of Jesus Christ, witnesses of His message, doers of His word.

The parish organist played Samuel J. Stone's *The Church's One Foundation* as St. John Paul II proceeded to the Chapel of Our Lady of Bethlehem, where he prayed before the image of *La Conquistadora*. He then went out into the courtyard and delivered another address from a raised platform, around which were seated 30 handicapped individuals. St. John Paul II personally greeted each one before he had lunch in the rectory with Bishop Shubsda and a small party of 14 clergy, after which he took a brief siesta before departing at 4pm aboard the *Marine Corps One* helicopter for San Francisco.

Saint John Paul II presented a chalice and paten bearing his coat of arms to San Carlos Cathedral. The cathedral also received the chair that was used by St. John Paul II, while the parish of Saint Francis Xavier in Seaside received the altar and ambo that were constructed especially for the papal Mass.

With happy memories of my pastoral visit to your diocese I wish to express my deep gratitude to you and your people for the warm reception and many kindnesses extended to me. May the faith that united us in the celebration of the Eucharist continue to inspire the Church in Monterey in the service of Christ and His Gospel. With affection in the Lord I cordially impart my apostolic blessing.

POPE ST. JOHN PAUL II

The Beatification
of Fray Junípero Serra

On September 25, 1988, in Saint Peter's Square, Pope St. John Paul II beatified Fray Junípero Serra Ferrer, OFM, along with five other Servants of God. In his homily, St. John Paul II said:

In *Fray Juniper Serra,* a priest of the Order of Friars Minor, we find a shining example of Christian virtue and the missionary spirit. His great goal was *to bring the Gospel to the Native Peoples of America,* so that they too might be "consecrated in the truth." For many years he devoted himself to this task in Mexico, in the Sierra Gorda, and in California. He sowed the seeds of Christian faith amid the momentous changes wrought by the arrival of European settlers in the New World. It was a field of missionary endeavor that required patience, perseverance and humility, as well as vision and courage. Relying on the divine power of the message he proclaimed, Father Serra led the Native Peoples to Christ. He was well aware of their heroic virtues—as exemplified in the life of Blessed Kateri Tekakwitha—and he sought to further their authentic *human development* on the basis of their *new-found faith as persons* created and redeemed by God. He also had to admonish the powerful, in the spirit of our second reading from James, not to abuse and exploit the poor and the weak. In fulfilling this ministry, Father Serra showed himself to be a true son of Saint Francis. Today, his example inspires in a particular way the many Serra Clubs throughout the world, the members of which do so much praiseworthy work in fostering vocations.[48]

The Loma Prieta Earthquake

On October 17, 1989, the Loma Prieta earthquake occurred in northern California at 5:04pm. The 6.9 quake was responsible for 63 deaths and 3,757 injuries in the affected areas. Several parish churches in the diocese were damaged, including Christ Child in Los Gatos, Holy Cross and Our Lady, Star of the Sea, both in Santa Cruz, Holy Eucharist in Corralitos, Our Lady, Help of Christians (Valley Church) in Watsonville, Saint John in Felton, Saint Michael in Boulder Creek, Saint Patrick in Watsonville and Sacred Heart in Hollister. The parish hall of Saint Michael in Boulder Creek was used as a temporary shelter for earthquake victims.

The official portrait for the 1988 beatification of St. Junípero Serra was painted by Lorenzo Ghiglieri. It "portrays a young Junípero Serra at the turning point of his life at thirty-five years of age, as he is embarking upon his Missionary career... the background is a nostalgic potpourri of California. In the right hand corner at Serra's feet he has painted a rose of Castile, which so moved Serra when he first entered California on July 1, 1769. The cross Serra is wearing is the reliquary type, popular on the island of Mallorca, Spain, of his day, and with which he was buried."

A replica of this painting hung over the portico of Saint Peter's Basilica for the Mass of Beatification. The original painting is in Mission Santa Barbara in the Archdiocese of Los Angeles.

> 48 SAINT JOHN PAUL II, *Homily,* 25 September 1988, n. 5: *Acta Apostolicae Sedis,* vol. 81 (1989), pp. 165-166; Copyright 1988, *Libreria Editrice Vaticana.*

Diocesan Priest becomes Bishop

On December 27, 1988, the Rev. Msgr. Tod D. Brown was appointed the seventh Bishop of Boise (Idaho) by Pope St. John Paul II. Born in San Francisco on November 15, 1936, Bishop Brown had been ordained a priest of the Diocese of Monterey-Fresno on May 1, 1963 after studying at Ryan College in Fresno, St John's College in Camarillo, and the North American College in Rome.

From 1977 until 1982, Bishop Brown had been the sixth pastor of Saint Francis Xavier in Seaside until he was appointed 3rd chancellor in 1982. He also served as the vicar for clergy (1981-1983) and vicar general (1983-1988), as well as chairman of the Divine Worship Commission, chairman and member of the Presbyterial Council and Priests Pension Committee, and member of the Diocesan Board of Education. He was ordained bishop on April 3, 1989. The principal consecrator was the Most Rev. William J. Levada, 4th Archbishop of Portland in Oregon. The co-consecrators were the Most Rev. Sylvester W. Treinen, Bishop Emeritus of Boise, and the Most Rev. Thaddeus A. Shubsda, 2nd Bishop of Monterey. On June 30, 1998 he was appointed 3rd Bishop of Orange in California. He resigned on September 21, 2012.

THE 1990S

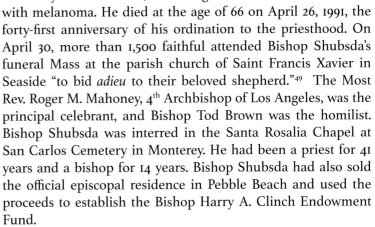

SEDE VACANTE: THE SEE OF MONTEREY IS VACANT

In September of 1990, the Most Rev. Thaddeus A. Shubsda, 2nd Bishop of Monterey in California, was diagnosed with melanoma. He died at the age of 66 on April 26, 1991, the forty-first anniversary of his ordination to the priesthood. On April 30, more than 1,500 faithful attended Bishop Shubsda's funeral Mass at the parish church of Saint Francis Xavier in Seaside "to bid *adieu* to their beloved shepherd."[49] The Most Rev. Roger M. Mahoney, 4th Archbishop of Los Angeles, was the principal celebrant, and Bishop Tod Brown was the homilist. Bishop Shubsda was interred in the Santa Rosalia Chapel at San Carlos Cemetery in Monterey. He had been a priest for 41 years and a bishop for 14 years. Bishop Shubsda had also sold the official episcopal residence in Pebble Beach and used the proceeds to establish the Bishop Harry A. Clinch Endowment Fund.

With the death of Bishop Shubsda, the Episcopal See of Monterey in California became vacant. In accordance with the *Code of Canon Law* (Latin: *Codex Iuris Canonici*), the diocesan board of consultors, which consisted of eleven diocesan priests, gathered at the rectory of San Carlos Cathedral within the designated time required to elect a temporary administrator for the diocese. The Rev. Charles G. Fatooh, who had been the moderator of the curia and chancellor for the diocese since April of 1989, was elected as the diocesan administrator, "to oversee the work of the diocese during the waiting period for a new bishop."[50] In this capacity, Fr. Fatooh performed all of the ministerial duties that are normally performed by a bishop, including confirmations, pastoral visitations, and public appearances at religious functions.

> 49 *The Observer*, May 9, 1991, vol. 23, no. 8.
> 50 *Ibid.*, p. 3.

The Third Bishop of Monterey in California
His Excellency the Most Rev. Sylvester D. Ryan

"I have no agenda except the Gospel of Jesus Christ."[51]

The *sede vacante* came to an end on January 28, 1992, when Pope St. John Paul II appointed the Most Rev. Sylvester D. Ryan as the third bishop of Monterey in California. Solemn Vespers was celebrated at Carmel Mission Basilica on March 18, with the installation Mass taking place the following day at the parish church of Saint Francis Xavier in Seaside. About 1,200 faithful were in attendance, as well as His Eminence Roger Cardinal Mahoney, 4th Archbishop of Los Angeles, the Most Rev. John R. Quinn, 6th Archbishop of San Francisco, and the Bishop Emeritus of Monterey, Harry A. Clinch.

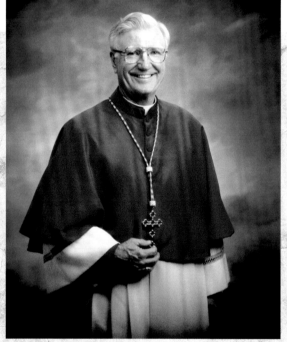

Sylvester Donovan Ryan was born and raised in the City of Avalon on Santa Catalina Island on September 3, 1930. He entered St. John's Seminary College after graduating from Long Beach City College in 1949. He was ordained a priest of the Archdiocese of Los Angeles on May 3, 1957 by James F.A. Cardinal McIntyre, 2nd Archbishop of Los Angeles († 1979).

He served as an assistant pastor at two parishes in Los Angeles and Long Beach, as a pastor at a parish in Tujunga, as director of Paraclete High School in Lancaster, as principal of Saint Paul High School in Santa Fe Springs and as Chaplain at Mount St. Mary's College in Los Angeles.

He obtained a bachelor's degree in philosophy from St. John's Seminary, a master's degree in religious education from Immaculate Heart College in Los Angeles, and attended the University of Southern California for his doctoral studies. He taught in the University of San Francisco's master's program in Catholic School Administration in Los Angeles and been on the boards of Catholic Charities in Los Angeles and Notre Dame High School in Sherman Oaks. He served as the rector and president of St. John's Seminary College in Camarillo from 1986 to 1990.

He was appointed Auxiliary Bishop of Los Angeles in California and Titular Bishop of Remesiana on February 17, 1990 and ordained (consecrated) bishop on May 31, 1990. The principal consecrator was the Most Rev. Roger M. Mahony, 4th Archbishop of Los Angeles; the principal co-consecrators were Bishop John J. Ward († 2011) and Bishop George P. Ziemann († 2009), both auxiliary bishops of the archdiocese. Like Bishop Clinch, the episcopal lineage of Bishop Ryan includes the Rt. Rev. John Carroll, SJ († 1815), the first Archbishop of Baltimore and cousin of Charles Carroll († 1832), who was the only Catholic to sign the Declaration of Independence.

> 50 *The Monterey County Herald,* January 29, 1992.

Bishop Ryan's Pastoral Letters

In June of 1995, the Most Rev. Sylvester D. Ryan, 3rd Bishop of Monterey in California, issued his first pastoral letter, *The Eucharist: The Church's Sacred Banquet.*

> The paschal meal in which the institution of the Eucharist took place, marked the Eucharist forever as a sign and sacrament of the death of the Lord until He comes. The Eucharist is a sacrifice, the sacrifice of the cross as well as the triumph of the resurrection, renewed for us through the offering of the Body and Blood of Christ under the appearance of bread and wine.[52]

In February of 1999, Bishop Ryan issued his second pastoral letter, this time on the Sacrament of Reconciliation, *Celebrating the Richness of God's Mercy.*

> The Church especially invites us to the sacrament in those times and occasions in our life, when burdened by sin, we need to feel the merciful love of God the Father, Son and Holy Spirit. We are all aware that the practice and frequency of the sacrament has dropped off in the past several years. We need to appropriate once again in our Catholic life this sacrament of healing, forgiveness, and conversion—the very gifts of God's grace that comprise the heart of the Gospel and the Church's mission. [53]

> 52 THE MOST REV. SYLVESTER D. RYAN, 3rd Bishop of Monterey in California, *Pastoral Letter on the Eucharist: The Church's Sacred Banquet,* Corpus Christi Sunday, June 18, 1995.
> 53 IBID., *Pastoral Letter on the Sacrament of Reconciliation: Celebrating the Richness of God's Mercy,* February 1999.

Ad limina 1998

The Most Rev. Sylvester D. Ryan, 3rd Bishop of Monterey in California, made his ad limina visit to Pope St. John Paul II in the fall of 1998. On September 29, the Holy Father "spoke directly with each bishop, and when he spoke the name, Diocese of Monterey, his face lit up. He said, 'I remember being in Monterey,' and did so with evident delight. As usual, he also recalled the name of Bishop Shubsda whom he remembers with real warmth." On October 2, the bishops concelebrated Mass with St. John Paul II in his private chapel on October 2 (*The Observer,* November 1998, vol. 30, no. 10, pp. 1-2).

THE 2000S

The Great Jubilee

Pope St. John Paul II opened the Great Jubilee on December 25, 1999, the solemnity of the Nativity of the Lord (Christmas), in Saint Peter's Basilica in Rome. He closed the Great Jubilee on January 6, 2001, the solemnity of the Epiphany of the Lord. Throughout the history of the Church, jubilee years have been celebrations of the mercy of God and the forgiveness of sins.

The Diocese of Monterey in California observed the Great Jubilee with various events including special jubilee days for various ministries, prayer gatherings, and musical concerts, including the veneration of the relics of Saint Thérèse of Lisieux on January 11 at Saint Francis Xavier in Seaside, Carmel Mission Basilica, and the Carmelite Monastery, where Bishop Ryan celebrated Mass on January 12.

The official logo of the Great Jubilee of 2000 featured its Latin motto: *Christus heri, hodie, semper* (Christ Yesterday, Today, Forever), which was taken from the Letter to the Hebrews: "Jesus Christ is the same yesterday and today and forever [*Iesus Christus heri et hodie idem, et in sæcula*] (13:8).

The diocese also took part in RENEW 2000, "is a thorough spiritual renewal and evangelization process designed for parish life in the 21st century". The RENEW program incorporated themes suggested by Pope St. John Paul II for pastoral life in the new millennium and implemented his call for a "New Evangelization".

"Festival 2000" was the Diocese of Monterey's "major celebration of the Great Jubilee Year 2000." "Festival 2000" was held at Cal Poly's Performing Arts Center in San Luis Obispo on the afternoon May 21 and at Sherwood Hall in Salinas on the evening of May 22. Bishop Ryan led the faithful in the "Jubilee Pledge for Charity, Justice, and Peace." The pledge contained aspects of the themes of the Great Jubilee and Christian evangelization. The "Festival 2000" celebration included story-telling, music, and dance.[54]

Jubilee Pledge for Charity, Justice, and Peace

As disciples of Jesus in the new millennium, I (we) pledge to:

- PRAY regularly for justice and peace.
- LEARN more about Catholic Social Teaching and its call to protect human life, stand with the poor, and care for creation.
- REACH across boundaries of religion, race, ethnicity, gender, and disabling conditions.
- LIVE justly in family life, school, work, the marketplace, and political arena.
- SERVE those who are poor and vulnerable, sharing more time and talent.
- GIVE more generously to those in need at home and abroad.
- ADVOCATE for public policies that protect human life, promote human dignity, preserve God's creation, and build peace.
- ENCOURAGE others to work for greater charity, justice, and peace.

"A Dark Shadow
on the Priesthood in Our Time" [55]

In early 2002, *The Boston Globe* covered the criminal prosecutions of five priests that had sexually abused children, setting off a national scandal as other victims began to come forward with allegations of abuse, revealing a pattern of cover-ups. In April 2002, Saint John Paul II summoned all of the American cardinals to Rome, telling them adamantly that "there is no place in the priesthood or religious life for those who would harm the young" (April 23, 2002). The meeting's participants drew up a final statement, calling for a set of national standards for dealing with sexual abuse of minors by priests and new procedures for dismissing from the clerical state those found guilty of such crimes. "Well before the Boston incidents garnered media attention, the Diocese of Monterey had complied with state mandated finger printing for those who work with children." [56]

On June 14, 2002, the United States Conference of Catholic Bishops (USCCB) promulgated the *Charter for the Protection of Children and Young People,* which was later amended in November of the same year. In compliance with the USCCB's national charter, the Diocese of Monterey revised its *Criminal Background Check Policy* for both volunteers and employees (October 22, 2003), followed by the *Safe Environment Program* (May 6, 2008) and the *Policy Against Sexual Misconduct* (May 16, 2012).

To the Victims of Abuse and their Families...

You have suffered grievously and I am truly sorry. I know that nothing can undo the wrong you have endured. Your trust has been betrayed and your dignity has been violated. Many of you found that, when you were courageous enough to speak of what happened to you, no one would listen...

It is understandable that you find it hard to forgive or be reconciled with the Church. In her name, I openly express the shame and remorse that we all feel. At the same time, I ask you not to lose hope. It is in the communion of the Church that we encounter the person of Jesus Christ, who was Himself a victim of injustice and sin. Like you, He still bears the wounds of His own unjust suffering. He understands the depths of your pain and its enduring effect upon your lives and your relationships, including your relationship with the Church. I know some of you find it difficult even to enter the doors of a church after all that has occurred. Yet Christ's own wounds, transformed by His redemptive sufferings, are the very means by which the power of evil is broken and we are reborn to life and hope. I believe deeply in the healing power of His self-sacrificing love—even in the darkest and most hopeless situations—to bring liberation and the promise of a new beginning.

Speaking to you as a pastor concerned for the good of all God's children, I humbly ask you to consider what I have said. I pray that, by drawing nearer to Christ and by participating in the life of His Church—a Church purified by penance and renewed in pastoral charity—you will come to rediscover Christ's infinite love for each one of you. I am confident that in this way you will be able to find reconciliation, deep inner healing, and peace.

POPE BENEDICT XVI
Pastoral Letter to the Catholics of Ireland
(19 March 2010), n. 6

> 55 THE MOST REV. SYLVESTER D. RYAN, 3rd Bishop of Monterey in California: *The Observer,* March 2002, vol. 34, no. 3, p. 2.
> 56 *The Observer,* May 2002, vol. 34, no. 5, p. 1.

The Death of the First Bishop of Monterey in California

On March 8, 2003, the Most Rev. Harry A. Clinch, the first Bishop of Monterey in California, died at the age of 94. The bishop emeritus had been residing at a retirement community in Santa Cruz. Bishop Clinch ordained 22 priests and established five new parishes (Resurrection in Aptos, Holy Eucharist in Corralitos, Saint Joseph in Nipomo, San Agustin in Scotts Valley, and Saint Joseph in Spreckels). He was a priest for over 66 years and a bishop for 46 years. At the time of his death, Bishop Clinch was believed to be the oldest Catholic bishop in the country and the last surviving participant of the Second Vatican Council in the United States.

The funeral rites were celebrated at Carmel Mission Basilica, beginning with the recitation of the rosary on the afternoon of March 13, followed by a vigil later that evening. The following day, Bishop Clinch's solemn funeral Mass was attended by "some 500 people, including scores of priests from around the state."[57] Roger Cardinal Mahoney was the principal celebrant and Bishop Tod D. Brown was the homilist. Bishop Clinch was interred in the Santa Rosalia Chapel at San Carlos Cemetery in Monterey.

SERVANTS OF CHRIST

The death of Bishop Harry Clinch, D.D., the first bishop of the present Catholic Diocese of Monterey, marks a closure to the special history of the Diocese and the territory of Monterey. In becoming the first Bishop of the restored Diocese of Monterey, Bishop Clinch in his own way imitated Father Junípero Serra as a leader and pioneer of the Church here on the Central Coast. Those whom Bishop Clinch served as priest and bishop remember him as a gentle and compassionate Shepherd. He became a precious friend and counselor to me, as he was for many others. We who knew him are deeply grateful for his example as a faithful servant of Christ and one who generously spent his life to serve others. He leaves a great legacy to us all.

The Most Rev. Sylvester D. Ryan, D.D.
3rd Bishop of Monterey in California
The Observer, vol. 35, no. 4

> 57 *The Observer*, vol. 35, no. 4, p. 10.

The Fourth Bishop of Monterey in California
His Excellency the Most Rev. Richard J. Garcia

"Work with me, minister with me, collaborate with me, build with me, and love with me." [58]

In September of 2005, Bishop Ryan submitted his resignation to the Holy See upon his 75th birthday, in accordance with the *Code of Canon Law*. He remained the apostolic administrator of the diocese until December 19, 2006, when Pope Benedict XVI appointed the Most Rev. Richard J. Garcia, an auxiliary bishop of the Diocese of Sacramento, as the fourth Bishop of Monterey. He was solemnly installed in Monterey on January 30, 2007, in the presence of His Eminence Roger Cardinal Mahoney, 4th Archbishop of Los Angeles and Metropolitan of the Province of Los Angeles, the late Archbishop Pietro Sambi, Apostolic Nuncio to United States, and the Most Rev. Sylvester D. Ryan, Bishop Emeritus of Monterey.

"More than 1,900 people gathered in the Monterey Conference Center to welcome their new shepherd and participate in a festive liturgy radiant with color and multicultural tradition... Joining in the celebration were 40 archbishops and bishops... More than 200 priests attended" from the Diocese of Monterey and beyond... "Ten representatives from each of the Monterey Diocese's 46 parishes also attended." [59]

Richard Joseph Garcia was born in San Francisco on April 24, 1947 to Manuel Garcia and Anita Maria Adame, who immigrated in the 1920s to California from Jalisco, Mexico. He received his first Holy Communion at St Joseph's School "in the City" and he later earned a bachelor and a master's degree from St. Patrick Seminary in Menlo Park.

On June 15, 1973, he was ordained to the priesthood for the Archdiocese of San Francisco at Sacred Heart Church in the City of San Jose. He served as associate pastor at St Catherine in Morgan Hill from 1973 to 1977 and pursued doctoral studies in dogmatic theology in Rome from 1980-1984.

Following the creation of the Diocese of San Jose from the Archdiocese of San Francisco in 1981, he taught at St. Patrick and St. Joseph seminaries from 1985 to 1992 and served as the pastor of St. Leo the Great parish in San Jose from 1995 to 1997.

On November 25, 1997, Pope St. John Paul II appointed him Auxiliary Bishop of Sacramento and Titular Bishop of Bapara, being ordained (consecrated) bishop on January 28, 1998. The principal consecrator was the Most Rev. William K. Weigand, 8th Bishop of Sacramento; the principal co-consecrators were the Most Rev. John R. Quinn, 6th Archbishop of San Francisco, and the Most Rev. R. Pierre DuMaine, 1st Bishop of San Jose. The episcopal lineage of Bishop Garcia includes Pope Blessed Pius IX († 1878), Pope Pius VIII († 1830), Pope Benedict XIV († 1758), and the Servant of God Pope Benedict XIII († 1730).

> 58 THE MOST REV. RICHARD J. GARCIA, 30 January 2006: *The Observer*, vol. 39, no. 3, p. 11.
> 59 *The Observer*, March 2007, vol. 39, no. 3, p. 12.

The Mass of Installation was preceded with the celebration of the solemn Vespers the evening before in San Carlos Cathedral in Monterey.

Photo courtesy of Jonabel O. Perez, January 29, 2007.

Bishop Garcia standing beside the original *cathedra* of the Bishops of Monterey in California in San Carlos Cathedral.

Photo courtesy of Jonabel O. Perez, January 29, 2007.

The concelebrant bishops of the Installation Mass of the Most Rev. Richard J. Garcia, 4th Bishop of Monterey in California.

Photo courtesy of Jonabel O. Perez, January 30, 2007.

The Pro-Cathedrals

On April 2, 2007, the Most Rev. Richard J. Garcia, 4th Bishop of Monterey in California, designated two parish churches to be pro-Cathedrals of the diocese: Old Mission San Luis Obispo and Madonna del Sasso in Salinas. A pro-cathedral is a parish church that is temporarily serving as the cathedral or co-cathedral of a diocese. A co-cathedral is a cathedral church which shares the function of being a bishop's seat or *cathedra* with another cathedral.

The Final Issue of *The Observer*

In September of 2008, the final issue of *The Observer,* "the official newspaper of the Diocese of Monterey in California," was published.

> As so much of the printed media—newspapers throughout our country have ceased publication, we know it is time to update and to move to a more contemporary way of 'Evangelization', getting out the word of God as our Mission as a Diocese to our People. Thus, with this issue, the *Observer* as you have known it for thirty-nine years is ending. We know how accustomed you have become to seeing and reading it. For this we are all most grateful. [60]

Bishop Garcia's First Pastoral Letter

At Easter 2009, the Most Rev. Richard J. Garcia, 4th Bishop of Monterey in California, issued his first pastoral letter, *Hope and Opportunity,* addressing the Great Recession of 2007-2009.

> It may seem incongruous or disingenuous to speak of hope in the midst of a crisis, but sometimes crisis can become a powerful stimulus for reforming our lives and changing what needs to be changed. It is difficult for us to change the economy, but we can change how we react to the challenges of our lives and how we take advantage of 'opportunities' that come packaged as significant hardship for our families, our communities and ourselves. [61]

> 60 THE MOST REV. RICHARD J. GARCIA, 4th Bishop of Monterey in California: *The Observer,* September 2008, vol. 40, no. 9, p. 3.
> 61 IBID., *Pastoral Letter on the Current Economic Crisis: Hope and Opportunity,* Easter 2009.

The Desecration
of the Portolá – Crespi Cross

On September 19, 2009, the Portolá-Crespi Cross that had been hewn and erected by Harry Downie in 1969 was vandalized and cut down during the previous night. As the City of Monterey was planning to repair and re-erect the cross, it came to light that the American Civil Liberties Union (ACLU) was in the process of challenging the legality of the cross because it was on public property. A heated debate soon followed. On October 7, the Monterey City Council voted to replace the cross, with the stipulation that a legal defense fund of $50,000 be established with private donations before proceeding. After raising only about $5,000 for the legal defense fund, it was decided on February 26, 2010, that the fund would be abandoned. On March 1, 2010, the Diocese of Monterey in California and the City of Monterey announced that the cross would be turned over to the Church and placed in San Carlos Cemetery in Monterey.

Statement of the Diocese of Monterey in California

The Diocese believes that the cross was a gift from it to the City of Monterey to mark the site of the original landing party of the Portolá Expedition in 1769. Now, the cross is coming home to the Diocese of Monterey so that it can stand in a place free from the controversy that surrounded it in its location on Del Monte Beach. In this way, those interested in this important part of Monterey's history will continue to be able to view the cross.

We are hopeful that this solution will resolve the controversy over the placement of the cross. The Diocese of Monterey hopes that all who visit the cross in its new location will remember that it is now located on consecrated ground and that many of the founders of Monterey rest at San Carlos Cemetery as well as so many of our beloved dead. The diocese is asking that whoever cut down the cross now leave it in the peace it deserves in its new home.

The Portolá – Crespi Cross was re-erected in a simple ceremony of blessing led by Bishop Garcia on Good Friday, April 2, 2010.
Photo courtesy of Agnieszka A. Klasa, August 19, 2015.

THIS CROSS IS KNOWN AS THE PORTOLA-CRESPI CROSS. IT IS A REPLICA OF THE ORIGINAL CROSS PLACED ON THE BEACH BY THE PORTOLA EXPEDITION SENT TO SEARCH FOR MONTEREY IN 1769. THIS REPLICA WAS DEDICATED ON DECEMBER 9, 1969 DURING MONTEREY'S YEAR-LONG 200TH BIRTHDAY CELEBRATION. IN SEPTEMBER 2009, VANDALS CUT DOWN THE CROSS, AND IT WAS RELOCATED HERE AND BLESSED BY THE MOST REVEREND RICHARD J. GARCIA, BISHOP OF MONTEREY, ON GOOD FRIDAY, APRIL 2, 2010.

The plaque marking the new home of the Portola-Crespi Cross at San Carlos Cemetery in Monterey.
Photo courtesy of Geoffrey Lopes da Silva, August 19, 2015.

The Bishop's Covenant for Peace

At Easter 2010, the Most Rev. Richard J. Garcia, 4th Bishop of Monterey in California, issued his second pastoral letter, *They Are Our Children*, which addressed the problems of gang violence in the local community. "The bishop acknowledged epidemic levels of drug-related violence in parts of the diocese, and offered suggestions for strengthening families, parishes and communities in response." [62]

> There are four key building blocks that I hope will help us begin to put an end to gang violence. These building blocks are prayer, strengthening families, providing healthy alternative activities for teens and young people and improving our communities' relationship with law enforcement. [63]

On March 23, 2010 Bishop Garcia, in partnership with COPA, a regional non-profit organization in Monterey, Santa Cruz, and San Benito Counties, publicly launched the Bishop's Covenant for Peace and Gang Violence Prevention at the parish of St. Mary of the Nativity in Salinas at the conclusion of a 5,000-person "Procession for Peace." The Bishop's Covenant called on all parishes to implement strategies to: connect children and parents with each other and the Church, promote trust between communities and those responsible for public safety, create new healthy activities and environments where young people can relate in healthy ways, and bring the power of prayer to this work. This initiative expanded to include institutions of all religious denominations, leading to the Procession for Building Peace that took place October 20, 2012 and Peace, Power and Youth: A Community Conversation that took place on March 23, 2013.

Bishop Garcia's Third Pastoral Letter

At the end of Easter Time 2011, the Most Rev. Richard J. Garcia, 4th Bishop of Monterey in California, issued his third pastoral letter, *Through the Shadow of the Cross Shines the True Light,* which addressed the "dark night of the soul" that had been the sexual abuse crisis.

> Jesus suffered a painful and humiliating death for us and he asks us to follow in his footsteps by picking up the crosses that we all have. The crosses may be different to some degree, but individually and collectively, they are at their core the same: the predominance of the individual self over our concern for others. Jesus asked us to follow him and so we must pick up these crosses and journey toward the painful "crucifixion" of those attachments. This crucifixion gives way to the hope in the resurrection and sharing in God's very life. [64]

> 62 *EWTN News,* "Soccer league is bishop's first step for stopping gang violence" (14 December 2010): http://www.ewtnnews.com/catholic-news/US.php?id=2306.
> 63 THE MOST REV. RICHARD J. GARCIA, 4th Bishop of Monterey in California, *Pastoral Letter on Gang Violence: They Are Our Children,* Easter 2010.
> 64 IBID., *Through the Shadow of the Cross Shines the True Light,* Easter 2011.

Another Local for Sainthood

On February 15, 2011, Bishop Garcia opened the cause of beatification and canonization of Mrs. Cora L. Evans († 1957), a former Mormon who was baptized into the Roman Catholic Church in 1935. Wife, mother, and mystic, she is said to have received visions of Christ Jesus and the Blessed Virgin Mary. She promoted the "Mystical Humanity of Christ."

On March 29, 2012, the Holy See approved the cause (*nihil obstat*), giving her the posthumous title of Servant of God, in a Latin decree signed by Angelo Cardinal Amato, SDB, prefect of the Congregation for the Causes of Saints. On May 13, 2014, Bishop Garcia authorized an investigation into a reported miracle due to the intercession of the Servant of God Cora Evans. One miracle is required for beatification, followed by a second for canonization.

Prayer for the Intercession of the Servant of God Cora L. Evans

This prayer was composed by Rev. Frank Parrish, SJ, who was the spiritual director of the Servant of God Cora L. Evans. The Most Rev. George Niederauer, 8th Archbishop of San Francisco, granted the *Imprimatur* on February 18, 2011.

Dear Jesus,
You blessed Cora Evans
with many supernatural mystical gifts
as a means of drawing us to a deeper
and more intimate union
with Your Sacred Heart
through Your Divine Indwelling,
Your Mystical Humanity.
I ask You through her intercession
to help me in my special request (*name the favor*)
and my efforts to do Your will here on earth
and be with You,
Your Blessed Mother,
Saint Joseph
and the whole Court of Heaven forever.

Say three times: the *Our Father, Hail Mary, Glory be to the Father.*

Ad limina 2012

The bishops of the United States began their *ad limina* visits in November of 2011. Bishop Garcia and the other bishops of California, as well as those of Nevada and Hawaii, went to Rome "*vidére Petrum*... to see Peter" [*Galatians* 1:18], meeting with His Holiness Pope Benedict XVI in the Apostolic Palace on April 20, 2012. Bishop Garcia can be seen on the right, fifth bishop farthest from the Pope. *Photo courtesy of the USCCB.*

The bishops of California pictured with the Vicar of Christ on April 20, 2012.

Photo courtesy of the USCCB.

From left to right:

1. The Most Rev. Robert H. Brom, 4th Bishop of San Diego
2. The Most Rev. Gerald R. Barnes, 2nd Bishop of San Bernardino
3. The Most Rev. Tod D. Brown, 3rd Bishop of Orange in California
4. The Most Rev. Armando X. Ochoa, 5th Bishop of Fresno
5. The Most Rev. Oscar A. Solis, Auxiliary Bishop of Los Angeles
6. The Most Rev. Thomas J. Curry, Auxiliary Bishop of Los Angeles
7. The Most Rev. José H. Gómez, 5th Archbishop of Los Angeles
8. His Holiness Pope Benedict XVI, 265th Bishop of Rome
9. His Eminence Roger M. Cardinal Mahoney, Archbishop Emeritus of Los Angeles
10. The Most Rev. Gerald E. Wilkerson, Auxiliary Bishop of Los Angeles
11. The Most Rev. Edward W. Clark, Auxiliary Bishop of Los Angeles
12. The Most Rev. Alexander Salazar, Auxiliary Bishop of Los Angeles
13. The Most Rev. Richard J. Garcia, 4th Bishop of Monterey in California
14. The Most Rev. Dominic M. Luong, Auxiliary Bishop of Orange in California
15. The Most Rev. Rutilio del Riego Jáñez, Auxiliary Bishop of San Bernardino,
16. The Most Rev. Cirilo B. Flores, Coadjutor Bishop of San Diego

Pope Benedict XVI "was most gracious and attentive to our presentations" (Bishop Garcia, *What's Happening in the Diocese of Monterey?*, May 2012).

While in Rome, the bishops of California, Nevada, and Hawaii (conference region XI) celebrated Holy Mass in the Papal Basilica of Saint Mary Major. The image of the Blessed Virgin Mary as the *Salus Populi Romani*, Latin for Protectress, Salvation, or Health of the Roman People, can be seen above them.

The *Annus Fidei* – Year of Faith

On October 11, 2011, Pope Benedict XVI promulgated the apostolic letter *Porta Fidei,* declaring that a "Year of Faith" would begin on October 11, 2012, the fiftieth anniversary of the opening of the Second Vatican Council and the twentieth anniversary of the publication of the *Catechism of the Catholic Church.* During the Year of Faith, Catholics were asked to study and reflect on the documents of Vatican II and the catechism, so that they may deepen their knowledge of the Faith. In preparation for the Year of Faith, the Most Rev. Richard J. Garcia, 4th Bishop of Monterey in California, issued his fourth pastoral letter, *Connecting our Hearts and Spirits to the Year of Faith.*

> Jesus opens the Door of Faith to us in many ways which may be different for each of us. By studying the teachings of the Church our intellect is engaged, by receiving the Sacraments of the Church, our spirituality is engaged and by listening to the yearnings of our hearts to be one with God, we come to believe and to grow in our faith so that we can share it with others.[65]

Immaculate Heart Radio

Immaculate Heart Radio Comes to the Diocese

Immaculate Heart Radio was founded in 1997 in answer to Saint John Paul II's call for a "New Evangelization." Immaculate Heart Radio "is bound to accurately and fully transmit the Faith as proposed by the Magisterium and documented in the *Catechism of the Catholic Church*" *(IHR: Business Overview).*

On December 1, 2011, Immaculate Heart Radio was officially launched in the Diocese of Monterey in California. The event was held in the Serra Ballroom of the Monterey Conference Center, where the Most Rev. Richard J. Garcia, 4th Bishop of Monterey in California, celebrated Mass and then ceremonially "flipped the switch," bringing Catholic radio to the Diocese on 1240 AM KNRY, a 1,000 Watt AM station based on Cannery Row in Monterey. On April 19, 2013, Immaculate Heart Radio began broadcasting on 1200 AM KYAA, a new 25,000 Watt AM station based in Salinas and a gift from Joe C. Rosa of People's Radio, Inc. The new Salinas station provided significantly better coverage up and down the coast, from Monterey into San Jose and the South Bay Area. On January 15, 2013, Immaculate Heart Radio was officially launched on 890 AM KIHC, bringing Catholic radio to the Central Coast, from Santa Maria to Paso Robles.

"Conversations with Bishop Garcia" airs on the first Monday of the month on *Immaculate Heart Radio's* KIHC 890 AM and KYAA 1200 AM.

> 65 The Most Rev. Richard J. Garcia, 4th Bishop of Monterey in California, pastoral letter, *Connecting our Hearts and Spirits to the Year of Faith,* 2012.

From left to right: Most Rev. Tod D. Brown, Bishop Emeritus of Orange in California, Most Rev. Richard J. Garcia, 4th Bishop of Monterey in California, Most Rev. Sylvester D. Ryan, Bishop Emeritus of Monterey in California, Most Rev. Stephen E. Blaire, 5th Bishop of Stockton, and His Eminence Roger M. Cardinal Mahony, Archbishop Emeritus of Los Angeles, *in choro*.

Photo courtesy of Jonabel O. Perez.

Bishop Garcia's Fifth Pastoral Letter

At Easter 2014, the Most Rev. Richard J. Garcia, 4th Bishop of Monterey in California, issued his fifth pastoral letter, *The Poor: Are They Not Our Brothers and Sisters?*

I am asking you in this Pastoral Letter to reflect on what I have said and to begin to give up the ways of materialism and individualism and to find a way to be in solidarity with the poor in our society. Today, it is easy for us to put ourselves first. Our world rewards such behavior. It is important that we take our theological option for the poor and translate it into a reality to assist our brothers and sisters in need.[66]

The Silver Jubilee of Bishop Ryan

On June 1, 2015, the Most Rev. Sylvester D. Ryan, Bishop Emeritus of Monterey, celebrated the 25th anniversary of his episcopal ordination with a Mass celebrated at Madonna del Sasso Pro-Cathedral in Salinas. Bishop Ryan was the principal celebrant and homilist, while concelebrants included the Most Rev. Richard J. Garcia, 4th Bishop of Monterey in California, the Most Rev. Tod D. Brown, Bishop Emeritus of Orange in California, and the Most Rev. Stephen E. Blaire, 5th Bishop of Stockton. His Eminence Roger M. Cardinal Mahony, Archbishop Emeritus of Los Angeles, attended the Mass *in choro* (in choir). It was Cardinal Mahoney who had ordained both Bishop Ryan and Bishop Blaire as auxiliary bishops of the Archdiocese of Los Angeles 25 years earlier, on May 31, 1990, the feast of the Visitation of the Blessed Virgin Mary.

Using the Votive Mass of the Visitation of the Blessed Virgin Mary in both English and Spanish and some Latin, Bishop Ryan's homily was devoted to the Joyful Mysteries of the Rosary. James E. Moore, Jr.'s *Taste and See (Gusten y Vean)* was used for the Communion Hymn at this Mass and at the original ordination Mass 25 years earlier. A reception followed in the parish hall.

The Canonization of Saint Junípero Serra

On September 23, 2015, at the Basilica of the National Shrine of the Immaculate Conception in Washington, DC, Pope Francis canonized Fray Junípero Serra Ferrer, OFM, reciting the solemn formula of canonization in Latin:

For the honor of the most holy and undivided Trinity, for the exaltation of the Catholic faith and the increase of the Christian life, by the authority of our Lord Jesus Christ, the blessed Apostles Peter and Paul, and Our own, after mature deliberation and having many times implored the divine assistance, and the counsel of many of our brothers, we declare and define Blessed Junípero Serra to be a Saint and we inscribe him among the Saints, decreeing that he is to be venerated with pious devotion by the universal Church. In the name of the Father, and of the Son, and of the Holy Spirit. Amen.

In his homily, the Holy Father said:

Today we remember one of those witnesses who testified to the joy of the Gospel in these lands, Father Junípero Serra. He was the embodiment of "a Church which goes forth," a Church which sets out to bring everywhere the reconciling tenderness of God. Junípero Serra left his native land and its way of life. He was excited about blazing trails, going forth to meet many people, learning and valuing their particular customs and ways of life. He learned how to bring to birth and nurture God's life in the faces of everyone he met; he made them his brothers and sisters. Junípero sought to defend the dignity of the native community, to protect it from those who had mistreated and abused it. Mistreatment and wrongs which today still trouble us, especially because of the hurt which they cause in the lives of many people.

Father Serra had a motto which inspired his life and work, not just a saying, but above all a reality which shaped the way he lived: *siempre adelante!* Keep moving forward! For him, this was the way to continue experiencing the joy of the Gospel, to keep his heart from growing numb, from being anesthetized. He kept moving forward, because the Lord was waiting. He kept going, because his brothers and sisters were waiting. He kept going forward to the end of his life. Today, like him, may we be able to say: Forward! Let us keep moving forward![67]

> 66 THE MOST REV. RICHARD J. GARCIA, 4th Bishop of Monterey in California, *Pastoral Letter on the Poor: Are They Not Our Brothers and Sisters?*, Easter 2014.
> 67 POPE FRANCIS, *Homily*, 23 September 2015. Copyright 2015, Libreria Editrice Vaticana.

The Most Rev. Richard J. Garcia, 4th Bishop of Monterey in California, led a contingent of both clergy and lay faithful from the Diocese to Washington, DC, for the Mass of Canonization.

On September 24, Pope Francis became the first pope to address a joint meeting of Congress. Bishop Garcia attended the address as the personal guest of Congressman Sam Farr, the U.S. Representative for California's 20th congressional district. Following the address, Congressman Farr gave a brief tour of the House, including the part of Statuary Hall containing the statue of Saint Junípero Serra.

Back row, from left to right: Nicholas Belli, Deacon William Ditewig, the Most Rev. Richard J. Garcia, Bishop of Monterey in California, Congressman Sam Farr, the Most Rev. Sylvester Ryan, Bishop Emeritus of Monterey in California, the Rev. Fredy Calvario, Wayne Shaffer, and Ron Johnson. Front row, from left to right: Diane Belli, Jo Shaffer, and Clare Johnson.

Photo courtesy of Deacon William Ditewig, September 24, 2015.

The visit of our Holy Father, Pope Francis, to Washington, DC, New York and to Philadelphia was a moving and transforming experience for so many of us. Pope Francis' messages, homilies and visits all opened our hearts to listen to him and to also commit ourselves to help make changes in the way we follow God's plan for us.

THE MOST REV. RICHARD J. GARCIA
4th Bishop of Monterey in California

Having been in Washington, D.C. for the Mass of Canonization of now St. Junípero Serra was a dream come true for so many. I thank you for joining me today as we celebrate our new Saint, here at home.

THE MOST REV. RICHARD J. GARCIA
4th Bishop of Monterey in California

The Diocese Celebrates the Canonization

The canonization of Saint Junípero Serra was officially celebrated by the Diocese of Monterey in California on the afternoon of October 24, 2015, with a solemn Pontifical Mass at Carmel Mission Basilica.

Bishop Garcia was the principal celebrant, with over a dozen bishops concelebrating, including the Most Rev. Carlo Maria Viganò, Titular Archbishop of Ulpiana and Apostolic Nuncio to United States, the Most Rev. Salvatore J. Cordileone, 9th Archbishop of San Francisco, the Most Rev. Sylvester D. Ryan, Bishop Emeritus of Monterey in California, and the Most Rev. Tod D. Brown, Bishop Emeritus of Orange in California. His Eminence William J. Cardinal Levada, Prefect Emeritus of the Congregation for the Doctrine of the Faith and Archbishop Emeritus of San Francisco, and His Eminence Roger M. Cardinal Mahoney, Archbishop Emeritus of Los Angeles, attended Mass *in choro*. Clergy, religious, officials, and dignitaries from throughout California were also present.

Front row, from right to left:

1. The Most Rev. Ignatius Chung Wang, Auxiliary Bishop Emeritus of San Francisco
2. The Most Rev. Sylvester D. Ryan, Bishop Emeritus of Monterey in California
3. The Most Rev. Carlo Maria Viganò, Titular Archbishop of Ulpiana and Apostolic Nuncio to United States
4. His Eminence Roger M. Cardinal Mahoney, Archbishop Emeritus of Los Angeles
5. The Most Rev. Richard J. Garcia, 4th Bishop of Monterey in California
6. His Eminence William J. Cardinal Levada, Prefect Emeritus of the Congregation for the Doctrine of the Faith and Archbishop Emeritus of San Francisco
7. The Rev. John S. Hardin, OFM, Minister Provincial of the Franciscan Friars of the St. Barbara Province
8. The Most Rev. John S. Cummins, Bishop Emeritus of Oakland

Back row, from right to left:

1. The Most Rev. Patrick J. McGrath, 2nd Bishop of San Jose in California
2. The Most Rev. Myron J. Cotta, Auxiliary Bishop of Sacramento
3. The Most Rev. Stephen E. Blaire, 5th Bishop of Stockton
4. Mr. Ivan Arevalo, seminarian, cross-bearer for the Mass
5. The Most Rev. George Hugh Niederauer, Archbishop Emeritus of San Francisco
6. The Most Rev. Carlos A. Sevilla, SJ, Bishop Emeritus of Yakima
7. The Most Rev. Tod D. Brown, Bishop Emeritus of Orange
8. The Most Rev. Salvatore J. Cordileone, 9th Archbishop of San Francisco
9. The Most Rev. Alexander Salazar, Auxiliary Bishop of Los Angeles in California
10. The Most Rev. Jaime Soto, 9th Bishop of Sacramento
11. The Most Rev. Rutilio del Riego Jáñez, Auxiliary Bishop of San Bernardino

Photo courtesy of Jonabel O. Perez.

From left to right: Archbishop Carlo Maria Viganò, Apostolic Nuncio to United States, Deacon Warren Hoy, the Most Rev. Richard J. Garcia, 4th Bishop of Monterey in California, the Most Rev. Sylvester D. Ryan, Bishop Emeritus of Monterey, the Most Rev. Salvatore J. Cordileone, 9th Archbishop of San Francisco, the Rev. Paul P. Murphy, Pastor of Carmel Mission Basilica, and Deacon Bill Reichmuth.

Photo courtesy of Jonabel O. Perez.

Mr. Tony Cerda, Headman of the Costanoan-Rumsen Carmel Tribe, with other members. www.CostanoanRumsen.org.

Photo courtesy of Jonabel O. Perez.

Special wine glasses were made to commemorate the canonization.

Photo courtesy of Jonabel O. Perez.

Lord, renew Your Church which is in Monterey
by the light of the Gospel.
Strengthen the bond of unity
between the faithful and the pastors of Your people,
together with Francis our Pope,
Richard our Bishop,
and the whole Order of Bishops,
that in a world torn by strife
Your people may shine forth
as a prophetic sign of unity and concord. [68]

Mass was followed by a reception in the large courtyard.

Photo courtesy of Jonabel O. Perez.

> 68 Cf. *The Roman Missal, Third Edition* (2010), Appendix to the Order of Mass, Eucharistic Prayer for use in Masses for Various Needs: The Church on the Path of Unity, n. 7.

RELIGIOUS LIFE IN THE DIOCESE

"From the God-given seed of the counsels a wonderful and wide-spreading tree has grown up in the field of the Lord, branching out into various forms of the religious life lived in solitude or in community. Different religious families have come into existence in which spiritual resources are multiplied for the progress in holiness of their members and for the good of the entire Body of Christ."

SECOND VATICAN COUNCIL
Dogmatic Constitution on the Church
Lumen Gentium, n. 43
21 November 1964

In 2013, Pope Francis proclaimed a Year of Consecrated Life to be celebrated by the Church, beginning on November 30, 2014, the First Sunday of Advent, and closing on February 2, 2016, the World Day of Consecrated Life. The diocesan celebration took place with a Mass celebrated by Bishop Garcia at Carmel Mission Basilica on Sunday, January 11, 2015. *Photo courtesy of Jonabel O. Perez.*

The **Order of Discalced Carmelites** (Latin: *Ordo Fratrum Discalceatorum B. Mariae V. de Monte Carmelo;* **OCD**) is an institute of consecrated life and a mendicant order with roots in the eremitic tradition of the Desert Fathers. The order was established in 1568 by Saint John of the Cross († 1591) and Saint Teresa of Ávila († 1582), both formerly of the Carmelite Order of the Ancient Observance. All Carmelites dedicate themselves to a life of prayer, with Carmelite nuns living in cloistered monasteries.

The **Carmelite Monastery of Our Lady, Mediatrix of All Graces, and Saint Thérèse** can trace its origins to 1925, when the Rt. Rev. Bernard MacGinley, 1st Bishop of Monterey-Fresno, attended the canonization of Saint Thérèse of Lisieux in Rome. Greatly inspired, Bishop MacGinley petitioned Pope Pius XI for permission to establish a Carmelite monastery in his diocese in honor of the new saint. With papal permission granted, Bishop MacGinley contacted Mother Augustine of the Carmelite monastery in Santa Clara. He asked her if she would consider establishing a new monastery in Carmel. Five nuns volunteered and they established the new community in a temporary monastery on Carmel Point on October 23, 1925.

In early 1931, plans were made for the construction of a permanent monastery on Highway One just north of Point Lobos and the cornerstone was laid on March 19. The entire project was financed with funds inherited by Mother Agnes née Ada Sullivan, Prioress of the Santa Clara Monastery, from her father. Mr. Francis J. Sullivan († 1930) was interred beneath the side altar of Saint Joseph in the monastery's chapel.[69] The architecture of the monastery is Lombardy Romanesque and much of the interior of the chapel, along with the altar, are made from specially imported Italian marble. The Stations of the Cross were carved in Geneva. The building project provided much needed work in the early years of the Great Depression.[70]

The interior of the Carmelite monastery's chapel during the Funeral Mass of the Most Rev. John B. MacGinley, 1st Bishop of Monterey-Fresno, who died in October of 1969.
Photo by Patricia Rowedder and courtesy of the diocesan archives.

The Carmelite Monastery of Our Lady, Mediatrix of All Graces, and Saint Thérèse on Highway One in Carmel, circa 1973.
Photo courtesy of the diocesan archives.

Carmelite Monastery of Our Lady and Saint Thérèse
27601 Highway One, Carmel
www.CarmeliteSistersByTheSea.org

> 69 "Carmel of Our Lady and Saint Therese", by Carol Card, *What's Doing,* January 1947, p. 23.
> 70 "The Carmelite Monastery: Where Cloistered Nuns Sing God's Praises and Pray for a Troubled World, by Bonnie Gartshore, *The Herald Weekend Magazine,* November 9, 1975, p. 13.

The **CONGREGATION OF THE CAMALDOLESE HERMITS OF MOUNT CORONA** (Latin: *Congregatio Eremitarum Camaldulensium Montis Coronae;* **OSB CAM.**) is an institute of consecrated life founded by Saint Romuald († 1025-1027) at the beginning of the eleventh century.

The **New Camaldoli Hermitage** in Big Sur can trace its origins to 1957, when the superior of the order came to the United States to explore the possibility of establishing a community in the United States. The following year, two monks from Camaldoli in Italy were sent. They discovered an ideal location for a hermitage that overlooked the Big Sur coast. Land and resources were donated by a generous benefactor and construction took eight years.

New Camaldoli Hermitage
62475 Highway One (Lucia), Big Sur
www.contemplation.com

The **ORDER OF OUR LADY OF MOUNT OLIVET,** popularly known as "Olivetans", is a branch of the Order of Saint Benedict founded in 1313 by Saint Bernardo Tolomei († 1348). The Order of Saint Benedict (Latin: *Ordo S. Benedicti;* **OSB**), popularly known as "Benedictines," is an institute of consecrated life founded around 529 A.D. by Saint Benedict of Nursia († 543 or 547). The Olivetan Congregation has been a part of the Benedictine Confederation of the Order of Saint Benedict (Latin: *Confœderatio Benedictina Ordinis Sancti Benedicti*) since 1960.

The **Monastery of the Risen Christ** in San Luis Obispo can trace its origins to 1987 as a "mission monastery" under the auspices of Our Lady of Guadalupe Abbey in the Pecos River Canyon in New Mexico. In March of 1992, the independent monastery was established, continuing "most of the ministry of the Pecos Monastery which was basically apostolic in nature and quite diversified." The monastery's Holy Spirit Chapel was dedicated by Bishop Ryan on July 11, 2004. Around 2012, the monastery began to decline as a consequence of loss of membership and lack of resources and in March of 2013, the Olivetan Congregation decided to close the monastery. Negotiations began with the New Camaldoli Hermitage in Big Sur for a transfer of the monastery to the Camaldolese Hermits of Mount Corona, which is expected to take place within three years.

Monastery of the Risen Christ
2308 O'Connor Way, San Luis Obispo
www.MonasteryRisenChrist.com

The **ORDER OF SAINT CLARE** (Latin: *Ordo Sanctae Clarae;* **PCC Colletines**) is an institute of consecrated life founded on Palm Sunday in 1212 by Saint Clare of Assisi and Saint Francis of Assisi. Also known as the Poor Clares, the order was organized after the Order of Friars Minor (the first Order).

The Poor Clares first came to the United States in 1877, when a small group of Colettine nuns arrived from Düsseldorf, Germany, seeking a refuge after having been expelled from their monastery by the government policies of the *Kulturkampf.* They established a monastery in Cleveland, Ohio. The Poor Clares came to Oakland in 1921, where they remained until moving to Capitola in 1940, where they established a house for 19 nuns. In 1954, the need arose for the community to require a proper monastery with a papal enclosure, which they established in Aptos. They remained there until the fall of 1990, when the **Saint Joseph's Monastery of the Poor Clares** in Aptos was moved to its current location.

St. Joseph's Monastery of the Poor Clares
1671 Pleasant Valley Road, Aptos
www.PoorClaresOfAptos.org

The **CONFEDERATION OF THE ORATORY OF ST. PHILIP NERI** (Latin: *Confoederatio Oratorii S. Philippi Nerii;* **CO** or **Cong. Orat.**), also known as the "Oratorians" or "Oratorian Fathers," is a society of apostolic life founded in 1564 by Saint Philip Neri, the "Apostle of Rome" († 1595). The confederation is made up of autonomous congregations of secular priests living in community under obedience but without vows. Blessed John Henry Cardinal Newman († 1890) first brought the Oratorians to England in 1849.[71] The Oratorians first arrived in the United States in 1934 (Rock Hill, South Carolina).

The Oratorians were founded in the City of Monterey on Christmas Day of 1967. On dedicating its public oratory, the Most Rev. Harry A. Clinch, 1st Bishop of Monterey in California, gave it the name **Holy Spirit Chapel**, in accord with the renewed devotion to the Holy Spirit that had been promoted by the Second Vatican Council. The chapel serves the diocese and beyond by being a center for the celebration of the sacraments, prayer, reflection on the word of God, and spiritual guidance. The priests of the Oratory, together with consecrated lay people, dedicate themselves to the purposes of the chapel under the spiritual mantle of the spirituality of St. Philip Neri. Originally, members studied for graduate degrees in religious education (catechesis) and served in the diocese as catechists. In addition to pursuing professional qualification as psychological counselors, they also served the local military community as chaplains.

The Oratorian community in Monterey also oversees the **Monterey Newman Institute for Historical and Religious Studies.** Named in honor of Blessed John Henry Newman, the institute is the largest theological library on the Central Coast. The Holy Spirit Chapel is also the principle seat of **New Pentecost Catholic Ministries**, a covenant of both clergy and lay leaders in several countries dedicated to service in healing, teaching, prayer, and evangelization ministries.

Holy Spirit Chapel
302 High Street, Monterey
www.NewPentecost.org

The **CONGREGATION OF CHRISTIAN BROTHERS** (Latin: *Congregatio Fratrum Christianorum;* **CFC**), also known as the "Edmund Rice Christian Brothers" and the "Irish Christian Brothers" is a worldwide religious community founded in 1802 by Blessed Edmund Ignatius Rice († 1844). The Christian Brothers primarily work for the evangelization and education of youth, but are involved in many ministries, especially with the poor. Their first school was opened in Waterford, Ireland, in 1802.

Palma Community of Edmund Rice Christian Brothers
263 W. Acadia Street, Salinas
www.cfcvocations.org

The **CONGREGATION OF THE MISSIONARIES OF SAINT CHARLES BORROMEO** (*Congregatio Missionariorum a S. Carolo;* **CS**), also known as the Scalabrinian Missionaries, is an institute of consecrated life that was founded in 1887 by Blessed Giovanni Battista Scalabrini († 1905), 31st Bishop of Piacenza, Italy, to "maintain Catholic faith and practice among Italian emigrants in the New World." Today, they minister to migrants, refugees, and displaced persons. Three Scalabrinian Fathers served as pastors of the parish of Saint John the Baptist in King City from 1968 to 1992.

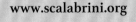

www.scalabrini.org

> 71 Cf. DONALD ATTWATER, *A Catholic Dictionary* (1958), p. 356

The **CONGREGATION OF THE MOST HOLY REDEEMER** (Latin: *Congregatio Sanctissimi Redemptoris; C.Ss.R*), also known as "Redemptorists", was founded in 1732 at Scala, near Amalfi, Italy, by Saint Alphonsus Maria de' Liguori († 1787). Redemptorists are "devoted to giving missions and retreats, anywhere and everywhere, but particularly to the poor."[72] The Most Rev. Aloysius Joseph Willinger, 3rd and last Bishop of Monterey-Fresno, was a Redemptorist.

www.cssr.com

The **MISSIONARY OBLATES OF MARY IMMACULATE (OMI)** was founded in 1816 by Saint Eugene de Mazenod († 1861), 18th Bishop of Marseille. The work of the Oblates in the United States began over 150 years ago and today is involved in parish ministry, schools, retreat centers, shrines and much more. Today nearly 4,000 Oblate priests and brothers serve God and His people in more than 60 countries.

www.oblatesUSA.org

The **OBLATES OF SAINT JOSEPH** (Latin: *Congregatio Oblatorum S. Ioseph, Astae Pompejae;* **OSJ**) also known as the "Josephines of Asti," is an institute of consecrated life and clerical religious congregation founded in 1878 by Saint Joseph Marello († 1895), 21st Bishop of Acqui.

The **Shrine of St. Joseph, Guardian of the Redeemer** in Santa Cruz can trace its origins to 1931, when two priests of the Oblates of St. Joseph came to the west coast to minister to the large number of Italian immigrants present in the diocese and throughout California. In 1933, a house was purchased in Santa Cruz to be used as a seminary. In March 1949, the Oblates prayed a novena to Saint Joseph. A benefactor appeared on December 8, 1949, and deeded a parcel of bayside property to them to be used for religious purposes. Ground-breaking for the construction of a seminary and chapel took place on September 30, 1951. By July 29, 1952, the first Mass was celebrated in the chapel. In March of 1952, Bishop Willinger granted permission for pilgrimages to this shrine and he blessed the chapel on August 31, 1952, as a "semi-public oratory dedicated to Saint Joseph."

The long held dream to construct a large national shrine dedicated to Saint Joseph was realized in late 1992, when extensive remodeling began on the chapel. On November 3, 1993 the chapel was dedicated by Bishop Ryan and declared to be a diocesan shrine in accordance with the Code of Canon Law. A relic of St. Joseph Marello was also placed within the altar. The name of the shrine was chosen in honor of St. John Paul II's 1989 apostolic exhortation on the person and mission of St Joseph in the life of Christ and of the Church, which was titled *Redemptoris custos*, Latin for "Guardian of the Redeemer."

Shrine of St. Joseph, Guardian of the Redeemer
544 West Cliff Drive, Santa Cruz
www.osjusa.org

Shrine of Saint Joseph, Guardian of the Redeemer.
Photo courtesy of Brandon Blackburn, May 2012.

> 72 DONALD ATTWATER, *A Catholic Dictionary* (1958), p. 421.

The **Order of Friars Minor** (Latin: *Ordo Fratrum Minorum*), popularly known as "Franciscans," is an institute of consecrated life founded in 1209 by Saint Francis of Assisi († 1226). The Franciscans are divided into three distinct and independent branches: Friars Minor (**OFM**), Friars Minor Conventual (*Ordo Fratrum Minorum Conventualium*; **OFM Conv.**), and Friars Minor Capuchin (*Ordo Fratrum Minorum Capuccinorum*; **OFM Cap.**).[73]

In 2009, the Franciscans Order celebrated the 800th anniversary of their founding. The Most Rev. Richard J. Garcia, 4th Bishop of Monterey in California, "led a pilgrimage novena to each of the seven historic missions as well as two other parishes and offered a plenary indulgence in accordance with the requirements of the Sacred Penitentiary for participation in all the days of the novena as well as the other requirements for reception of the indulgence." [74]

www.ofm.org
www.ofmconv.net

Franciscan Friars
www.SBFranciscans.org

St. Joseph Cupertino Friary (OFM Conv.)
1352 Dale Avenue, Arroyo Grande

St. Francis Retreat Center (Franciscan Friars)
549 Mission Vineyard Road, San Juan Bautista
www.StFrancisRetreat.com

The **Society of Saint Francis de Sales** (Latin: *Societas S. Francisci Salesii;* **SDB**) is an institute of consecrated life and clerical religious congregation founded by Saint John Bosco in 1854 in Turin, Italy. Also known as **the Salesians of St. John Bosco,** the objective of the society is "the Christian perfection of its members through the exercise of spiritual and corporal works of mercy especially among the young and the poor. The principal work of the society is education of all kinds— elementary, secondary, technical, agricultural, and social. It also undertakes foreign missions." [75]

In January of 1921, Our Lady Help of Christians (Valley Church) parish and school in Watsonville was assigned to the care of the Salesians of St. John Bosco by the Rt. Rev. John J. Cantwell, 5th and last Bishop of Monterey-Los Angeles. In 2000, the Salesians entered into a joint venture with the Diocese of Monterey in California and established the **Saint Francis Central Coast Catholic High School** in the City of Watsonville.

2401 East Lake Avenue, Watsonville
www.sdb.org
www.DonBoscoWest.org

The **Society of Jesus** (Latin: *Societas Iesu;* **SJ**), popularly known as "Jesuits," is an institute of consecrated life and order of clerics regular founded in 1534 by Saint Ignatius Loyola († 1556). While the primary mission of the Jesuits "is to be at the call of the pope for whatever work is required, its chief apostolic labors are the education of youth and foreign missions." The Society of Jesus is divided throughout the world into provinces, governed by provincials under the father general residing in Rome.

www.SJWeb.info

> 73 Donald Attwater, *A Catholic Dictionary* (1958), p. 200.
> 74 *Quinquennial Report 2003-2011*, p. IV-10.
> 75 Donald Attwater, *A Catholic Dictionary* (1958), p. 446.
> 76 Ibid., p. 266

The **Society of Mary** of Lyons (Latin: *Societas Mariae*; **SM**), also known as "Marist Fathers," is an institute of consecrated life and clerical religious congregation founded in 1816 in Lyons, France by the Venerable Jean-Claude Colin († 1875). "The Marists profess, besides the three simple and perpetual vows of poverty, chastity, and obedience, common to all similar institutes, a spirit of special devotion to Mary, absolute loyalty to the Holy See, reverence for the hierarchy, and the love of the hidden life, conformably to their motto: *Ignoti et quasi occulti in hoc mundo*",[77] Latin for "hidden and even unknown in this world".

In 1995, the parish of Our Lady, Star of the Sea in Santa Cruz, was assigned to the Marist Fathers, as well as responsibility for Hispanic ministry in the Santa Cruz area, along with partial responsibility for campus activities at University of California, Santa Cruz, Cabrillo College, and California State University, Monterey Bay. The Marist community moved into the former parish convent. On August 1, 2004, due to a shortage of personnel, the Marist order returned responsibility for the parish to the diocese.

The **Society of Mary** of Paris (Latin: *Societas Mariae;* **SM**), also known as "Marianists" and "Brothers of Mary," is a religious congregation founded in 1817 in Bordeaux, France by Blessed William Joseph Chaminade († 1850). The Marianists "make the usual simple vows of poverty, chastity, and obedience, to which at the time of their final profession they add the fourth vow of stability in the service of the Blessed Virgin."[78] Its members are officially designated by the Roman Curia as Marianists, to distinguish them from the Marists of the Society of Mary of Lyons, founded at Lyons in 1816. In 1928, the Marianists began teaching at Holy Cross parish school in Santa Cruz. In 1930, the Marianists opened **Chaminade High School** in Santa Cruz, which closed in 1940.

www.Marianist.org

695 Cerro Romauldo Avenue, San Luis Obispo
www.SocietyOfMaryUSA.org

Chaminade High School in Santa Cruz, circa 1940.
Photo courtesy of the diocesan archives.

> 77 Joseph Sollier, *The Catholic Encyclopedia*, vol. 9 (1910).
> 78 George Meyer, *The Catholic Encyclopedia*, vol. 9 (1910).

The Company of the **DAUGHTERS OF CHARITY OF SAINT VINCENT DE PAUL** (Latin: *Societas Filiarum Caritatis a S. Vincentio de Paulo*; **DC**), also known in as the Sisters of Charity, is a society of apostolic life co-founded in 1633 by Saint Vincent de Paul and Saint Louise de Marillac († 1660) dedicated to serving Christ in the "poorest of the poor" through corporal and spiritual works of mercy.

www.filles-de-la-charite.org

The Congregation of the **DAUGHTERS OF MARY AND JOSEPH (DMJ)** was founded in 1817 in Aalst, Belgium, by Constant G. van Crombrugghe († 1865). Members are called to be "instruments of mercy in God's hand" and to have an "unlimited devotion to Jesus Christ, to His Church, and to all living beings". The Daughters of Mary and Joseph first arrived in the United States in 1926 at the invitation of the Rt. Rev. John J. Cantwell, 5th and last Bishop of Monterey-Los Angeles and 1st Bishop of Los Angeles-San Diego.

www.DaughtersOfMaryandJoseph.org

The **CONGREGATION OF THE MOST HOLY NAME OF JESUS**, also known as the **Dominican Sisters of San Rafael (OP)** can trace their origins to August of 1850, when the Rt. Rev. Joseph Alemany, OP, 1st Bishop of Monterey, travelled to Europe in search of "religious women to provide a Catholic education for young women in a very wild and uncivilized California... of the Gold Rush days." Bishop Alemany arrived in San Francisco on December 6, 1850, along with Sr. Mary of the Cross Goemaere, OP. Sr. Mary settled in Monterey in the spring of 1851 and "became prioress of the first group of women religious in the new state, and opened a Catholic school for girls, **Santa Catalina**, with the financial help of local residents" and Bishop Alemany. Within three years, nine women had joined the Rev. Mother Mary to form the new Congregation of the Most Holy Name of Jesus. The Dominican Sisters moved from Monterey to Benicia in 1854. Today, the "Dominican Sisters of San Rafael teach, administer schools, care for the sick, work with the materially poor, do social service, missionary work, and are engaged in a variety of other ministries. At its height in 1965, the congregation numbered 376 women religious" and presently number 101 sisters "who continue to minister primarily in California and Nevada."

www.SanRafaelOp.org

The **DOMINICAN SISTERS OF THE CONGREGATION OF THE MOST HOLY ROSARY**, also known as the **ADRIAN DOMINICAN SISTERS**, is a religious institute of Dominican sisters in the United States. The Dominicans, officially known as the Order of Preachers (Latin: *Ordo Praedicatorum*; **OP**), was founded in 1215 by Saint Dominic de Guzmán († 1221) "for the salvation of souls, especially by means of preaching. They are mendicant friars whose active work is rooted in monastic observance, and whose preaching of truth involves commensurate study. The order is the guardian of scholastic theology and philosophy... There are also nuns of the order and a third order."[79]

The Dominican Sisters of the Congregation of the Most Holy Rosary of Adrian, Michigan, trace their origins to Holy Cross Convent in Regensburg (*Ratisbon*), Bavaria, which was established in 1233. In 1853, three sisters from this convent were sent to New York to provide religious education for German immigrant children. In 1869, a separate foundation was established at Newburgh in New York. From this congregation, sisters were sent to the parish of Saint Mary in 1879 and the parish of Saint Joseph in 1880 in Adrian, Michigan. They were joined in 1884 by sisters sent to establish a hospital for injured railroad workers. Adrian became a province of the Newburgh congregation.

www.AdrianDominicans.org

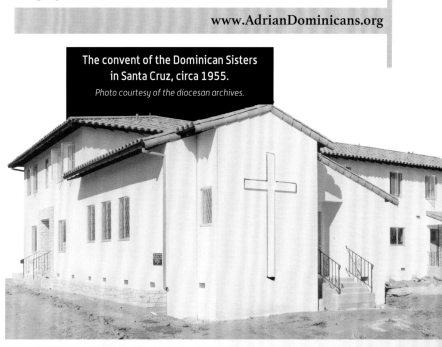

The convent of the Dominican Sisters in Santa Cruz, circa 1955.
Photo courtesy of the diocesan archives.

> 79 DONALD ATTWATER, *A Catholic Dictionary* (1958), p. 156.

The **Congregation of the Sisters of Saint Joseph** of Carondelet (**CSJ**) is an institute of consecrated life founded in 1650 in Le Puy-en-Velay, France, by the Rev. Jean Paul Médaille, SJ († 1689). [*Nota bene:* Some identify his older brother, Jean Pierre Médaille († 1669), as the founder of the Order.] The Sisters of St. Joseph of Carondelet "strive to serve all realms of human life, with a special care for the poor" (*Mission Statement*). There are approximately 14,000 members worldwide: about 7,000 in the United States and 2,000 in France. The Sisters are also active in fifty other countries.

www.CSJCarondelet.org
www.csjla.org

The **Franciscan Hospitaller Sisters of the Immaculate Conception** (**Fhic**) was co-founded in 1871 in Portugal by the Rev. Raimundo dos Anjos Beirao († 1878) and Mother Maria Clara do Menino Jesus († 1899). Members of the order follow the Rule of the Third Order Regular of St. Francis, with an emphasis on hospitality and service under the model of the Good Samaritan, particularly in health care. Members daily attend Mass, make a Eucharistic holy hour, pray the Liturgy of the Hours, and recite the Rosary. The Franciscan Hospitaller Sisters first came to the United States in 1960 to aid Portuguese immigrants and are currently located only in the dioceses of San Jose, Fresno, and Monterey.

www.confhic.com

The **Franciscan Missionary Sisters of Our Lady of Sorrows** (**Osf**) was founded in 1939 in China by Bishop Raffaele A. Palazzi († 1961), an Italian Franciscan missionary "as a Community founded in the Missions and for the Missions." Following the advent of Communism, the Sisters were forced to leave their motherhouse in Hengyang, Hunan, and fled to Hong Kong. After several years as refugees, the Sisters travelled to the United States and opened retreat houses in California and Oregon. Around 1958, the Sisters resumed their original missionary work for China by opening schools in Hong Kong and later in Taiwan. The spirituality of the community is centered on the Gospel imitation of Christ, particularly in His poverty and in His self-surrender, in the spirit of St. Francis of Assisi. The Sisters also have a special devotion to the Blessed Virgin Mary as co-redemptrix with Christ at the foot of the Cross.

In 1954, the Franciscan Missionary Sisters established **Saint John the Baptist Elementary School,** the parish school of Saint John the Baptist in King City. The nucleus of the campus was the old church building, which was moved from Bassett and Russ Streets, and the former rectory became the convent. In 1956, a new wing of the school was constructed. The school closed in 1986 due to funding problems.

St. Clare's Retreat & Convent in Soquel was established in 1950 as "an oasis of peace, stillness, and silence for all those seeking to nurture a life of prayer and respond to Jesus' invitation to 'come apart for a while and rest.'"

St. Clare's Retreat & Convent
2381 Laurel Glen Road, Soquel
www.StClaresRetreatCenter.com

The Congregation of the **FRANCISCAN SISTERS OF MARY IMMACULATE AND SAINT JOSEPH FOR THE DYING (OSF)** was unique in its service to the Diocese of Monterey-Los Angeles, the Diocese of Monterey-Fresno, and then finally the Diocese of Monterey in California. The order's origins can be traced to 1918, when the Rt. Rev. John J. Cantwell, 5th Bishop of Monterey-Los Angeles, approved the rule of the order, which had been written by the Rev. Mother M. Ottilia († 1954), the foundress of the order. The special aim of this community was "to lead a life of atonement and intercession for the Salvation of the Poor Dying Sinners, especially, those Dying Sinners, who are in the greatest and immediate danger of being lost forever."[80]

In 1928, the community witnessed the dedication of its **Saint Joseph's Convent** in the City of Monterey, which served as the motherhouse of the order. In 1936, a house on Webster Street was purchased in order to accommodate additional vocations.

In 1954, the Congregation constructed the **Ave Maria Convalescent Hospital and Convent** on Josselyn Canyon Road (now known as the **Ave Maria Senior Living**). On January 31, 1972, a lay Franciscan auxiliary was established to assist the work of the Sisters at Saint Joseph's convent and at the convalescent home. In 1996, the Saint Joseph's Convent was purchased by the diocese and plans were made to convert the building into a conference center, offices, and archives. The remaining sisters moved to the Ave Maria Convalescent Hospital and Convent.

The Congregation ceased to exist on August 29, 2012, when its last living member, Sister M. Agnes Zwolenik, OSF, died at the age of 94. Her Funeral Mass was celebrated by Bishop Garcia on September 6 at the Ave Maria Chapel in Monterey. She had been admitted to the order in 1953 and made her perpetual vows in 1957. From the order's founding in 1918 to the death of its last member, the order existed for 96 years.

83

The interior of the chapel of the old Saint Joseph's Convent, circa 1946.

Photo courtesy of the diocesan archives.

> 80 *Constitutions for the New Community* (November 4, 1918), n. 4.

The **Immaculate Heart Sisters of Africa (IHSA)** is an institute of consecrated life founded in 1955 by the Rev. Msgr. J. Gerald Grondin, MM († 1966). The first members were mentored and advised by the Maryknoll Sisters until 1969, when the first mother general was elected from the congregation. The motherhouse is located in the Diocese of Musoma, Tanzania, in East Africa. The charism of the Immaculate Heart Sisters of Africa is conversion, according to the words of Christ: "Let your light so shine before men, that they may see your good works and give glory to your Father who is in heaven" (*St. Matthew* 5:16). The Immaculate Heart Sisters work to fulfill this charism by serving in Tanzanian in the dioceses of Musoma, Shinyanga, Singida, Geita, Mwanza, Dodoma, and Dar es Salaam. In the United States, they can only be found in the Diocese of Monterey in California.

www.IHSistersOfAfrica.org

Bishop Garcia with the Immaculate Heart Sisters of Africa.
Photo courtesy of Jonabel O. Perez, September 13, 2009

The **Our Lady of Victory Missionary Sisters (OLVM)**, also known as the Victory Noll Sisters, was founded in 1922 by the Rev. John J. Sigstein. In 1934, the Missionary Sisters of Victory Noll were placed in charge of religious education program at the parish of **Saint Angela in Pacific Grove** for children attending public schools. In 1939, Mrs. Eva Bennett George gave her house and land on Laine Street in New Monterey to the diocese to be used as a residence for the Victory Noll Sisters.

www.olvm.org

The Institute **Religious of the Sacred Heart of Mary (RSHM; RSCM)** was co-founded in 1849 in Béziers, France, by the Venerable Jean Gailhac († 1890) and Mother St. Jean Pelissier Cure († 1869). The mission of members is "to know and love God, to make God known and loved."

www.rshm.org

The **Salesian Sisters of Saint John Bosco (FMA)**, also known as the Daughters of Mary, Help of Christians, were founded in 1872 in Italy by Saint John Bosco († 1888) and Saint Mary D. Mazzarello († 1881). The Salesian Sisters are committed "to the new evangelization of youth" by educating, while striving to live by St. John Bosco's original constitutions. The first Salesian Sisters arrived in the United States in 1908 and eventually divided into three provinces: Canadian, Eastern U.S., and Western U.S. The Salesian Sisters established their first foundation on the west coast in Watsonville on May 14, 1921, when they began assisting at the first Saint Francis School. In 1960, they opened the **Mary, Help of Christians Juniorate** in Aptos, a high school for aspirants. They also assisted in catechetical work and other apostolic activities in the area.

605 Enos Lane, Corralitos
www.SalesianSistersWest.org

The **School Sisters of Notre Dame (SSND)** is an international congregation of women religious founded in 1847 in Bavaria by Blessed Maria Theresa of Jesus née Gerhardinger († 1879). The first sisters arrived in North America that same year.

www.ssnd.org
www.AtlanticMidWest.org

The Servants of the Blessed Sacrament (SJS) was founded in 1859 in France by St. Peter Julian Eymard († 1868), the "Apostle of the Eucharist," as a contemplative, but not cloistered, congregation of sisters with a focus on Eucharistic adoration. The congregation was approved by Blessed Pius IX in 1871 and Sr. Marguerite Guillot was the first Superior General. In April of 1947, the first house in the United States was established in Waterville, Maine, by six sisters from the Canadian foundation. In June of 1956, a second American foundation was established in Pueblo, Colorado.

www.SisterServantSSJS.org

The Institute of the Sisters of Charity of Saints Bartolomea Capitanio and Vincenza Gerosa (SCCG), also known as the Sisters of Maria Bambina and the **Sisters of Charity of the Infant Mary (IM)** was founded in 1832 in Lovere, Italy by St. Bartolomea Capitanio († 1833) and St. Vincenza Gerosa († 1847). The Sisters of *Maria Bambina* express the love of God through prayer and the works of mercy in a variety of countries and ministries, particularly in the areas of education, health care, and pastoral care, helping anyone in need: the youth, the elderly, the sick, the poor—anyone rejected and marginalized by society. In 1967, the Sisters of the Infant Mary were installed in a new convent in Soledad for catechetical work including migrant workers.

Sisters of Charity of the Infant Mary Capitanio Convent
512 Fairview Drive, Gonzales
www.SuoreDiMariaBambina.org
www.sccg.in

The Sisters of Mercy (RSM) is an institute of consecrated life founded in 1827 in Dublin by the Venerable Catherine Elizabeth McAuley († 1841) "for the practice of all the works of mercy, spiritual and corporal, elementary, secondary and private schools, homes of rest for women, hostels for business girls and domestic servants, training homes for girls, night-refuges, hospitals."[81] The Sisters of Mercy opened the first house of the congregation in the United States in 1843. In 1854, the Rev. Hugh Gallagher visited Kinsale Convent in Ireland on behalf of the Rt. Rev. Joseph Alemany, 1st Bishop of Monterey, to procure the Sisters of Mercy for his diocese of San Francisco, California.[82]

www.SistersOfMercy.org

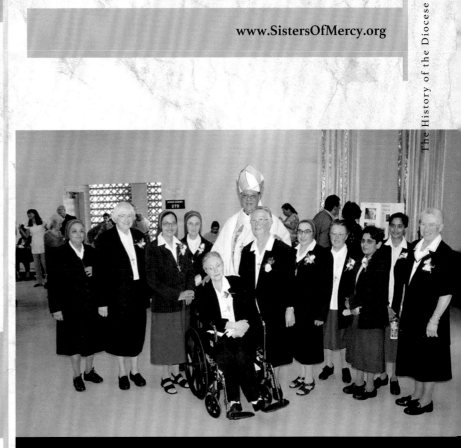

Bishop Garcia with the Sisters of the Infant Mary, on the occasion of their 50th anniversary serving in the Diocese of Monterey in California.
Photo courtesy of Jonabel O. Perez, September 13, 2009.

> 81 Donald Attwater, *A Catholic Dictionary* (1958) p. 466.
> 82 Cf. Mary Stanislas Austin, *The Catholic Encyclopedia*, vol. 10 (1911).

85

The History of the Diocese

The Congregation of the **SISTERS OF NOTRE DAME DE NAMUR (SNDdeN)** was founded in 1803 in Amiens by Saint Julie Billiart († 1816) and Françoise Blin de Bourdon, Baroness of Gézaincourt († 1838). The bishop opposed missions outside of his diocese, and so the headquarters was moved to then French Namur in 1809, from which it spread to become a worldwide organization. Dedicated to providing education to the poor, the Sisters of Notre Dame de Namur now have foundations in five continents and in 20 countries.

The Villa Angelica and House of Prayer in Carmel, circa 1968.

Photo courtesy of the diocesan archives.

Villa Angelica and House of Prayer
27951 Highway One, Carmel
www.sndden.org

The **SISTERS OF SAINT FRANCIS** of Assisi (OSF) can trace their origins to 1849 when a small group of secular Franciscans left Bavaria to minister to immigrants in Milwaukee, Wisconsin. The Rt. Rev. John M. Henni, 1st Archbishop of Milwaukee († 1881), asked the sisters to assist at the Saint Francis Seminary in Milwaukee, which had been constructed for German-speaking seminarians. In 1873, Mother Antonia, believing that working in a seminary was not an appropriate ministry for her sisters, asked the sisters in Milwaukee to discontinue that work. 37 sisters chose to remain in seminary ministry, and they became the first Sisters of Saint Francis of Assisi.

www.SistersOSF.org

The Congregation of the **SISTERS OF SAINT MARY OF NAMUR (SSMN)** was co-founded by Dom Nicholas-Joseph Minsart († 1837) and Mother Claire of Jesus († 1861) in Namur, Belgium. In 1819, Dom Minsart, sought to restore the Christian spirit among the working families of his parish and to ensure that "underprivileged youth find bread for their souls as well as nourishment for their bodies." He opened up a sewing room where poor children of the local area came to learn the trade and also to be catechized. In 1831, Mother Claire of Jesus joined the community, becoming its head in 1835.

In 1863, the Sisters of St. Mary of Namur arrived in the United States to work as missionaries to the American Indians. Due to the confusion of the Civil War, the Sisters never reached the missions, but ended up in Lockport, New York, where they established a school for immigrant children. The Congregation continued to grow throughout the country, requiring the establishment of the Western Province of the Sisters of St. Mary in 1921.

In September of 1930, the Sisters of St. Mary of Namur came to the Diocese of Monterey-Fresno to provide instruction at **Sacred Heart School** in the City of Hollister. During their time of over 50 years in Hollister, the Sisters took part in many other activities outside of their work in the school, i.e., visiting rest homes, taking Holy Communion to the sick (after that was permitted), teaching catechism in the nearby labor camp for boys, training altar boys, helping immigrants learn English, etc.

The Sisters of St. Mary of Namur in Hollister, circa 1940s, during a visit by the superior general, who would visit each house once every six years.

Photo courtesy of the archives of the Sisters of St. Mary of Namur.

The eight grade class of Sacred Heart School in Hollister, from 1954, with their teacher, Sr. Mary Ellen Williams, wearing a modified habit.

Photo courtesy of the archives of the Sisters of St. Mary of Namur.

On November 7, 1985, "the Sister's car was struck by another vehicle and one of the Sisters was dead on arrival at the hospital. Another Sister died a month later. At the time, there were no Sisters free to replace them, so the remaining Sisters were forced to return to Texas" (*Archives of the Sisters of St. Mary of Namur*).

www.SSMNwestern.com

The SISTERS OF THE DIVINE SAVIOR (SDS), also known as the Salvatorian Sisters, was co-founded in 1888 in Tivoli by Blessed Maria of the Apostles († 1907) and the Venerable Francis Mary of the Cross Jordan († 1918). Salvatorian Sisters "strive to make known the goodness and kindness of the Savior through prayer, apostolic ministry and advocacy."

www.SistersOfTheDivineSavior.org

The Congregation of the SISTERS OF THE HOLY CROSS (CSC) was founded in 1841 in Le Mans, France, by Blessed Basil A. Moreau, CSC († 1873), who also founded the Congregation of Holy Cross (Latin: *Congregatio a Sancta Cruce; CSC*). The Sisters of the Holy Cross first arrived in the United States in 1843 to assist Holy Cross priests in establishing what would become the University of Notre Dame du Lac (Latin: *Universitas Dominae Nostrae a Lacu*) in Indiana. "Throughout the 20th century, the sisters also would found colleges in Salt Lake City, Utah, Washington, D.C., and Brookline, Massachusetts, which were later closed. During this time the sisters also operated schools and orphanages from California to New York and South Dakota to Texas." `

www.CSCSisters.org

The Congregation of the SISTERS OF THE HOLY FAMILY (SHF) was founded in 1872 in San Francisco by the Rev. John J. Prendergast († 1914) and Sr. M. Dolores Armer († 1905) in order to provide charitable aid for families of the working poor. Between 1948 and 1958, the Sisters of the Holy Family, "the only religious community of women founded in the United States west of the Mississippi," relocated their motherhouse from San Francisco to the City of Fremont in the Diocese of Oakland. Between 1907 and 1908, the Sisters of the Holy Family commuted from San Jose to teach catechism to the children of the parish of Saint Michael in Boulder Creek. They would travel the relatively long distance through a long and mountainous trip by train every weekend. In 1941, the Sisters of the Holy Family began their catechetical work in the parish of Saint Joseph in Capitola and elsewhere in the diocese. In 1955, the Holy Family Guild of Santa Cruz County was founded to assist the work of the Holy Family Sisters as catechists and social workers throughout the local area.

www.HolyFamilySisters.org

The **Sisters of the Holy Names of Jesus and Mary** (French: *Sœurs des Saints Noms de Jésus et de Marie*; **SNJM**) was founded in 1843 in Québec, Canada, by Blessed Marie-Rose Durocher († 1849) for the Christian education of young girls. Since 1843, the order's mission has extended beyond Québec into other Canadian provinces, as well as internationally in the United States, Lesotho, and South America. The motto of the order is "*Jésus et Marie, ma force et ma gloire,*" French for "Jesus and Mary, my strength and my glory."

www.snjm.org/en
www.snjmusontario.org

The **Sisters of the Immaculate Heart of Mary (IHM)**, originally known as the Daughters of the Most Holy and Immaculate Heart of the Blessed Virgin Mary, was founded in 1848 in Spain by the Rev. Joaquin Masmitjá de Puig († 1886) as a means of rebuilding society through the education of young women. In 1869, the Rt. Rev. Thaddeus Amat y Brusi, CM, the second and last Bishop of Monterey, was visiting Spain and asked his friend, Fr. Masmitjá, to send some sisters to California. In 1871, nine sisters arrived under the leadership of Mother Raimunda Cremadell and established two houses: one in Gilroy and the other in San Juan. On August 2, 1876, eight Sisters (then called Daughters) arrived in San Luis Obispo from their house in Gilroy to staff the **Academy of the Sacred Heart or Academy of the Immaculate Heart** of Mary (now the site of **Mission College Prep**). In 1924, the Rt. Rev. John J. Cantwell, 1st Bishop of Los Angeles-San Diego, assisted the community in separating from the Spanish community. In 1963, the Convent of Immaculate Heart Sisters on Broad Street in San Luis Obispo was enlarged to accommodate 13 faculty members.

www.SistersOfTheImmaculateHeartOfMary.com

The **Society of the Atonement (SA)**, also known as the Graymoor Friars and Sisters, is a Franciscan religious congregation that was founded in 1898 as a religious community of the Protestant Episcopal Church in the United States and dedicated to the Blessed Virgin Mary under the title of Our Lady of Atonement. The Society preached the primacy of the Roman pontiff, while keeping its allegiance to the Episcopal Church, working to bring about a corporate reunion between the two bodies. Due to this, the Society came to find themselves not only criticized but ostracized by their fellow Episcopalians who saw them as walking an impossible tightrope. In 1909, the Society sought full communion with the Holy See and the Roman Catholic Church. In October of 1909, the Holy See took the unprecedented step of accepting the members of the Society as a corporate body, allowing its members to remain in their established way of life. Now in full communion union with the Bishop of Rome, the Friars and Sisters of the Atonement continue their work of ecumenism, advocating the reconciliation and eventual reunion of the various Christian communities.

In 1937, the Sisters of the Atonement established a convent in Soledad with additional catechetical centers in King City, Greenfield, Gonzales, and Salinas. In 1950, sisters from the Delano community of the Franciscan Sisters of the Atonement and from Arroyo Grande replaced the Maryknoll Sisters in catechetical work at Mission San Juan Bautista. The Graymoor Sisters also served at the parish of Saint Mary of the Nativity in Salinas (1976).

408 Second Street, San Juan Bautista
www.AtonementFriars.org

CAMALDOLESE BENEDICTINE OBLATES are extended members of the Camaldolese family that seek to share in the monastery's way of living the Christian life in a unique way compatible with their own state in life. To this end, the Rule of Saint Benedict, the Camaldolese Constitutions, and the rich and ancient Camaldolese traditions are adapted especially for oblates. The heart of Camaldolese-Benedictine spirituality is the seeking of God and the following of Christ's two-fold command of love in the natural rhythms of daily life. The celebration of the Eucharistic liturgy, the Liturgy of the Hours, and the practice of *Lectio divina,* as well as silence, solitude, and work, are all means which enable Camaldolese Oblates to seek and find God with a pure heart.

www.camaldolese.com

The **SECULAR ORDER OF DISCALCED CARMELITES** (Latin: *Ordo Carmelitarum Discalceatorum Saecularis;* **OCDS**) is a religious association composed primarily of lay persons, but also secular clergy. Secular Carmelites are an integral part of the Discalced Carmelites, being juridically dependent upon the friars and in "fraternal communion" with them and the cloistered nuns of the Order. Secular Carmelites share the same charism according to his particular state of life. Secular Discalced Carmelites follow the Rule of St. Albert, their own Constitutions, and the Provincial Statutes. They endeavor to spend 30 minutes in mental prayer, recite Lauds and Vespers, wear the Brown Scapular, attend Mass, and recite the Rosary or practice some other Marian devotion every day. Members are also encouraged to frequent the Sacrament of Penance and Reconciliation regularly, take part in an active apostolate, and fast in preparation for liturgical feasts that are proper to the Carmelite calendar. Local members of the Secular Order of Discalced Carmelites meet regularly at the Carmelite Monastery of Our Lady and Saint Thérèse in Carmel.

www.SecularCarmelite.com

The **THIRD ORDER OF OUR LADY OF MOUNT CARMEL,** sometimes also known as Lay Carmelites, is an association of laity who choose to live the Gospel in the spirit and under guidance of the Carmelite Order of the Ancient Observance, which is different than the Discalced Carmelites. Local Lay Carmelites meet regularly at the parish of Saint Angela Merici in Pacific Grove for prayer, sharing, and discussion, while maintaining a special devotion to Our Lady of Mount Carmel.

www.carmelnet.org/toc/html/about.htm

The **SECULAR FRANCISCAN ORDER** (Latin: *Ordo Franciscanus Saecularis*; **OFS**) is a community of men and women in the world "who seek to pattern their lives after Christ in the spirit" of Saint Francis of Assisi. Secular Franciscans are tertiaries or members of the Third Order of Saint Francis which was founded in 1233 by Saint Francis of Assisi, and with the permission of Pope Innocent III, as "the Brothers and Sisters of Penance." It is comprised of lay men and women, as well as secular priests, who make a commitment to follow the Gospel according to Rule of the Secular Franciscan Order.

The **St. Junípero Serra Fraternity of Carmel of the Secular Franciscan Order** was established in 1956 at Saint Clare's Retreat House in Soquel and is one of 25 local fraternities of the St. Junípero Serra Regional Fraternity of Northern and Central California and Northern Nevada. The Secular Franciscan Order in the United States is governed by the National Fraternity of the Secular Franciscan Order. The St. Junípero Serra Fraternity meets at the St. Francis Retreat Center in San Juan Bautista.

www.JuniperoSerraSFO.org

The **Order of Malta**, formally known as the Sovereign Military Hospitaller Order of Saint John of Jerusalem, of Rhodes, and of Malta (Latin: *Supremus Ordo Militaris Hospitalis Sancti Ioannis Hierosolymitani Rhodius et Melitensis*; Italian: *Sovrano Militare Ordine Ospedaliero di San Giovanni di Gerusalemme di Rodi e di Malta*; Spanish: *Soberana Orden militar y hospitalaria de San Juan de Jerusalén, de Rodas y de Malta*; **SMOM**) is unique among the Church's religious orders as it is a lay religious order of chivalry. Founded in 1099 by Blessed Gerard Thom († 1120), membership in the order is divided into three classes which are further subdivided into several categories. The head of the order is officially known as His Most Eminent Highness the Prince and Grand Master of the Sovereign Military Hospitaller Order of St. John of Jerusalem, of Rhodes and of Malta, Most Humble Guardian of the Poor of Jesus Christ. The Order's motto, *Tuítio fídei et obséquium páuperum*, is Latin for "Defense of the faith and assistance to the poor." Membership is by invitation. The Order has three national associations in the United States: the Federal Association, the American Association, and the Western Association, which was established in 1953 and now has more than 800 members.[83]

Each member of the Order takes an oath to practice and defend the Catholic faith and to serve the poor and the sick. The Order's invested members are supported in these efforts by hundreds of auxiliary members—men, women, and young adults who share the Order's mission.

The Western Association runs free medical clinics in Los Angeles and Oakland for the poor and uninsured. The Western Association also provides nursing services to parish communities in Los Angeles, Orange County, Phoenix, and San Francisco. Every spring, members of the Order from around the world, including roughly 250 from the Western Association, travel to Lourdes to care for men, women, and children facing serious and often life-threatening illness.

www.OrderOfMalta.int
www.OrderOfMaltaUSAWestern.org

Mr. Patrick T. Kraft, KM, and Mr. Harry N. How II, KM, at Carmel Mission Basilica on April 27, 2014.

Photo courtesy of Jonabel O. Perez.

> 83 H.E. Richard J. Dunn, BGC and Jon L. Rewinski, KM, "The Western Association at 60", *The Journal of the Order of Malta, Western Association USA*, vol. 25.2, autumn 2013, p. 4.

> *"In some ways lay associations have always been present throughout the Church's history as various confraternities, third orders and sodalities testify even today. However, in modern times such lay groups have received a special stimulus, resulting in the birth and spread of a multiplicity of group forms: associations, groups, communities, movements. We can speak of a new era of group endeavours of the lay faithful."*

SAINT JOHN PAUL II
Post-synodal apostolic
exhortation
Christifideles laici, n. 29
30 December 1988

The CITY OF THE LORD, a Catholic Charismatic Covenant Community, was founded in 1984 when the Los Angeles and Phoenix branches of the Catholic Charismatic Renewal movement merged. The San Diego branch joined in 1986 and the Monterey Bay branch joined in 1988. In 1990, the City of the Lord became one of the twelve founding members of the Catholic Fraternity of Charismatic Covenant Communities and Fellowships, an International Association of the Faithful under the auspices of the Pontifical Council for the Laity. The City of the Lord has established or worked with numerous outreaches and ministries. Their founding charism is "Receptivity and Commitment to the Person and culture of the Holy Spirit, particularly Covenant Love". Members seek to serve the Church with their gifts and talents, and bring all the faithful to a greater awareness of the centrality of Jesus as Lord and the power of the Holy Spirit.

www.CatholicFraternity.net
www.CityOfTheLord.org

The LEGION OF MARY (Latin: *Legio Mariae;* Spanish: *Legión de María*) was founded in 1921 in Ireland by the Servant of God Francis M. "Frank" Duff († 1980) "as a new form of apostolate, paying visits to the sick and needy in twos, like the Disciples. Prayer in common, apostolic work, and the weekly meeting which all the members are required to attend, have been typical features of the Legion from the beginning."[84] The Legion of Mary is a lay apostolate with the primary purpose of membership being the personal sanctification of each member. Members hold the Blessed Virgin Mary as their model, endeavoring to imitate her virtues, particularly her faith, charity, and humility. The spirituality of the Legion of Mary is based on the classic book *True Devotion to Mary* by Saint Louis-Marie Grignion de Montfort († 1716). "The Legion of Mary presents the true face of the Catholic Church" (Pope St. John XXIII).

The Legion of Mary is present in a large number of countries in every continent and consists of both active and auxiliary members. The basic unit of the Legion is a *praesidium* which consists of 3 to 20 members and is ordinarily based at a parish. The *praesida* of a diocese collectively make up a *curia.* The Monterey Curia falls under the San Francisco Senatus of the Legion of Mary.

Praesidium	Parish	Established
Madonna del Sasso	Madonna del Sasso in Salinas	1973
Our Lady of Fátima	Sacred Heart in Salinas	1991
Our Lady, Help of Christians	Our Lady, Help of Christians in Watsonville	1997
Our Lady of Bethlehem	Carmel Mission Basilica	2000
Our Lady of Lourdes	San Carlos Cathedral in Monterey	2002 / 2003
Our Lady of Good Success	Monterey Bay Traditional Latin Mass Community	2015

Praesidia formerly existed in the parishes of Sacred Heart in Hollister, Saint Angela Merici in Pacific Grove, Saint Mary of the Nativity in Salinas, Saint Joseph in Spreckels, and Saint Francis Xavier in Seaside, as well as three in Santa Cruz.

www.LegionOfMary.ie
www.SFSenatus

> 84 PONTIFICAL COUNCIL FOR THE LAITY, *Directory of the International Associations of the Faithful.*

The **National Catholic Committee on Scouting (NCCS)** is the national branch of the International Catholic Conference of Scouting (ICCS), an international association of the faithful under the auspices of the Pontifical Council for the Laity, "committed to promoting and supporting Catholic Scout associations and to be a link between the Scout movement and the Catholic Church. Its headquarters is located in Rome, Italy." The Diocese of Monterey in California falls under Region II of the NCCS.

www.cics.org
www.nccs-bsa.org

The **Society of Saint Vincent de Paul (SSVP)**, also known as the "Vincentians," can trace its origins to 1833, when Blessed Frederic Ozanam († 1853) and five of his friends founded the "Conference of Charity," whose purpose was to assist the poor. After drawing up their first rule in 1835, the name was changed to the Society of Saint Vincent de Paul in honor of their patron. The SSVP obtained the recognition of the Holy See in 1845 and was established in the United States that same year at the Basilica of Saint Louis, King of France in Saint Louis, Missouri.

www.svdpusa.org

THE **World Organization of the Cursillo Movement** (Spanish: *Organismo Mundial de Cursillos de Cristiandad; OMCC*) was founded in 1980 as an organization to coordinate the *Cursillos de Cristiandad* Movement that was founded in the late 1940s in Spain by a small group of priests and laymen who felt the need to provide religious instruction in order to enable people to restore a Christian impetus to a life that had ceased to be Christian. Convinced that the lay faithful have a specific role to play in the mission of evangelization through the strength of the sacraments of Baptism and Confirmation, Cursillo Movement strives to set up groups of baptized Christians that can act as leaven for the evangelization of the places in which they live and work.[85] The OMCC is present in 63 countries and was officially recognized by the Pontifical Council for the Laity in 2004.

www.orgmcc.org

The **Worldwide Marriage Encounter (WWME)** can trace its origins to 1952 Spain, when the Rev. Gabriel Calvo began developing a series of conferences for married couples, focusing on developing an open and honest relationship within marriage and learning to live out a sacramental relationship in the service of others. The weekend conferences soon spread throughout Spain, followed by Latin America and then to Spanish-speaking couples in the United States by the mid-1960s. By the summer of 1968, 50 couples and 29 priests were presenting weekends in the United States and by January of 1969, a national executive board was formed to coordinate the development of the Movement in both the United States and Canada. In the fall of 1971, the WWME began to spread to other parts of the world. Marriage encounter weekends are now offered in numerous languages in nearly 100 countries. *Encuentro Matrimonial* is the Spanish language arm of the WWME.

www.WWME.org
www.EncuentroMatrimonial.com

> 85 Pontifical Council For The Laity, *Directory of the International Associations of the Faithful.*

"From all the missions we in California have received our originating faith. In Monterey it is a faith enriched and enlivened with the influx of so many groups: the California Indians, Hispanics, Portuguese, Croatians, Irish, Korean and Filipino, to name a few."

THE MOST REV. SYLVESTER D. RYAN, D.D.
3rd Bishop of Monterey in California
March 19, 1992
(*The Californian*, March 20, 1992, p. 1c)

The *FEDERACIÓN MARIANA GUADALUPANA* was founded in the late 1950s in the Diocese of Monterey-Fresno to honor Our Lady of Guadalupe, provide spiritual growth for its members, develop the spirit and practice of the Roman Catholic faith among its members, preserve respect and love for Mexican traditions while at the same time studying and learning about American traditions, and promote among its members the spirit of fraternal love and mutual help.

The **PORTUGUESE HOLY SPIRIT SOCIETY, INC.** in San Luis Obispo was founded in 1931 and hosts the Portuguese Festa Parade in downtown San Luis Obispo every June. In 1931, the *Socieda do Divino Espirito Santo* (Society of the Divine Holy Spirit) constructed a social hall on property belonging to the parish of Our Lady Help of Christians (Valley Church) in Watsonville.

The *FESTAS DO ESPÍRITO SANTO*, Portuguese for "Feasts of the Holy Spirit", are annual festivals in honor of the Holy Spirit and Queen Saint Isabel of Portugal († 1336), observed annually by the local Portuguese community, the majority of which originate from the Azores—nine volcanic islands located in the north Atlantic, roughly 850 miles (1,360 kilometers) west of continental Portugal.

To perpetuate their traditional customs, the local Portuguese community in Hollister organized a *festa* (festival) to be held annually on Pentecost Sunday, around 1897. In 1924, the local Portuguese community in Salinas observed their first annual Holy Ghost Festival on July 27. The local Portuguese community in Santa Cruz did the same in 1928.

Festa do Divino Espírito Santo

MONTEREY

The **F.D.E.S. PORTUGUESE HALL OF MONTEREY,** located at the top of Casanova Street in the City of Monterey, was established in 1943, the same year that the first local *Festa do Divino Espirito Santo* (Feast of the Divine Holy Spirit) was held. A chapel was added in 1952. The annual *Festa do Divino Espirito Santo* is held every July, which includes a small parade or procession in downtown Monterey, followed by Mass in Portuguese.

The **Our Lady of Fátima Society** was founded in 1950 at the parish of Saint Angela Merici in Pacific Grove and continues to sponsor an annual celebration at the parish every August.

www.fdesMonterey.org

The ITALIAN CATHOLIC FEDERATION (ICF) was founded in 1924 in San Francisco by the Rev. Albert R. Bandini and Mr. Luigi Providenza as a lay apostolate to unite Catholic Italians in their faith, community, and pride in their shared heritage. The Central Coast District of the ICF has eight branches.

Branch No.	Branch Name	Parish	City	Established
21	*Nostra Signora del Soccorso*	Holy Cross	Santa Cruz	1929
25	*Nostra Signora del Sasso*	Sacred Heart	Salinas	1930
26	*Santa Barbara*	Sacred Heart	Hollister	1930
36	*Santa Rosalia*	San Carlos Cathedral	Monterey	1931
51	*Santa Caterina da Siena*	Our Lady of Refuge	Castroville	1935
227	*Saint Joseph*	Saint Joseph	Capitola	1968
291	*Saint Patrick*	Saint Patrick	Arroyo Grande	1974
354	*Saint Rose*	Saint Rose	Paso Robles	1991

www.icf.org
www.MontereyICF.org

The *FESTA ITALIA SANTA ROSALIA* FOUNDATION was incorporated as a non-profit corporation in 1997. Its purpose is to plan and implement the annual Santa Rosalia Fisherman's Festival, "along with several other fund raising events throughout the year." The Santa Rosalia Festival, also known as the Monterey Fisherman's Festival, is held every September. (The liturgical feast day of Saint Rosalia is September 4.)

The tradition of the blessing the local fishing fleet and praying for the fishermen was begun in Monterey in 1933, its first organizers being Francesca (Ferranti) Giamona, Giovanna Balbo, Rosa Ferrante and Domenica Enea, and under the auspices of The Royal Presidio Chapel of San Carlos. The Festival has taken many forms over the years, including parades, dances, outdoor Masses, Benediction of the Blessed Sacrament, and festival queens. The festival always concludes with "the procession to the water front and the blessing of the fleet."

www.FestaItaliaMonterey.org

The FILIPINO-AMERICAN CATHOLIC ASSOCIATION OF THE MONTEREY PENINSULA can trace its origins to 1961, when the first local association in the area was founded with the support of Msgr. Thomas J. Earley, V.G., P.A., 8th pastor of Sacred Heart in Salinas. In 1976, the Marina branch was founded and immediately began fundraising (including bingo) for a variety of parish and diocesan causes.

The FILIPINO-CATHOLIC ASSOCIATION OF WATSONVILLE was founded on October 12, 1959.

The **APOSTLESHIP OF PRAYER** can trace its origins to 1844, when a group of Jesuit seminarians at Vals, France established what would become a worldwide association of Catholics and other Christians who strive to make their ordinary, everyday lives apostolically effective. Through the Apostleship of Prayer, His Holiness the Pope gives his monthly prayer intentions to the entire Church. For this reason, the Apostleship of Prayer came to be known as "the Pope's own prayer group." The Apostleship of Prayer has always operated under the auspices of the Society of Jesus (Jesuits). The morning offering and prayers are the basic membership requirements, and in many countries the apostleship has no registration, no groups, no fees, and no special meetings. By the year 2000, the Apostleship of Prayer had over 40 million members.

www.ApostleshipOfPrayer.org

CATHOLIC CHARISMATIC RENEWAL is a movement within the Church that incorporates aspects of both Catholic and charismatic practice. It places an emphasis on having a personal relationship with Christ Jesus and expressing the gifts of the Holy Spirit. Communities that practice charismatic worship usually hold prayer meetings outside of Mass and feature such gifts as prophecy, faith healing, and glossolalia. The CCR exists in over 230 countries in the world and has over 160 million members and falls under the auspices of the **International Catholic Charismatic Renewal Services (ICCRS)**, a private association of the faithful, recognized as such by the Holy See's Pontifical Council for the Laity in 1993. Headquartered in Rome, the ICCRS serves as a link between the CCR movement and the Holy See.

www.iccrs.org

CATHOLIC CHARITIES was founded in 1910 as the National Conference of Catholic Charities, changing its name to Catholic Charities USA (CCUSA) in 1986. Catholic Charities USA, the national office of more than 160 local Catholic Charities agencies nationwide that serve millions of people each year, is a member of **Caritas International,** an international federation of Catholic social service organizations. **Catholic Charities of the Diocese of Monterey** was founded in 1984 as a faith-based non-profit social service agency providing aid to individuals and families throughout the diocese, focusing on mental health counseling, immigration and citizenship and family supportive services.

Catholic Charities
Diocese of Monterey
Providing Help. Creating Hope.

www.CatholicCharitiesCentralCoast.org

CATHOLIC DAUGHTERS OF THE AMERICAS (CDA), originally known as the National Order of the Daughters of Isabella, was founded in in Utica, New York, in 1903 and "is one of the largest women's organizations in the Americas." Headquartered in New York City, "the purposes of the organization are to participate in the religious, charitable and educational Apostolates of the Church. Catholic Daughters of the Americas engages in creative and spiritual programs which provide its members with the opportunity to develop their God-given talents in meaningful ways that positively influence the welfare of the Church and all people throughout the world. Catholic Daughters of the Americas strives to embrace the principle of faith working through love in the promotion of justice, equality and the advancement of human rights and human dignity for all" *(CDA Mission Statement).*

Court No.	Name	Established
686	Salinas	1921
1162	San Luis Obispo	1930
1505	Ramon Mestres in Monterey	1949
1532	Saint Angela in Pacific Grove	1950
2563	John Paul II in Salinas	2006

www.CatholicDaughters.org
www.CatholicDaughtersCalifornia.org

Diocesan Council of Catholic Women is the local branch of the **National Council of Catholic Women** (NCCW) which was founded in 1920 by the bishops of the United States in order "to support, empower, and educate all Catholic women in spirituality, leadership, and service. NCCW programs respond with Gospel values to the needs of the Church and society in the modern world." The Monterey Council of Catholic Women is the local branch of the NCCW.

www.nccw.org

Engaged Encounter "is an in-depth, private, personal, marriage preparation experience within the context of Catholic faith and values. Catholic Engaged Encounter is a weekend retreat away with other engaged couples with plenty of time alone together to dialogue honestly and intensively about their prospective lives together—their strengths and weaknesses, desires, ambitions, goals, their attitudes about money, sex, children, family, their role in the church and society—in a face to face way. The weekend is open to any engaged couple wanting to prepare for a deeper, more meaningful life together in a marriage recognized by the Catholic Church according to its Church law."

www.EngagedEncounter.org
http://mcee.org

Friends of
JOHN PAUL II FOUNDATION, INC.
WASHINGTON, D.C. CHAPTER

The **Friends of John Paul II Foundation** of Northern California, Inc., a local chapter of the Pope John Paul II Foundation based in Rome, was founded in April of 1990. Bishop Shubsda was the first honorary chairman and the late Dr. Stefan Kaminski, K.C.S.S. († 2015), was the first president.

The purpose and scope of activities will be to conduct religious, cultural, educational, humanitarian, and fund raising programs in close cooperation with the Vatican... The foundation will devote special attention to studies of Pope John Paul II's teachings by sponsoring lectures and seminars... and to popularize John Paul through exhibitions, films, symposia, and similar projects to deepen the knowledge and understanding of the true meaning of John Paul II.[86]

www.jp2friends.org

> 86 *The Monterey Bay and Pacific Grove / Pebble Beach Tribune*, April 19, 1990.

The **KNIGHTS OF COLUMBUS** is the world's largest Catholic fraternal service organization. Founded in 1882 in New Haven, Connecticut, by the Venerable Michael J. McGivney († 1890), it was named in honor of the mariner Christopher Columbus. Originally serving as a mutual benefit society to low-income immigrant Catholics, it developed into a fraternal benefit society dedicated to providing charitable services, promoting Catholic education and actively defending the Catholic faith in various nations.

There are more than 1.85 million members in nearly 15,000 councils, with nearly 200 councils on college campuses. Membership is limited to "practical" Catholic men aged 18 or older. ("A practical Catholic is one who lives up to the Commandments of God and the Precepts of the Church.") Membership consists of four different degrees, each exemplifying a different principle of the Order.

Council No.	Name	Established
958	Watsonville	1905
971	Santa Cruz	1905
1271	San Luis Obispo	1907
1375	Arroyo Grande	1909
1465	San Carlos Cathedral in Monterey	1910
1792	San Benito	1915
1948	Salinas	1919
3648	Santa Lucia	1953
3815	Southern Monterey	1954
4593	Carmel Mission Basilica	1958
5140	Madonna del Sasso in Salinas	1961
5175	Our Lady of Good Counsel	1961
5210	Charles T. Kerfs	1961
5261	St. Francis Xavier in Seaside	1962
5736	Mission de la Soledad	1965
7155	St. Jude in Marina	1978
8177	St. Joseph	1982
8762	St. Maximillian Kolbe	1984
9162	Los Padres	1986
9486	Sacred Heart in Seaside / Fort Ord	1987
9580	Resurrection in Aptos	1987
9951	Cristo Rey in Salinas	1988
11804	Mary, Help of Christians	1996
12888	Greenfield	2001
15705	Scotts Valley	2013

The Santa Rosalia Assembly (no. 77) consists of fourth degree knights from the five local councils of the Monterey Peninsula of the Junípero Serra Province in Central California. The five local councils are council nos. 1465, 4593, 5261, 7155, and 9486.

www.kofc.org
www.CaliforniaKnights.org
www.kc1465.org

MAGNÍFICAT OF MONTEREY BAY is the local chapter of *Magníficat:* **A Ministry to Catholic Women,** which can trace its origins to 1981, when a group of Catholic women from the Archdiocese of New Orleans observed a need among Catholic women for a faith-sharing experience in a relaxed social setting. Under the inspiration of the Most Rev. Stanley J. Ott, Auxiliary Bishop of New Orleans, and with the encouragement of the Most Rev. Philip Hannan, Archbishop of New Orleans, its first prayer breakfast on October 7. Archbishop Hannan would eventually approve the statutes of *Magníficat* as a private association of the faithful. Local chapters function with the permission of the local ordinary, and is incorporated in its respective state. *Magníficat* was born out of the Catholic Charismatic Renewal and has been nurtured by it.

www.Magnificat-Ministry.net

The History of the Diocese

RETROUVAILLE OF SANTA CRUZ / MONTEREY, French for "rediscovery," is a program that "consists of a weekend experience combined with post-weekend sessions. It is designed to provide the tools to help put your marriage in order again. The main emphasis of the program is on communication between husband and wife. It will give you the opportunity to rediscover each other and to examine your lives together in a new and positive way."

www.retrouvaille.org
www.retroca.com

The **SERRA CLUB OF THE DIOCESE OF MONTEREY** is the local representation of **Serra International,** which was founded in 1935 in Seattle, Washington, under the patronage of Saint Junípero Serra. The mission of Serra International is "to foster and promote vocations to the ministerial priesthood in the Catholic Church as a particular vocation to service, and to support priests in their sacred ministry; to encourage and affirm vocations to consecrated religious life in the Catholic Church; to assist its members to recognize and respond in their own lives to God's call to holiness in Jesus Christ and through the Holy Spirit." Serra International has chartered 1,170 Serra Clubs in 46 countries on six continents.

www.SerraInternational.org

The **YOUNG LADIES' GRAND INSTITUTE (YLI)** was founded in 1887 in San Francisco by Mrs. Annie M. Sweeney († 1925), Mrs. Mary E. Richardson († 1925), and Mrs. Emily Coogan († 1892), as an organization of Catholic women dedicated to the Christian principles of charity and love. The history of the YLI "reflects a sisterly care and concern for each other and for those in need" and the purpose of the YLI is to help fellow members, and members of the Church and the community. There are approximately 8,500 members in California, Oregon, Washington, and Hawaii, comprising women of all ages. District #12 of the YLI was officially organized in 1930 and consists of the counties of Santa Cruz, Monterey, and San Benito. District #12 currently consists of six local chapters or institutes:

Institute No.	Institute Name	City	Organization Date
83	Victory	Soledad	1919
85	Ignatius	Salinas	1919
95	Santa Cruz	Santa Cruz	1921
138	El Pajaro	Watsonville	1930
172	El Gabilan	Hollister	1946
240	Our Lady of Bethlehem	Seaside	1985

Former local institutes:

Institute No.	Institute Name	City	
12	Agnes	Santa Cruz	1889 – 1908 / 1909
25	Watsonville	Watsonville	1890 – 1897
59	Annunciata	Castroville	1909 – 1917
99	San Carlos	Monterey	1921 – 1955
133	San Luis Obispo	San Luis Obispo	1930 – 2007
135	San Antonio	King City	1930 – 1931
232	Christ the King	King City	1974 – 1978

www.YLIonline.com

Papal honors or "pontifical decorations are the titles of nobility, orders of Christian knighthood and other marks of honor and distinction which the papal court confers upon men of unblemished character who have in any way promoted the interests of society, the Church, and the Holy See."[87]

Papal titles of nobility "range all the way from prince to baron inclusive, and are bestowed by the pope" as the temporal Sovereign of the State of the Vatican City (formerly the Papal States of the Church).[88] The most well-known American recipient of such an honor was Rose E. Fitzgerald Kennedy († 1995), mother of President John F. Kennedy, who in 1951 received the title of countess from Pope Venerable Pius XII in recognition of her "exemplary motherhood and many charitable works."[89] The Countess Kennedy was only the sixth woman from the United States to have the title bestowed upon her by the Holy See. The practice is now considered very rare. Papal honors also include Gentlemen of His Holiness (Italian: *Gentiluomo di Sua Santitá*) and recipients of the Golden Rose. Papal honors and awards are typically made based on recommendations from diocesan bishops or apostolic nuncios for specific services rendered to the Church. Many Catholic faithful in the Diocese of Monterey in California have received papal honors over the years.

The papal orders of knighthood, ranking according to their importance and dignity, are:

The **Supreme Order of Christ** (Latin: *Militia Domini Nostri Iesu Christi*) was founded in 1318 and is reserved for Catholic sovereigns and heads of state.

The **Order of the Golden Spur** (Latin: *Ordo Militia Aurata*) was founded in 332 and remained inactive for centuries until it was reactivated by Pope Paul III in 1539. The hereditary title of Palatine Count and Count of the Lateran Palace used to accompany this award until 1841. The order is now reserved for Catholic and non-Catholic heads of state. It is the only order to be under the patronage of the Blessed Virgin Mary.

The **Order of Pius IX** (Latin: *Ordo Pianus IX*) was founded in 1847 by Pope Blessed Pius IX in honor of his predecessor Pope Pius IV († 1565). The order is awarded upon the recommendation of the Secretariat of State or the local bishop and is open to both Catholic men and women. It is commonly awarded to retiring ambassadors accredited to the Holy See.

The **Order of Saint Gregory the Great** (Latin: *Ordo Sancti Gregorii Magni*) was founded in 1831 by Pope Gregory XVI in honor of his predecessor Pope St. Gregory the Great. "The Greg" was awarded to both Catholic and non-Catholic men until 1991, when Pope St. John Paul II opened the order to women.

The **Order of Saint Sylvester** (Latin: *Ordo Sanctus Silvestri*) was founded in 1841 by Pope Gregory XVI in honor of Pope Saint Sylvester I († 335) and is awarded to both Catholic and non-Catholic men "who by their examples in business, the professions, the military, and society have lived exemplary lives."[90]

> 87 P.M.J. Rock, *The Catholic Encyclopedia* (1908), vol. IV.
> 88 Ibid.
> 89 Christina Cox, *Images of America: Catholics in Washington*, DC (April 2015), p. 78.

> 90 James-Charles Noonan, Jr., *The Church Visible: The Ceremonial Life and Protocol of the Roman Catholic Church* (1996), p. 113.

Other permanent awards, ranking according to their importance and dignity, are:

The **Cross Pro Ecclesia et Pontifice** (Latin for "For Church and Pontiff") was established in 1888 by Pope Leo XIII and is bestowed on both clergy and laity.

The **Benemerenti Medal** (Italian for "Good Merit") was established in 1791 by Pope Pius VI and is awarded to both clergy and laity "who have merited special recognition by the Holy See." It was originally intended "as an award for military courage in the defense of" the Papal States of the Church. This was not changed until 1925.

The **Holy Land / Jerusalem Pilgrim's Cross** (Latin: *Signum Sacri Itineris Hierosolymitani*) was established in 1901 by Pope Leo XIII and is conferred in the name of His Holiness the Pope by the Custody of the Holy Land (*Custodia Terræ Sanctæ*) in Jerusalem to honor and endorse pilgrimage to the Holy Land.

The **Order of the Holy Sepulchre**, formally known as the Equestrian Order of the Holy Sepulchre of Jerusalem (Latin: *Ordo Equestris Sancti Sepulchri Hierosolymitani;* Spanish: *Orden de Caballería del Santo Sepulcro de Jerusalén*), is an order of knighthood under the protection of the Holy See. Founded in 1099 by Godfrey of Bouillon († 1100), Duke of Lower Lorraine and first ruler of the Latin Kingdom of Jerusalem following the First Crusade (1096-1099), membership in the Order is divided into several grades. The head of the order was the Pope himself from 1496 until 1949 when the office of Grand Master was filled by a cardinal appointed by the Pope. The Patriarch of Jerusalem of the Latins is the Grand Prior. The Order's motto, *"Deus lo vult,"* is Latin for "God wills it." The Order has 11 lieutenancies in the United States and the Western USA Lieutenancy had approximately 1,102 active Knights and Dames in 1998. The Western Lieutenancy provides funding for special projects in the Holy Land.

"The Order relives in a modern manner the spirit and ideal of the Crusades, with the arms of faith, of the apostolate, and of Christian charity. To this end the Order (a) fosters in its members the practice of the Christian life; (b) is zealous for the preservation and spread of the faith in Palestine; (c) champions the defense of the rights of the Catholic Church in the Holy Land, the cradle of the Order."[91]

www.eohsj.net
www.KHSWesternUSA.org

> 91 James-Charles Noonan, Jr., *The Church Visible: The Ceremonial Life and Protocol of the Roman Catholic Church* (1996), p. 164

"Education is integral to the mission of the Church to proclaim the Good News. First and foremost every Catholic educational institution is a place to encounter the living God who in Jesus Christ reveals His transforming love and truth (cf. Spe Salvi, 4)."

Pope Benedict XVI
Address to Catholic Educators,
Washington, D.C.
17 April 2008

The History of the Diocese

Early Childhood Education in the Diocese

Saint Angela's Preschool in the City of Pacific Grove is a parochial preschool, meeting "all education, catechetical, and security requirements of the Department of Catholic Schools," offering "programs ranging from a 3 half day schedule to a 5 full day schedule for pre-kindergarten and pre-school ages. The preschool "is an educational ministry" of the parish of Saint Angela Merici "that provides a child-centered environment for families where Christian community can be experienced through activities that support child development and family life" (*Mission Statement*).

136 Eighth Street, Pacific Grove
Monterey County
www.StAngelasPreschool.org

Nota bene: Several primary schools in the diocese also offer early childhood education. **Santa Catalina School** in the City of Monterey offers coed early childhood and primary education, along with secondary education for girls.

Primary or Elementary Schools in the Diocese

Good Shepherd School in the City of Santa Cruz is a coed parochial school (grades preschool through 8) founded in 1963 by the Rev. Francis Markey. The elementary school was a joint project with between the parishes of Saint Joseph in Capitola, Our Lady, Star of the Sea in Santa Cruz, and Resurrection in Aptos. In the fall of 1982, a kindergarten program was added. The school is designed to meet the needs of families who desire an affordable Catholic education for their children in the context of a challenging and values-based environment. Committed to academic excellence," the curriculum "is grounded in the teachings of the Roman Catholic Church".

2727 Mattison Lane, Santa Cruz
Santa Cruz County
www.GSSchool.org

Holy Cross School in City of Santa Cruz is a coed parochial school (grades preschool through 8) founded in 1862 by the **Daughters of Charity** originally as a school for girls and orphan asylum in the old Juzgado building at School and Emmett Streets. (A cholera epidemic had created a large number of  orphans.) In 1899, Holy Cross Orphan Asylum and School numbered 168 pupils. In 1943, the Daughters of Charity turned over the administration of the parochial school to the **Adrian Dominican Sisters.**

Holy Cross School in Santa Cruz, circa 1967.
Photo courtesy of the diocesan archives.

In 1970, grades 9 through 12 at Holy Cross School were discontinued due to a projected budget deficit. In 1976, grades 1 through 5 were located on Emmet Street and grades 6 through 8 were located on High Street. Students came from the surrounding parishes and the faculty was composed of both religious and laity. In early summer of 1977, ground was broken for an addition to the school. It was designed to bring 7th and 8th grades back into the building on a permanent basis. On January 29, 1978, the new school wing was blessed by Bishop Clinch. In the fall of 1982, a kindergarten program was added.

150 Emmet Street, Santa Cruz
Santa Cruz County
www.HolyCSC.org

Junípero Serra School (JSS) in the City of Carmel-by-the-Sea is a coed parochial school (grades preschool through 8) founded by the **Sisters of Notre Dame de Namur** on February 15, 1943, beginning in temporary quarters. In 1944, three acres on the south side of the property of Carmel Mission were purchased for the school from Alma Brooks Walter. In 1945, four classrooms were built using adobe bricks as part of the south wing. The new facilities were first used on September 24. In 1946, work on the school office was completed and in 1951, a cafeteria and an additional classroom were completed on the southwest wing. Between 1953 and 1955, three additional classrooms in the west wing were built.

In 1975, discussions were held to plan the future of Junípero Serra School following the announcement by the **Sisters of Notre Dame de Namur** that they would withdraw from the school. Tuition costs for an all-lay staff were explored. Eventually, the **Adrian Dominican Sisters** were selected to staff the school beginning in September of 1976.

In July of 1981, Junípero Serra School became the first Catholic school in the diocese to receive full accreditation from the Western Association of Schools and Colleges. In November of 1981, Bishop Clinch blessed the site for an addition to Junípero Serra School. It was to provide space for a kindergarten, a kitchen, workrooms, and a recreational / meeting center. Half of the financing was to be provided by the Coburn Charitable Trust. In the fall of 1982, the first kindergarten class began in the new multipurpose building and an After-School Care Program was initiated. The building was dedicated on October 17.

3090 Rio Road, Carmel
Monterey County
www.JuniperoSerra.org

Madonna del Sasso School in the City of Salinas is a coed parochial school (grades preschool through 8) that opened on September 10, 1957. Classes for grades 1 through 4 were held in the Portuguese Hall a few blocks east of the parish church, with two sisters of **Notre Dame de Namur** in charge. In 1958, the school moved to the current site and grade 6 was added. A total of 220 students were enrolled. In 1959, a school board was organized. By 1960, school enrollment had increased to 305. In 1964, the construction of the school was completed with eight co-educational grades being instructed. On March 1, 1981, a new Day Care Center was opened. It provided extended care hours to Madonna del Sasso School students. In September of 1983, a kindergarten class was added to the Day Care Center program.

20 Santa Teresa Way, Salinas
Monterey County
www.MadonnaDelSasso.com

MORELAND NOTRE DAME SCHOOL in the City of Watsonville is a private Catholic coed school for children in kindergarten through the eighth grade and "is an expression of the educational mission of the Catholic Church and the teaching ministry of the **Sisters of Notre Dame de Namur**. In keeping with the *Hallmarks of a Notre Dame de Namur Learning Community* Faculty and staff, in partnership with parents, work to provide students with the foundations of Christ-centered faith and life-long learning: love, hope, simplicity, a longing for justice and truth, a desire to serve others, the power of critical thinking, and a sense of wonder and awe" *(Statement of Mission)*.

MORELAND NOTRE DAME

In 1899, the **Sisters of Notre Dame** entered contract with the Rt. Rev. George T. Montgomery, 3rd Bishop of Monterey-Los Angeles, to conduct the Moreland Academy for girls and to include boys up to the age of 12. It was to include both boarders and parochial students. Funds for construction were donated by Mrs. Margaret S. Moreland in honor of her recently deceased daughter, Mary Josephine. Classes started on October 19. On March 7, 1900, Bishop Montgomery presided at the formal dedication ceremony.

Moreland Academy in Watsonville, circa pre-1963.
Photo courtesy of the diocesan archives.

In 1941, expansion of Moreland Notre Dame Academy by addition of a building was begun. The planning documents indicated that both boys and girls would be educated there at the elementary school level. The old building on the northeast corner of the property would remain. Total cost was estimated at $55,000. On September 13, 1942, the new **Notre Dame School** building was dedicated by the Most Rev. Philip G. Scher, 2nd Bishop of Monterey-Fresno. It included new classrooms and a library. Two additional rooms had also been added to the old building. The name Moreland Notre Dame Academy was reserved for the secondary division.

133 Brennan Street, Watsonville
Santa Cruz County
www.MNDSchool.org

SACRED HEART PARISH SCHOOL in the City of Hollister is a coed parochial school (grades preschool through 8) that was originally founded as a boarding and day school on August 8, 1891 by four **Daughters of Charity**. On April 18, 1906, both the school and convent were damaged by an earthquake. Classes were held in tents during the $5,000 reconstruction project. In 1927, construction began on new school ($75,000) and convent ($25,000), but work on the new school was soon halted due to funding problems. Ten years, later a new school was finally built at a reduced cost. In 1929, school enrolment was 135 in the grammar school and 31 in the high school. In 1930, the **Sisters of St. Mary of Namur** took over the stewardship of the school. In 1937, **Serra High School** closed. New grammar school dedicated on September 19. In 1948, two classrooms were added to the school. In 1972, a perpetual endowment fund for the school was established. The last religious community to direct the school was the **Adrian Dominican Sisters**. Since 1992, the school has been administered by lay leadership.

670 College Street, Hollister
San Benito County
www.SacredHeartSchool.org

SACRED HEART SCHOOL in the City of Salinas is a coed parochial school (grades transitional kindergarten through 8) that can trace its origins to 1886, when a school was founded by the Sisters of Loreto at the Foot of the Cross; however, they departed  the following year. In June of 1889, the **Sisters of Mercy** opened a parish school, but it too only last about one year. In 1906, both a school and a convent for seven sisters of **Notre Dame de Namur** were built. The new school opened in October with 143 students enrolled.

The current school structure was dedicated on September 20, 1942. In the early 1950s, enrollment increased rapidly and a kindergarten class was added, and the school had two classes of each grades from first to sixth. With the opening of **Saint Mary of the Nativity School** in East Salinas and **Madonna del Sasso School** in North Salinas in 1957, there was a subsequent decrease in enrollment, and Sacred Heart School now offered only one classroom of kindergarten through sixth grade. In 1959, the 4th through 8th grade classrooms, the library, and the parish hall were added. In 1960, in preparation for the opening of Notre Dame High School, the seventh and eighth grade girls returned to the Sacred Heart campus. In 1974, a Montessori program was initiated and in the fall of 1976, kindergarten was added. At the request of parents and upon the recommendation of the 1975 accreditation team, boys were once again admitted to the seventh and eighth grades in 1976. In 1998, planning for a school expansion project was initiated. An auditorium, a lab, and a media center were to be included.

In 1999, it was found that enrollment in the parish school had remained stable at 300-310 for five years. In 2003, a transitional kindergarten was added. In November of 2006, the centennial of the school was celebrated. A reception was held in the Cislini Youth Center attended by surviving alumni from each decade.

A preschool was founded in June of 2015 as "a free-standing and independently licensed preschool in Salinas," serving students from ages three to five between the hours of 7am and 5:30pm. Although the preschool operates independently from the elementary school, its curriculum will focus on creating a comfortable transition to the elementary school.

123 W. Market Street, Salinas
Monterey County
www.SHSchool.org

 SAINT PATRICK SCHOOL (STP) in the City of Arroyo Grande, a coed parochial school for preschool through the eighth grade, was established in August of 1963 when seven **Sisters of Mercy** arrived from Ennis, Ireland, at the invitation of the Rev. James Marron, 13th pastor of the parish of Saint Patrick in Arroyo Grande. The doors of Saint Patrick's Elementary School officially opened that September with 234 students. In June of 1966, the school celebrated its first graduating class of 33 students. In 1984, a multi-purpose building was constructed, which added a gymnasium, classrooms, kitchen, and offices to the grounds. In 1994, a modular building was purchased to house the seventh grade homeroom, which allowed for an entire classroom to be dedicated solely to the sciences. The following year, 1995, the convent chapel was expanded and converted into a kindergarten classroom. In 1998, the outdoor facilities were upgraded to include a track, an improved baseball diamond, and basketball courts. A need for increased space for the school's fine arts program lent to the purchase of another modular classroom in 2003. This building also provided office space for the school's counselor and bookkeeper. Between 2007 and 2008, the convent was renovated to include a preschool, conference rooms, offices, and a chapel. The groundbreaking took place on February 15, 2007, and the Most Rev. Richard J. Garcia, 4th Bishop of Monterey in California, blessed both the building and the grounds.

900 W. Branch Street, Arroyo Grande
San Luis Obispo County
www.StPatSchoolAg.com

SAINT ROSE SCHOOL in the City of Paso Robles is a diocesan coed school for children in preschool through the eighth grade. The school opened its doors on September 7, 1959 under the direction of the **Sisters of St. Joseph of Carondelet** from Wichita, Kansas. At first, only grades one through five were offered. Within three years, grades six, seven, and eight were added. In 1981, the Parish Center was constructed, which provides a venue for school-wide gatherings such as assemblies, plays, prayer services, and sporting events; it also houses our school library and computer lab. In 1983, a kindergarten and pre-school were added. In 1987, a new classroom, staff lounge, and staff workroom were added and between 1991 and 1993, two modular classrooms were added.

900 Tucker Avenue, Paso Robles
San Luis Obispo County
www.SaintRoseCatholicSchool.org

SALESIAN ELEMENTARY AND JUNIOR HIGH SCHOOL in Corralitos is a private Catholic coed school from kindergarten through the eighth grade that began in 1975, though it

can trace its origins to when the **Salesian Sisters of St. John Bosco** ran a high school and a summer camp out of the historic Sesnon-Porter home in Aptos. The Salesian Sisters sold the property to Cabrillo Community College and moved to Corralitos.

By 1976, the Salesian Sisters had established the **Mary, Help of Christians Youth Center**, consisting of four multipurpose cabins, a kitchen, a cafeteria, basketball and tennis courts, a swimming pool, and a playfield. A novitiate program and a summer camp were also established. The need for a Catholic school with grades kindergarten through eight arose, and by September 1, 1978, the Salesian Elementary and Junior High School was established and continues to be run by the Salesian Sisters.

605 Enos Lane, Corralitos
Santa Cruz County
www.SalesianSchool.org

SAN CARLOS SCHOOL in the City of Monterey is a coed parochial school (kindergarten through grade 8) that can trace its origins to 1894, when the parochial school was first founded. In 1897, the San Carlos elementary and secondary school was constructed, and it served 170 students. The school was officially dedicated on August 31, 1898, and was staffed by the **Sisters of Saint Joseph of Carondolet**. The school closed in 1915 and the Sisters departed. The school reopened between 1917 and 1919 as an elementary school under the **Franciscan Sisters of Mary Immaculate and Saint Joseph for the Dying**.

In 1971, the old San Carlos School building at Webster and Figueroa was demolished and the elementary school moved to the building of the former Junípero Memorial High School, which had been founded in 1949 and closed in 1970. In June of 1974, the Diocesan Board of Education voted to designate San Carlos School as a regional or inter-parish institution. In 1980, the **Franciscan Sisters** withdrew from the school which was then administered by an **Adrian Dominican Sister** until July of 2001. San Carlos School is now run as a parish ministry of San Carlos Cathedral by a lay principal and a committed, dedicated, professional lay faculty.

450 Church Street, Monterey
Monterey County
www.SanCarlosSchool.org

Nota bene: Old Mission School in San Luis Obispo is highlighted on page 108.

PALMA SCHOOL in the City of Salinas is a private Catholic school for boys in grades 7 through 12 owned and operated by the **Congregation of Christian Brothers** that was established in 1951 by Msgr. Thomas J. Earley and a group of dedicated community members. The Most Rev. Aloysius J. Willinger, 3rd Bishop of Monterey-Fresno, formally dedicated the school on December 11, 1953. With a reputation for excellence in academics, athletics, and the arts, Palma differentiates itself as the only school of its kind with a diverse student body that commutes from as far north as Gilroy, as far south as King City, west from the Monterey Peninsula and Santa Cruz, and from Hollister to the east.

919 Iverson Street, Salinas
Monterey County
www.PalmaSchool.org

Photo courtesy of John Glover, 2015.　　The Palma High School Chapel. Photo courtesy of John Glover, 2015.

NOTRE DAME HIGH SCHOOL in the City of Salinas is a diocesan secondary school for girls in grades 9 through 12 and was founded in 1951 as the girls division of Palma High School, under the direction of the Sisters of Notre Dame de Namur. "As a diocesan co-instructional school staffed by the Sisters of Notre Dame de Namur and the Congregation of Christian Brothers, the enrollment increased steadily." The schools separated during the 1964-1965 school year, with the girls moving to a new campus at its current location. "A close relationship continues to exist between the two schools. Activities, such as dances, extra-curricular activities, sports, homecoming, Associated Student Body (ASB), drama, band, yearbook and a yearly event are still conducted jointly between Palma and Notre Dame."

455 Palma Drive, Salinas
Monterey County
www.NotreDameSalinas.org

Photo courtesy of John Glover, 2015.

SAINT FRANCIS CENTRAL COAST CATHOLIC HIGH SCHOOL in the City of Watsonville is coed high school (grades 9 through 12) that was established in 2000 as a joint venture between the Diocese of Monterey in California and the Salesians of St. John Bosco. The first classes were held at Holy Cross parish church in Santa Cruz before moving to the permanent site, which is located across from the parish church of Our Lady, Help of Christians. In March of 2000, the first $1 million donation for the Saint Francis Central Coast Catholic High School was received from a local donor. On August 20, 2001, groundbreaking for the new high school took place. On September 19, 2004, the new Borina Athletic Center and Strawberry Fields were dedicated.

2400 East Lake Avenue, Watsonville
Santa Cruz County
www.StFrancisHigh.net

Photo courtesy of John Glover, 2015.

Photo courtesy of John Glover, 2015.

SANTA CATALINA SCHOOL in the City of Monterey is a private Catholic coed school from preschool through the eighth grade and for girls from the ninth through the twelfth grade.

SANTA
CATALINA
SCHOOL

The school can trace its origins to 1850, when the Rt. Rev. Joseph Alemany, OP, 1st Bishop of Monterey, and Sr. Marie Goemaere, OP, established the original Santa Catalina Convent in what is now downtown Monterey, but which was at that time the capital of California. The original Santa Catalina School was also established, which was the first non-mission Catholic school in California. Classes were conducted in Spanish for the daughters of local residents. In 1853, the state capital moved to the City of Benicia and by 1854, Mother M. Goemaere and her community of French Dominican sisters relocated their school to the new capital. The adobe building in Monterey became the new **Saint Catherine's Academy,** and educated American students whose families had moved west.

Almost a century later, Sr. Margaret Thompson, OP, Mother General of the **Dominican Sisters of San Rafael,** re-established Santa Catalina School for girls in Monterey on a 36-acre Spanish colonial estate previously owned by Colonel Harold L. Mack, officially re-opening in the fall of 1950. Sr. Mary Kieran, OP, served as the first principal until her death in 1965. She was succeeded by Sr. Carlotta O'Donnell, who served as principal for 35 years.

The school grew from the original hacienda to 14 classrooms, offices, dormitory buildings, the Rosary Chapel, an athletic field, swimming pool, and tennis courts. In 1970, a preschool and kindergarten program was established.

1500 Mark Thomas Drive, Monterey
Monterey County
www.SantaCatalina.org

The oldest school on the Central Coast...

On August 16, 1876, the **Sisters of the Immaculate Heart of Mary** opened the doors to the **Academy of the Sacred Heart,** now the site of **Mission College Preparatory Catholic High School (MCP).** Also known as the **Academy of the Immaculate Heart of Mary,** the three-story parish school with a convent offered both an elementary and secondary school education until 1886, when the high school had to be closed due to the need for the sisters to staff the new Cathedral School in Los Angeles.

Sometime before 1924, the 3-story building was nearly destroyed in a fire and the sisters scrambled for other space to teach the grammar school students. In 1924, under the guidance of the Rev. Daniel J. Keenan, 38th pastor of Old Mission San Luis Obispo, plans were made for a new parochial elementary and secondary school. Construction was funded from a grant by the Hearst family. Bishop MacGinley and Archbishop Hanna of San Francisco dedicated the new **Mission School** on August 19, 1926, the fiftieth anniversary of the founding of the original **Academy of the Immaculate Heart.** The grammar school occupied the ground floor and the high school occupied the second floor.

The task of providing separate facilities for the grammar school and the high school began in 1957 with the construction of **Mission Grammar School** on Broad Street, now the site of **Old Mission School.** The school on Palm Street then became **Mission Central Catholic High School.** In 1961, **Mission School Annex** was constructed on Daly Street, now the site of **Old Mission School's Nativity Campus.**

In 1964, Old Mission San Luis Obispo's mission station of the Nativity of Our Lady became a parish in its own right. Mission School Annex was re-named **Nativity Grammar School,** becoming a parochial school of the new parish. In 1968, Mission Grammar School and Nativity Grammar School were consolidated and renamed **Mission-Nativity Elementary School,** with both parishes subsidizing the new school.

Photo courtesy of John Glover, 2015.

In June 1970, **Mission Central Catholic High School** was closed and **Mission-Nativity Elementary School** was expanded to include the ninth grade, eventually taking over the former **Mission High School** building for its junior high school. The school now had three campuses: Broad Street, Daly Street, and Palm Street.

In September of 1971, a morning preschool and kindergarten program was begun at the **Nativity** campus and an afternoon program was added in the spring of 1972. Between 1974 and 1975, the consolidated school resumed the name Mission School. From 1981 to 1984, the preschool and kindergarten programs were relocated to the building on Palm Street, sharing the space with the junior high.

In September of 1983, the doors of the new **Mission College Preparatory Catholic High School** were opened. Because of its endowment fund, the new high school was able to offer a total of $20,000 in financial aid to its students the first year.

With the reopening of the old high school on Palm Street as **Mission College Preparatory School**, Old Mission School's seventh and eighth grades were moved to the campus on Broad Street, with the ninth grade once again becoming part of the high school. In 1984, the preschool and kindergarten programs returned to the campus on Daly Street, officially becoming **Old Mission School's Nativity Campus.**

In 1999, a building project began to more than double the size of **Mission College Preparatory Catholic High School** and to provide state-of-the-art science classrooms, computer facilities, cafeteria, gymnasium and locker rooms, professional space, and underground parking. The new building was completed in time for the 2004'2005 school year. In 2008, construction began to provide seismic upgrades and renovations to the historic building that has served the school since 1926.

Mission College Preparatory Catholic High School
682 Palm Street, San Luis Obispo
www.MissionPrep.org

Old Mission School
761 Broad Street, San Luis Obispo

Old Mission School's Nativity Campus
221 Daly Street, San Luis Obispo

www.OldMissionSchool.com

Mora Central High School
1957 – 1970

The former **Mora Central High School** on Arthur Road in Watsonville can trace its origins to 1956, when land for the school was purchased for $30,000. A $300,000 fundraising campaign to build a central Catholic high school soon began and groundbreaking took place on September 23. The school officially opened in September of 1957.

In 1963, revenue from plot sales in the Pajaro Valley Public Cemetery was used to reduce the debt from the construction of Mora High and a cafeteria was added. In February of 1969, parishioners voted to keep the school open with an all-lay staff after the staff of religious sisters withdrew from the school. Due to low enrollment and a projected budget deficit, Bishop Clinch closed Mora Central High School in 1970.

"Just as the human body deserves to be treated with respect and dignity in life, so should they be treated in death. The Catholic Cemeteries of the Diocese of Monterey exist to meet the needs of individuals and families in preparation for, in time of, and following the event of death. Our primary focus continues to be the comforting of the bereaved. We strive to serve as a symbol of the extended community of the Church—a community unbroken by death" (Mission Statement).

www.CemeteriesDOM.org

Active Cemeteries

CALVARY – SACRED HEART CEMETERY is located in the southeast part of Hollister and was established in 1874 in order to meet the needs of Sacred Heart parish. Measuring 12.67 acres, five acres in the rear of the cemetery remained undeveloped until recently. The chapel mausoleum complex was constructed in 1999. The cemetery currently serves the parishes of Sacred Heart in Hollister, Immaculate Conception in Tres Piños, and Old Mission San Juan Bautista.

1100 Hillcrest Road, Hollister
San Benito County

HOLY CROSS CEMETERY was established in 1943 in order to supplement the depleted space of the Old Holy Cross Cemetery that had been established in 1873, which is located just around the block. The cemetery began and continues to be a flush monument only (no upright headstones, though mausoleum complexes began being added in the 1950's. The newest addition was completed in 1997 and surrounds the chapel mausoleum complex, featuring murals depicting scenes from the life of Christ. The cemetery currently serves the parishes of Holy Cross in Santa Cruz, Saint Joseph in Capitola, Resurrection in Aptos, Our Lady, Star of the Sea in Santa Cruz, as well as the nearby parishes of Holy Eucharist in Corralitos, Our Lady, Help of Christians and Saint Patrick in Watsonville, Saint John in Felton, and San Agustín in Scotts Valley.

2271 Seventh Avenue, Santa Cruz
Santa Cruz County

OLD MISSION CEMETERY is located two miles south of Old Mission San Luis Obispo and was established in 1877, measuring 9.2 acres. Various beautification projects began in 1964, including paving, new plantings, and an irrigation system. Between 1971 and 1972, the Mary Gate of Heaven Mausoleum was constructed, which consists of a chapel with room for 640 internments. The mausoleum was dedicated on October 28, 1972. The cemetery currently serves the parishes of Old Mission San Luis Obispo, Nativity of Our Lady, Saint William in Atascadero, Saint Rose of Lima in Paso Robles, Saint Patrick in Arroyo Grande, Saint Joseph in Nipomo, and Saint Timothy in Morro Bay.

101 Bridge Street, San Luis Obispo
San Luis Obispo County

QUEEN OF HEAVEN CEMETERY was established in January of 1964 by Msgr. Thomas Earley as the parish cemetery for Sacred Heart in Salinas. Measuring 30 acres, 12 remain undeveloped. The cemetery is considered one of the most attractive in Monterey County, with its beautifully landscaped environment and recent plant renovations. On May 13, 2015, the Memorial of Our Lady of Fátima, Bishop Garcia blessed newly-constructed statues of Our Lady of Fátima, the Servant of God Lúcia dos Santos († 2005), Blessed Francisco Marto († 1919), and Blessed Jacinta Marto († 1920). While still a Catholic cemetery, Queen of Heaven also serves the needs of much of the community in the greater Salinas area.

18200 Damian Way, Salinas
Monterey County

SAN CARLOS CEMETERY is located in central Monterey across from Dennis the Menace Park and was established in in 1832, when the cemetery was transferred to the lagoon area from the vicinity of the Royal Presidio Chapel—though the official date for the founding of the cemetery is sometimes cited as 1834. On June 31, 1839, a 60 x 60 *varas* area of "*el campo santo*" was blessed for burials. In 1851, a 7-acre site was established, half of which was transferred for a "Protestant cemetery," which later became *El Encinal*, the cemetery of the City of Monterey. Many of the founding members of the local community rest in this cemetery, making it truly historic.

Construction on the Our Lady of Bethlehem Mausoleum began in 1970. On Palm Sunday, April 4, 1971, the new mausoleum was blessed, in addition to the Santa Rosalia Chapel, garden crypts, and the office. Another dedication was celebrated on May 29, 1972. A number of outdoor crypts were built in the last four decades. The largest, Our Lady of Angels, which contains 1,000 crypts, was constructed in 1993. In 2007, an additional 400 crypts were added.

San Carlos Cemetery currently serves eight parishes: San Carlos Cathedral in Monterey, Carmel Mission Basilica, Saint Angela's in Pacific Grove, Our Lady of Mount Carmel in Carmel Valley, Saint Jude in Marina, Saint Francis Xavier in Seaside, Our Lady of Refuge in Castroville, and Saint Joseph in Spreckels.

**792 Fremont Street, Monterey
Monterey County**

RESURRECTION CEMETERY, formerly known as Our Lady of Mount Carmel Cemetery, in Aptos was officially established in 1875 when five month old Josefa Arano was interred on September 14. Land for a church and cemetery had been donated in 1868 by Rafael de Jesus Castro († 1878) and construction of the church was completed in October of 1875. Both the church and cemetery were dedicated in honor of Our Lady of Mount Carmel. Cypress trees were planted around the cemetery and down the Santa Cruz Watsonville Road (Soquel Drive) the following year.

**7600 Soquel Avenue, Aptos
Santa Cruz County**

Inactive Cemeteries

The OLD CALVARY CEMETERY in Salinas in Monterey County was established in 1870 on two acres of land belonging to Mr. George N. Graves († 1889), a farmer who had settled in the Salinas Valley in 1855. Graves set aside a place for private burials on his ranch, upon the death of some of his young children. He soon saw the need for a community cemetery, and deeded the site to the diocese. The cemetery was closed to further burials in 1960. As the cemetery is the resting place of many Salinas Valley pioneers and their descendants, the first restoration effort was undertaken in 1975 by the Knights of Columbus (council no. 1948). In 2003, the Old Calvary Cemetery Restoration Committee was founded to make necessary repairs and establish an endowment fund. In 2008, the committee reported that it had raised $100,000 and that renovation work was 80% complete. The Monterey County Historical Society was also seeking an official Historical Landmark designation.

The OLD HOLY CROSS CEMETERY in Santa Cruz was established in 1873 on 6.8 acres of land that was purchased by the Diocese of Monterey-Los Angeles from Mr. Frederick A. Hihn († 1913). In 1866, it had become apparent that the Santa Cruz mission cemetery was too overcrowded following the following the influx of miners, settlers, and immigrants that the California Gold Rush and subsequent statehood had brought to the area. The new cemetery was blessed by the Rt. Rev. Francisco Mora, 2nd Bishop of Monterey-Los Angeles, on October 12, 1873. The first two burials occurred later that afternoon and the cemetery would go on to serve the Catholic faithful of the Santa Cruz area for the next 75 years before it too became overcrowded. In 1943, ground was broken for the new Holy Cross Cemetery a block away. Following the Second World War, Old Holy Cross Cemetery fell into ruin as little money was available for its upkeep. It has recently been restored and beautified by the Friends of Old Holy Cross Cemetery.

The OLD SANTA ROSA CEMETERY in Cambria in San Luis Obispo County was established, along with the Old Santa Rosa Chapel, in 1871. Dedicated to St. Rose of Lima, both were on land that was originally part of Mission San Miguel. After the construction of the larger Santa Rosa parish church in the 1960s, the chapel and adjacent cemetery fell to ruin by vandals. In 1978, a committee was formed to save both the chapel and the cemetery. In 1982, both were listed on the National Register of Historic Places.

SAINT PATRICK CEMETERY in Arroyo Grande in San Luis Obispo County was established in 1887, when Mr. John M. Price († 1902) sold the property to the Diocese of Monterey-Los Angeles for use as a cemetery. The last burial occurred in 1981. The cemetery would soon fall prey to both weather and vandalism. Various local organizations attempted to maintain the historic site until the cemetery had to be fenced off in order to protect the graves from any further vandalism. Restoration and beautification efforts are currently underway.

The SANTA RITA CEMETERY in Salinas in Monterey County was active from the 1890s to the 1960s, and is part of the grounds of the Our Lady of Guadalupe or Santa Rita Chapel, currently a mission station of the parish of Madonna del Sasso. The cemetery is the final resting place of many Salinas Valley pioneers and their descendants. Like the chapel, the cemetery would fall into a poor state. The first renovation effort began in 1972 and the last burials in the cemetery took place in the 1980's. In 2004, the Santa Rita Chapel Renovation Fund launched a project to locate relatives and descendants of those who were interred in Santa Rita Cemetery. The Monterey County Historical Society estimated that there were 490 graves in the cemetery. In 2005, small markers to identify anonymous graves were planned and regular maintenance of the cemetery began.

There are also eight inactive mission cemeteries:

1. Mission San Carlos Borromeo del Rio Carmelo (Carmel Mission Basilica)
2. Mission San Antonio
3. Mission San Juan Bautista
4. Mission San Luis Obispo
5. Mission San Miguel
6. Mission Santa Cruz
7. Mission Soledad

AVE MARIA SENIOR LIVING was originally founded in 1954 by the Congregation of the **Franciscan Sisters of Mary Immaculate and Saint Joseph for the Dying** as the **Ave Maria Convalescent Home** for women. In 1965, the facility had grown to a 31-bed non-profit community that provides skilled nursing care. In 2010, the convent and chaplain's residence were converted "to residential care facilities for the elderly, providing assisted living care for seniors," continuing to serve as the motherhouse of the Franciscan Sisters of Mary Immaculate and Saint Joseph for the Dying until the death of its last sister in 2012.

> **1249 Josselyn Canyon Road, Monterey**
> **www.AveMariaMonterey.com**

DOMINICAN HOSPITAL can trace its origins to August of 1941, when the **Adrian Dominican Sisters** arrived at the request of the Diocese of Monterey-Fresno, and took over the Hanley Hospital located on West Cliff Drive in the City of Santa Cruz. On September 14, it re-opened as Santa Cruz Sisters Hospital.

> ### Mission, Vision, and Values
>
> Dignity Health and Dominican Hospital
> are committed to furthering the healing ministry of Jesus,
> and to providing high-quality,
> affordable healthcare
> to the communities we serve.

In 1949, the Adrian Dominican Sisters purchased Santa Cruz Hospital on Soquel Avenue from a physicians group. This 49-bed hospital was renamed Dominican Santa Cruz Hospital. The Adrian Dominican Sisters now operated two hospitals to meet the needs of the growing community. In 1951, Dominican Santa Cruz Hospital was dedicated by Bishop Willinger.

In 1967, a 17-acre site on the outskirts of the city was purchased and all Dominican Sisters hospital activities were moved to this new site on Soquel Avenue. The new hospital with 150 beds opened on December 26. On August 6, 1978, Msgr. Tod E. Brown blessed a new Outpatient Service Building.

In 1980, plans were made for a three-year project to expand Dominican Hospital by 114 beds. Groundbreaking took place on July 17, 1981, and the total cost was estimated at $17.6 million. On July 11, 1983, a new 28-bed Mental Health Unit was dedicated by Bishop Shubsda. The $3 million building was designed by architect Robert Radell. It was built to provide short-term acute care for Santa Cruz County, as well as private long-term services.

In 1990, Dominican Hospital purchased AMI Community Hospital on Frederick Street in Santa Cruz, which then became **Dominican Rehabilitation Services.** The two campuses provide a total of 379 acute care beds. In 2006, the Adrian Dominican Sisters celebrated 65 years in Santa Cruz. From its original five sisters, the local resources had grown to 14 sisters, with 500 medical staff, 1,700 employees, and 450 volunteers. The hospital had grown to 369 beds on two sites with a wide variety of services.

> **1555 Soquel Drive, Santa Cruz, CA. 95065**
> **www.DominicanHospital.org**

DOMINICAN OAKS, opened by Dominican Hospital in 1988, is a 206-apartment residential community for seniors with assisted living services for those residents that require them. Located in a quiet, wooded setting behind the hospital, "residents live a quality lifestyle and remain independent while receiving the unique benefits of congregate living."

> **3400 Paul Sweet Rd, Santa Cruz**
> **www.DominicanOaks.com**

NEWMAN CENTERS, also known as **Newman Clubs,** are ministry centers at non-Catholic universities and can be found throughout the world. The movement was inspired by Blessed John Henry Cardinal Newman († 1890), who encouraged societies for Catholic students attending secular universities. The very first Newman Club was established at Oxford in 1888. The first Newman Club in the United States was established at the University of Pennsylvania in 1893.

The Diocese of Monterey in California established the **Department of Campus Ministry** in 1970, and there are Newman Centers at the California State Polytechnic Institute / Cuesta College in San Luis Obispo, Cabrillo College in Santa Cruz, and the University of California at Santa Cruz.

www.sloNewman.org
www.newmanite.org

RETREAT HOUSES

"In the fever and agitation of modern life, the need of meditation and spiritual repose impresses itself on Christian souls who desire to reflect on their eternal destiny, and direct their life in this world towards God."[92]

Camp Saint Francis

2320 Sumner Avenue, Aptos
www.donboscowest.org/salesianym/campstfrancis

Saint Francis Retreat Center

549 Mission Vineyard Road, San Juan Bautista
www.StFrancisRetreat.com

Saint Clare's Retreat House

2381 Laurel Glen Road, Soquel
www.StClaresRetreatCenter.com

Villa Maria del Mar Retreat Center

21918 E. Cliff Drive, Santa Cruz
www.VillaMariadelMar.org

Nota bene:
The New Camaldoli Hermitage in Big Sur and the Monastery of the Risen Christ in San Luis Obispo also offer retreat services.

> 92 PAUL DEBUCHY, *The Catholic Encyclopedia*, vol. 12 (1911).

Heraldry is both art and science. It is a phenomenon very much a part of the legal and social structures of practically every continent on earth. It originated nearly a thousand years ago in Europe and has been carried throughout the world by both the migrating peoples of continental Europe and by the Church, which is represented in every corner of the globe.

JAMES-CHARLES NOONAN, JR.
The Church Visible (1996), p. 187

The Coat of Arms of the Diocese of Monterey in California

The coat of arms of the Diocese of Monterey in California consists of a red field (background) with a white mountain and a gold crown, representing Monterey, named in honor of Gaspar de Zúñiga Acevedo y Fonseca († 1606), 5th Count of Monterrey and Viceroy of New Spain, Monterrey (*Monterrei*) being Spanish for "mountain of the king." The colors of red and gold are those of the Count of Monterrey's home of Castile and León in Spain and the color white represents the sands of the beaches of Monterey and the gold cross standing between two mission bells represents Saint Junípero Serra, the Apostle of California. [93]

Blazon: Gules, issuing from a mount argent, a wooden Latin cross or, between two bells of the second, in base a crown proper.

The Coats of Arms of the Bishops of Monterey in California

Upon elevation to the episcopacy, all bishops are required to assume a personal coat of arms or heraldic achievement, which is a unique design on a shield that must conform to the rules of heraldry, as well as be simple and clear. Before 1960, the process of designing and displaying a bishop's coat of arms was "in the strict domain of the Heraldry Commission of the Roman Curia." [94] This office was abolished by Pope Saint John XXIII, requiring bishops to "assume" their heraldic achievement without the official mandate or advice of the Church.

Ecclesiastical heraldry is not determined by heraldic considerations alone but also by doctrinal, liturgical, and canonical factors. It not only produces arms denoting members of the ecclesiastical state but also shows the rank of the bearer. [95]

A complete heraldic achievement or coat of arms is generally composed of a shield (*escutcheon*) with its symbols (*charges*), a motto scroll, and external ornaments. The shield (*escutcheon*) is

the central and most important feature of any heraldic device and is always officially described (*blazoned*) in rather archaic 12th century terms. The external ornamentation for the coat of arms of a bishop "include a gold processional cross that is placed in back of the shield and which extends above and below the shield; and the pontifical hat, called a gallero, with its six tassels in three rows on either side of the shield, all in green—the heraldic insignia of a prelate of the rank of bishop." [96]

It is customary for diocesan bishops, particularly in the United States, to join their personal coat of arms with the arms of the diocese they head. The diocesan coat of arms appears on the left side (*dexter*) of the shield and the personal arms of the bishop appear on the right side (*sinister*) of the shield.

Papal coats of arms have their own unique customs, as do the heraldic achievements of deacons, priests, religious, parishes, dioceses, and religious orders.

> 93 Cf. *Observer,* March 2007, p. 28.
> 94 JAMES-CHARLES NOONAN, JR., *The Church Visible* (1996), p. 188.
> 95 BRUNO B. HEIM, *Heraldry in the Catholic Church* (1981), p. 43: JAMES-CHARLES NOONAN, JR., *The Church Visible* (1996), p. 188.
> 96 *Observer,* March 2007, p. 28.

The Coat of Arms
of the Most Rev. Harry A. Clinch

1st Bishop of Monterey in California

The coat of arms or heraldic achievement of Bishop Clinch was designed by William F.J. Ryan upon his elevation to the episcopacy as Auxiliary Bishop of Monterey-Fresno in 1956. The coat of arms of Bishop Clinch is based on the arms of the Clinch family of Ireland, which consist of three black lozenges on a gold field. The arms were differenced or personalized for Bishop Clinch by the addition of symbols or charges signifying Saint Anselm († 1109), Doctor of the Church and the baptismal patron of Bishop Clinch.

The open black book, leaved in gold and bearing the Greek letters *alpha* and *omega* in the same tincture "symbolizes the deep influence of St. Anselm on Catholic philosophy and theology. The black archiepiscopal cross that is above and below the book both represents St. Anselm as Archbishop of Canterbury and his membership in the Benedictine Order, which bears a similar cross in its coat of arms. Benedictines also wear the color black.

The episcopal motto of Bishop Clinch was "*salus animárum supréma lex,*" Latin for "the salvation of souls is the supreme law," a quotation from canon 1752 of the *Code of Canon Law*, referring "to the ultimate aim of the Church's canon law, which is for the aid of those in the Church to reach salvation. Thus, the principal aim of canon law is not meant to be essentially disciplinary but medicinal or nourishing."[97]

This motto was also the episcopal motto of Archbishop Thomas E. Molloy († 1956), 5th Bishop of Brooklyn, who died within hours of Bishop Clinch's appointment to the episcopate. Bishop Willinger, who consecrated Bishop Clinch, had been consecrated to the episcopacy by Bishop Molloy in 1929. "Thus the motto affords an estimable symbol of the Succession of the Apostles in our time from St. Peter, the first Bishop of Rome and the first Pope" (William F.J. Ryan, 22 November 1967).

Blazon: Impaled arms. Dexter: Gules, issuing from a mount argent, a wooden Latin cross or, between two bells of the second, in base a crown proper (Diocese of Monterey). *Sinister:* Or, an archiepiscopal cross surmounted by an open book sable, leaved and garnished and bearing Greek letters, alpha and omega, of the field, between three lozenges of the second.

> 97 James T. Bretzke, *Consecrated Phrases: A Latin Theological Dictionary* (1998), p. 215.

Blazon: Impaled arms. Dexter: Gules, issuing from a mount argent, a wooden Latin cross or, between two bells of the second, in base a crown proper (Diocese of Monterey). Sinister: The dove and blue background signifies the Bishop's devotion to the Holy Spirit and to Mary, the Blessed Mother of God.

The Coat of Arms
of the Most Rev. Thaddeus A. Shubsda

2nd Bishop of Monterey in California

The coat of arms or heraldic achievement of Bishop Shubsda was designed upon his elevation to the episcopacy as Auxiliary Bishop of Los Angeles in 1976. The coat of arms of Bishop Shubsda consists of a white dove on a blue shield. The white dove represents the Holy Spirit, the third person of the Blessed Trinity. The blue background represents the Blessed Virgin Mary.

The episcopal motto of Bishop Clinch was *"Imple supérna grátia,"* Latin for "fill with heavenly grace." These words are taken from the hymn *Veni, Creator Spiritus.* Attributed to Rabanus Maurus († 856), the hymn is used at Pentecost, the Dedication of a Church, the celebration of the sacraments of Confirmation and Holy Orders, and whenever the Holy Spirit is solemnly invoked. The popular English translation of this hymn traditionally translates this line as "come with Thy grace and heavenly aid."

The Coat of Arms
of the Most Rev. Sylvester D. Ryan

3rd Bishop of Monterey in California

The coat of arms or heraldic achievement of Bishop Ryan was designed by Paul J. Sullivan upon his elevation to the episcopacy as Auxiliary Bishop of Los Angeles in 1990. Bishop Ryan selected a design that brought together representations of his life as a priest, and then as a bishop. The background of the shield (or "field"), is white (silver) on which are displayed a broken ship's wheel, in red, which is the ancient symbol of Saint Catherine of Alexandria. This charge was employed to signify that Bishop Ryan was the first priest from Santa Catalina Island to be elevated to the episcopacy. It also honored Bishop Ryan's childhood parish of Saint Catherine. Above the wheel are two pairs of blue wings with a red rose between each. These charges are taken from the arms of the Archdiocese of Los Angeles.

The episcopal motto of Bishop Ryan is "Servants of Christ." These words are taken from the first and second verses of the fourth chapter of Saint Paul's First Letter to the Corinthians: " This is how one should regard us, as servants of Christ and stewards of the mysteries of God. Moreover it is required of stewards that they be found trustworthy; Latin: "*Sic nos existimet homo ut ministros Christi et dispensatores mysteriorum Dei. Hic iam quaeritur inter dispensatores, ut fidelis quis inveniatur.*"

Bishop Ryan's episcopal motto expresses "the ancient Christian belief that each of us, who has received the Faith, and especially the bishops, priests, and deacons of the Church, who have been entrusted with the preaching and teaching of the Faith, must live according to the charge they have been given in order to be found worthy of that great responsibility" (Paul J. Sullivan, 25 April 1990).

Blazon: Impaled arms. Dexter: Gules, issuant from a mount Argent a wooden Latin cross Or between two bells of the second; in base a crown Proper. Sinister: Argent, a broken ship's wheel Gules, below two pairs of wings Azure, between each wing a rose of the second, barbed and seeded Vert.

The Coat of Arms
of the Most Rev. Richard J. Garcia

4ᵗʰ Bishop of Monterey in California

Blazon: Impaled arms. Dexter: Gules, issuing from a mount argent, a wooden Latin cross or, between two bells of the second, in base a crown proper (Diocese of Monterey). *Sinister:* Argent, a semé of seven pointed stars Azure; per fess at the nombril point and tied at center a sash Gules below a California Golden Eagle Proper.

The coat of arms or heraldic achievement of Bishop Garcia was designed by Paul J. Sullivan upon his elevation to the episcopacy as Auxiliary Bishop of Sacramento in 1998. Bishop Garcia's coat of arms reflects the deep devotion of his California and Mexican-American heritage.

"The main body of the design is a variant on the mantle of Our Lady of Guadalupe, to whom Bishop Garcia has particular devotion. Here on a silver (white) field is a scattering (*semé*) of no specific number of blue stars as seen on Our Lady's mantle with the colors varied from gold on blue to blue on silver. Overall, at a point about one-third of the way up the shield, called the 'nombril point', is a tied red sash. This belt is seen in the portrait of Our Lady and was a classic accessory for a woman in the Mexican culture who was with child as Mary appeared to Saint Juan Diego at the time of Our Lady's appearance. The belt indicated that the Blessed Virgin was carrying the Divine Lord and that as His Mother she was and is our mother too.

"Above the belt, represented in its natural colors (Proper) is a California Golden Eagle, as taken from the Mexican flag. This bird, that is indigenous to the region, is of particular significance for The Bishop because he used "The Eagle" as the topic for his graduate dissertation, examining all the ways that the eagle, as referring to God, is recorded in Sacred Scripture, is used in religious art or in other culturally significant ways" (Deacon Paul J. Sullivan, heraldic artist).

The episcopal motto of Bishop Garcia is "*En El vivimos*," Spanish for "In Him we live" (Latin: *In ipso enim vivimus*). These words are taken from the twenty-eighth verse of the seventeenth chapter of the Acts of the Apostles: "In Him we live and move and have our being"; Latin: "*In ipso enim vívimus et movémur et sumus*" (*Nova-Vulgata*); Spanish: "*En él vivimos, nos movemos y existimos*" (*Traducción argentina, 1990*).

Bishop Garcia's episcopal motto expresses his "deep belief that the lives of Christians are ordered in such a way that 'for Him we live and move and have our being'" (*Observer*, March 2007, p. 28). Bishop Garcia's episcopal motto is also referenced in Preface VI of the Sundays in Ordinary Time: "For in You we live and move and have our being [*In quo vívimus, movémur et sumus*]" (*The Roman Missal*, Third Edition (2010), Order of Mass, n. 57).

Metropolitans of the Ecclesiastical Province of Los Angeles

1.	Most Rev. John J. Cantwell	1936 – 1947 †
2.	His Eminence James F. Card. McIntyre	1948 – 1970
3.	His Eminence Timothy Card. Manning	1970 – 1985
4.	His Eminence Roger Card. Mahony	1985 – 2011
5.	Most Rev. José H. Gómez	2011 –

Bishop of California

1.	Rt. Rev. Francisco José Vicente Garcia Diego y Moreno, OFM	1840 – 1846 †
	Rev. José Maria González Rúbio, OFM *administrator of the Diocese of California*	1846 – 1849

Bishops of Monterey

1.	Rt. Rev. Joseph Sadoc Alemany y Conill, OP	1850 – 1853
2.	Rt. Rev. Thaddeus Amat y Brusi, CM	1853 – 1873

Bishops of Monterey-Los Angeles

1.	Rt. Rev. Thaddeus Amat y Brusi, CM	1873 – 1878 †
2.	Rt. Rev. Francisco Mora y Borrell	1878 – 1896
3.	Rt. Rev. George T. Montgomery	1896 – 1902
4.	Rt. Rev. Thomas J. Conaty	1903 – 1915 †
	Rt. Rev. Peter J. Muldoon *(appointment never took effect)*	1917
5.	Rt. Rev. John J. Cantwell	1917 – 1922

Bishops of Monterey-Fresno

1.	John B. MacGinley	1924 – 1932
2.	Philip G. Scher	1933 – 1953 †
3.	Aloysius J. Willinger, C.Ss.R.	1953 – 1967

Bishops of Monterey in California

1.	Most Rev. Harry A. Clinch	1967 – 1982
2.	Most Rev. Thaddeus A. Shubsda	1982 – 1991 †
3.	Most Rev. Sylvester D. Ryan	1992 – 2007
4.	Most Rev. Richard J. Garcia	2007 –

Administration Assignments since December 13, 1967:

Vicar Generals

1.	Msgr. Thomas Earley	1967 – 1980
2.	Msgr. Thomas Neary	1981 – 1983
3.	Msgr. Philip Maxwell	1968 – 1983 †
4.	Msgr. Tod D. Brown	1983 – 1988
5.	Msgr. D. Declan Murphy	1989 – 2006
6.	Msgr. Charles G. Fatooh	2002 – 2003
7.	Very Rev. Peter Crivello	2003 –

Moderators of the Curia

1.	Msgr. Tod D. Brown	1985 – 1988
2.	Msgr. Charles G. Fatooh	1989 – 2006
3.	Rev. Roy Shelly, SDB	2007 – 2011
4.	Very Rev. Peter Crivello	2016 –

Episcopal Vicar

1.	Very Rev. James Henry	2003 – 2006

Chancellors

1.	Msgr. Thomas Neary	1967 – 1971
2.	Msgr. Philip Maxwell	1971 – 1982
3.	Msgr. Tod D. Brown	1982 – 1988
4.	Msgr. Charles G. Fatooh	1989 – 2001*
5.	Ms. Molly McDonald, Esq.	2001 – 2003
6.	Sr. Patricia Murtagh, IM	2003 –

Vice Chancellors

1.	Msgr. Philip Maxwell	1969 – 1970
2.	Rev. James Henry	1981 – 1982
3.	Br. John O'Brien, CFX	1995 – 2001

Vicars for Clergy

1.	Msgr. Thomas Neary	1972 – 1980
2.	Msgr. Tod D. Brown	1981 – 1983
3.	Rev. Michael Miller	1997 – 1999
4.	Rev. Jerry McCormick	2000 – 2006
5.	Rev. Paul P. Murphy	2007 –

Vicars for Religious

1.	Msgr. Tom Morgan	1969 – 1974
2.	Msgr. Thomas Neary	1974 – 1975
3.	Msgr. Philip Maxwell	1976 – 1983
4.	Rev. Victor Farrell	1984 – 1993
5.	Br. William Bolts, SM	1994
6.	Sr. Adrienne Piennette, OP	1994 – 1998
7.	Rev. Thomas Long CSV	1995 – 1996
8.	Sr. Gabriela Covi-Maffei, IM	1999 – 2006
9.	Sr. Sheila Novak, SDS	2007 – 2010
10.	Sr. Jean Fitzgerald, OP	2011 – 2014
11.	Sr. Gloria Loya, PBVM	2014 –

Vicars of Temporalities and Administration

1.	Mr. Thomas H. Riordan	2008 –

† = died in office

THE VICARIATES

The Diocese of Monterey in California is divided into seven vicariates. A vicariate, also known as a vicariate forane or deanery, is a region of a diocese that is headed by a vicar forane. A vicar forane is a priest appointed by the diocesan bishop and given a certain degree of leadership within his vicariate, traditionally in order to promote a common pastoral activity in a region of the diocese and to provide spiritual and pastoral counsel to other priests in that region. A priest who serves as a vicar forane uses the style "The Very Reverend." The canonical duties of a vicar forane are outlined in canon 555 of the *Code of Canon Law*. The dean of a deanery or vicariate where the diocesan bishop resides is a vicar urbane.

The Vicariate of the Monterey Peninsula

1. San Carlos Cathedral (*Monterey*)
2. Carmel Mission Basilica (*Carmel*)
   Mission Station: St Francis of the Redwoods (*Big Sur*)
3. Our Lady of Mount Carmel (*Carmel Valley*)
4. Saint Jude (*Marina*)
5. Saint Angela Merici (*Pacific Grove*)
6. Saint Francis Xavier (*Seaside*)
7. Saint Joseph (*Spreckels*)

The Vicariate of the Salinas Area

1. Madonna del Sasso Pro-Cathedral (*Salinas*)
   Mission Station: Santa Rosa Chapel (*Salinas*)
2. Our Lady of Refuge (*Castroville*)
3. Christ the King (*Salinas*)
4. Sacred Heart (*Salinas*)
5. Saint Mary of the Nativity (*Salinas*)

The Vicariate of the Salinas Valley

1. Saint Theodore (*Gonzales*)
   Mission Station: Capilla de Guadalupe (*Chular*)
2. Holy Trinity (*Greenfield*)
3. Mission San Antonio de Padua (*Jolon*)
   Mission Station: South Shore Lake San Antonio
4. Saint John the Baptist (*King City*)
   Mission Station: San Lucas
5. Our Lady of Solitude (*Soledad*)
   Mission Station: *Mission Nuestra Señora de la Soledad*

The Vicariate of San Benito County

1. Sacred Heart & Saint Benedict (*Hollister*)
2. Old Mission San Juan Bautista (*San Juan Bautista*)
3. Immaculate Conception (*Tres Piños*)

The Vicariate of San Luis Obispo County:
Southeast Vicariate

1. Old Mission San Luis Obispo Pro-Cathedral (*San Luis Obispo*)
2. Saint Patrick (*Arroyo Grande*)
   Mission Station: Saint Francis of Assisi (*Oceano*)

3. Saint Elizabeth Ann Seton (*Los Osos*)
4. Saint Joseph (*Nipomo*)
5. Saint Paul the Apostle (*Pismo Beach*)
6. Nativity of Our Lady (*San Luis Obispo*)
7. Santa Margarita de Cortona (*Santa Margarita*)

The Vicariate of San Luis Obispo County:
Southwest Vicariate

1. Saint William (*Atascadero*)
2. Santa Rosa (*Cambria*)
3. Saint Joseph (*Cayucos*)
4. Saint Timothy (*Morro Bay*)
5. Saint Rose of Lima (*Paso Robles*)
6. Old Mission San Miguel (*San Miguel*)
   Mission Station: Our Lady of Ransom (*San Ardo*)
   Mission Station: Our Lady of Guadalupe (*Bradley*)

The Vicariate of Santa Cruz County:
Northern Vicariate

1. Resurrection (*Aptos*)
2. Saint Michael (*Boulder Creek*)
3. Saint Joseph (*Capitola*)
4. Saint Vincent de Paul (*Davenport*)
5. Saint John (*Felton*)
6. Christ Child (*Los Gatos*)
7. Holy Cross (*Santa Cruz*)
   Mission Santa Cruz
8. Our Lady, Star of the Sea (*Santa Cruz*)
9. San Augustin (*Scotts Valley*)

The Vicariate of Santa Cruz County:
Southern Vicariate

1. Our Lady of Refuge (*Castroville*)
2. Holy Eucharist (*Corralitos*)
3. Our Lady, Help of Christians (*Watsonville*)
4. Our Lady of the Assumption (*Watsonville*)
5. Saint Patrick (*Watsonville*)

Year	Catholics	Total Population	Percent Catholic	Diocesan Priests	Religious Priests	Total Priests	Catholics per Priest	Permanent Deacons	Male Religious	Female Religious	Parishes
1970	99,645	498,223	20%	80	55	135	738.11	N/A	35	290	43
1980	131,805	659,025	20%	87	29	116	1,136.25	N/A	21	180	43
1990	168,452	842,262	20%	80	32	112	1,504.04	3	23	151	45
2000	192,121	960,604	20%	81	27	108	1,778.90	2	41	116	46
2010	201,039	1,005,193	20%	80	32	112	1,794.99	21	27	56	46
2015	208,100	1,040,498	20%	81	27	108	1,926.85	33	18	56	46

Part II

The Parishes of the Diocese

DIOCESE OF MONTEREY

JUNIPERO SERRA 1713-1784

MILES
0   5   10

CHAPEL SCHOOL PARISH
HOSPITAL CONVENT MISSION
CEMETERY ©2002 Las

N E S W

DIABLO RANGE

SAN ANDREAS RIFT ZONE

GABILAN RANGE

PINNACLES

SIERRA DE SALINAS

SANTA LUCIA

VENTANA WILDERNESS
TASSAJARA HOT SPRINGS
THE INDIANS

JUNIPERO SERRA PEAK 5862 FT

CALIF 25
SACRED HEART 1877
IMMACULATE CONCEPTION 1904
HOLLISTER   TRES PINOS

SAN JUAN BAUTISTA 1797
SA
OFM
SAN JUAN BAUTISTA
FREMONT PEAK 3171 FT

OUR LADY OF SOLITUDE 1933
SOLIDAD
HOLY TRINITY 1951
ST. JOHN THE BAPTIST 1891
KING CITY

HOLY EUCHARIST 1969
CORRALITOS
FMA
K-8

OUR LADY HELP OF CHRISTIANS 1854
K-8
SDB
PAJARO

OUR LADY OF THE ASSUMPTION 1953
US 101
SANTA RITA
CFC 9-12
SND

SAINT THEODORE 1893
RIVER
GREENFIELD
US 101

CHRIST CHILD 1983
CALIF 17
LOS GATOS

PCC POOR CLARES
SAINT PATRICK 1861
WATSONVILLE

MADONNA DEL SASSO 1960
ST. MARY OF THE NATIVITY 1447
SAINT JOSEPH 1969
CHUALAR
MISSION SOLEDAD 1791

ST. CLARE'S RETREAT
RESURRECTION 1968
OUR LADY OF REFUGE 1869
SALINAS
SALINAS
GONZALES

SAINT MICHAEL 1921 BOULDER CREEK
SAN AGUSTIN 1968
SAINT JOSEPH 1904
APTOS
CAPITOLA
CASTROVILLE
SACRED HEART 1876
SPREKLES
MT TORO

CALIF 9
OSF
OSA
OUR LADY STAR OF THE SEA 1947
K-8
SND

SCOTTS VALLEY
FELTON
SAINT JUDE 1963
CHRIST THE KING 1995

SAINT JOHN 1952
PS-8
HOLY CROSS
SANTA CRUZ
MARINA
SAINT FRANCIS XAVIER 1950
CALIF 68
OUR LADY OF MOUNT CARMEL 1953
CARMEL VALLEY

SAINT VINCENT DE PAUL 1935
CALIF 1
1791
OSJ
DAVENPORT

SAINT ANGELA 1928
PACIFIC GROVE
PT PINOS
SEASIDE
1770
MONTEREY

MISSION CARMEL BASILICA 1771
OCD
SND
PT LOBOS

BIXBY CREEK
OSB Cam
BIG SUR
PT SUR
CALIF 1

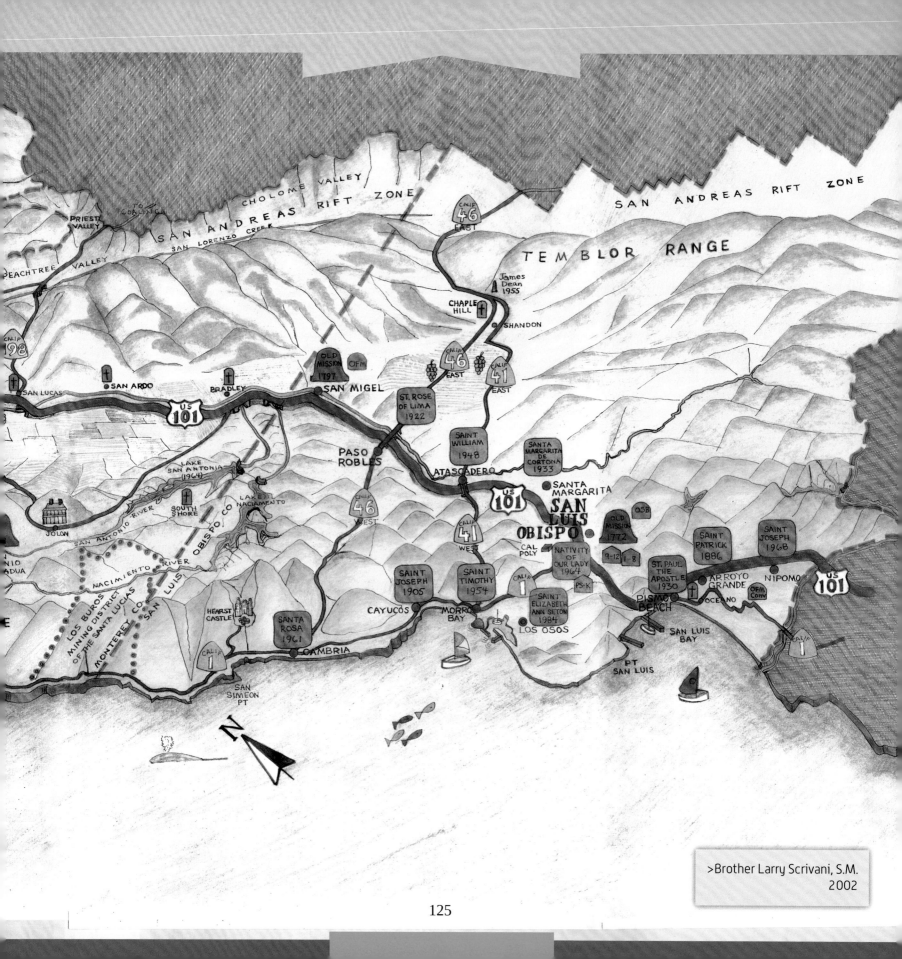

>Brother Larry Scrivani, S.M.
2002

San Carlos Cathedral

(The Royal Presidio Chapel)

500 Church Street, Monterey - Monterey County - www.SanCarlosCathedral.org

San Carlos Cathedral, also known as the Royal Presidio Chapel, was originally founded as *Mission San Carlos Borromeo de Monterey*, the second Spanish Mission in Alta California. On Pentecost Sunday, June 3, 1770, the area was claimed in the name of His Most Catholic Majesty the King of Spain. Saint Junípero Serra founded the mission "by erecting a cross, hanging bells from a tree, and saying Mass under the same venerable rock where Viscaíño's party celebrated it in 1602, 168 years before."[1]

Fray Francisco Palóu († 1789) described the day in these words:

On the third day of June, being the holy day of Pentecost, the whole of the officers of sea and land, and all the people, assembled on a bank at the foot of an oak, where we caused an altar to be erected, and the bells rang; we then chanted the *Veni Creátor*, blessed the water, erected and blessed a grand cross, hoisted the royal standard, and chanted the first Mass that was ever performed in this place; we afterwards sang the *Salve* to Our Lady before an image of the illustrious Virgin, which occupied the altar; and at the same time preached a sermon, concluding the whole with a *Te Deum*. After this the officers took possession of the country in the name of the King, our Lord, whom God preserve. We then all dined together in a shady place on the beach; the whole ceremony being accompanied by many volleys and salutes by the troops and vessels.[2]

Succession of Pastors		
1. Fr. Jose de Real	1840 – 1844
2. Fr. Antonio Real	1844 – 1845
3. Fr. Jose Antonio Anzar	1845 – 1846
4. Fr. Jose Real	1846
5. Rev. Doroteo Ambris	1846 – 1849
6. Fr. Ignacio Ramirez de Arellano	1849 – 1851
7. Rev. Doroteo Ambris, January – June	1851
8. Fr. Sadoc Villarasa, OP	1851 – 1854
9. Rev. Francisco Foretnic	1854
10. Rev. S. Filoteo	1854 – 1855
11. Rev. Cajetanus Sorentini	1855 – 1856
12. Rev. John Comellas	1859 – 1864
13. Rev. Michael Racca	1865 – 1869
14. (Very) Rev. Ángel Delfino Casanova	1870 – 1893
15. Rev. Ramon M. Mestres	1893-1930
16. Rev. Philip Scher	1930 – 1933
17. Rev. Gerald Gay	1933 – 1940
18. Rev. John Durkin	1940 – 1945
19. Rev. Leo Beacom	1945 – 1948
20. Very Rev. Msgr. John J. Ryan	1948 – 1969
21. Rev. Msgr. Brandan McGuinness	1969 – 1992
Rev. Ron Wiecek, CPPS, *administrator*	1992
22. Rev. Joseph L. Occhiuto	1992 – 2004
23. Very Rev. Peter A. Crivello, V.G.	2004 – 2016
24. Rev. Emil Robu	2016 –

1 • ELLIOTT & MOORE, *History of Monterey County, California, With Illustrations* (1881); reprinted by Valley Publishers, 1979, p. 15.

2 • IBID., p. 16.

> The sanctuary of the cathedral church. Frederick J. Blersh painted decorations and the two coats of arms in the sanctuary, one being the Coat of Arms of the Franciscan order and the other being the Coat of Arms of the Kingdom of Spain.

Photo courtesy of John Glover, 2015.

The Sacrament of Baptism was celebrated for the very first time on December 26, 1770, the feast of Saint Stephen, the first martyr (cf. *Acts of the Apostles*, 7:54-60). The presidio and mission of San Carlos Borromeo de Monterey was constructed on land that Saint Junípero Serra described as "pretty plain about a rifle shot from the beach."[3] He soon decided to sever the mission from the presidio, in order to "provide a less confining environment for the Indians away from the soldiers."[4] On December 24, 1771, Mission San Carlos Borromeo was moved to the mouth of Carmel River Valley, and is now popularly known as Carmel Mission Basilica. The former mission church of San Carlos Borromeo de Monterey became the presidio chapel and was re-named in honor of Saint Joseph, with the Franciscans continuing as chaplains.

"The first two chapels at the Presidio were of pole and brush (*palizada*) construction,"[5] and more than likely doubled as storerooms. The third and final flat-roofed adobe chapel was constructed in 1773 "of adobe with foundations of stone and lime".[6] In 1775, Monterey became the capital of the Viceroyalty of New Spain's Province of the Californias (*Provincia de las Californias*) and the presidio chapel received the designation of *royal*. In 1789, the Royal Presidio Chapel was destroyed by a fire caused by a misfired cannon and the construction of the fourth and final chapel by Manuel Ruiz began in 1791, with Fray Fermín de Lasuén blessing the cornerstone on July 7, 1793. Construction of the present stone structure was completed in 1794 and blessed in September of 1797.

When Mission San Carlos Borromeo in Carmel was secularized between 1834 and 1836, the Royal Presidio Chapel in Monterey became the parish church for the entire Monterey Peninsula. In 1835, the chapel was transferred from a military to a civil jurisdiction, thereby officially ceasing to be the Royal Presidio Chapel. In 1840, the titular patron of the parish was officially changed from Saint Joseph to Saint Charles Borromeo and the Bonifacio Adobe next to the chapel was purchased and used as the parish rectory.

On June 30, 1850, the parish church of San Carlos was designated a pro-cathedral of the original Diocese of Monterey by the Rt. Rev. Joseph Sadoc Alemany y Conill, 1st Bishop of Monterey. The parish ceased being a pro-cathedral in 1859, when the bishop's residence was relocated to Los Angeles and the name of the diocese was subsequently changed to Monterey-Los Angeles.

In 1869, a wooden rectory was built east of the church. In 1874, a whalebone paving was put down in front of the church. In 1893, the pyramidal roof of the bell tower was added and the parish altar society was founded. In 1894, the *espadaña* was extended as a complete second tier to the tower with a pyramidal tile roof. In the late 1890s, electricity was installed and a vestibule was constructed at the entrance.

Around 1900, the Rev. Ramon M. Mestres, 15th pastor of the parish, introduced "pew rent" and Sunday collection envelopes in order to obtain regular financial support for parish activities. In 1902, a new two-story parish rectory and office was constructed.

> The Royal Presidio Chapel, circa 1910.

Photo courtesy of the diocesan archives.

3 • SAINT JUNÍPERO SERRA (1784-1713): ANTONINE TIBESAR, ed., *Writings of Junípero Serra* (1955-1966), vol. 1, p. 171: MARTIN J. MORGADO, *Junípero Serra: A Pictorial Biography* (1991), p. 42.

4 • MARTIN J. MORGADO, *Junípero Serra: A Pictorial Biography* (1991), pp. 42-43.

5 • DONALD THOMAS CLARK, *Monterey County Place Names* (1991), p. 484.

6 • IBID.

> In 1921, the Lourdes grotto was built outside the entry area of the parish church.

Photo courtesy of Jonabel Perez, 2016.

> In 1932, the outdoor shrine honoring the Blessed Virgin Mary as **Queen of Heaven** was built at Church and Fremont Streets by Carlo Abbe. The statue was a reproduction made by Harry Downie.

Photo courtesy of Agnieszka A. Klasa, 2016.

> In 1942, this crucifix was placed above the altar in the sanctuary. Made in Barcelona in 1880, it had previously occupied other locations in the Royal Presidio Chapel.

Photo courtesy of Domina Nostra Publishing.

> In 1953, the Stations of the Cross were transferred from Santa Cruz to San Carlos church. They had been painted in Rome in 1890.

Photo courtesy of Agnieszka A. Klasa, 2016.

The boundaries of the parish were defined by decree of the Most Rev. John B. MacGinley, 1st Bishop of Monterey-Fresno, on January 1, 1927. They were later modified by the Most Rev. Philip G. Scher, 2nd Bishop of Monterey-Fresno, on October 26, 1933.

In 1935, the parish church was re-roofed with tile. In 1938, a parish hall was constructed at Figueroa and Church Streets and a major rehabilitation of the church was planned. That same year, a group of artists researched the church's art and architecture as part of the Federal Art Project. They stripped away layers of whitewash and paint to disclose many original details of decoration.

In 1942, the parish sold land at Webster and El Estero to the U.S. government for the purposes of the United Service Organizations (U.S.O.). That same year, an extensive restoration of the interior of the church occurred, under the direction of Harry Downie. The parish church was re-dedicated with a solemn consecration by the Most Rev. Philip G. Scher, 2nd Bishop of Monterey-Fresno, on June 3, 1942. At least 32 priests attended and took part in a procession accompanied by buglers from Fort Ord. In 1953, pews were installed in the transepts. In 1956, a new parish rectory was built east of the church.

In 1961, the parish church building was designated a National Historic Landmark by the National Park Service. In 1962, further changes in the interior decoration were made. In 1966, the parish church building was listed on the National Register of Historic Places.

The parish church of San Carlos Borromeo was officially designated the cathedral of the new Diocese of Monterey in California by Pope Blessed Paul VI (Apostolic Constitution *Montereyensis-Fresnensis*, October 6, 1967). In December 1969, the sanctuary of the church was remodeled and the interior was repainted and a wave-shaped *dado* was added.

In 1980, a new parish hall was constructed. The Spanish colonial style building was completed in September and blessed by the Most Rev. Harry A. Clinch, 1st Bishop of Monterey in California, on October 19. It provided 10,000 flexible square feet for either banquets or general meetings. The old parish hall building was moved next to U.S.O. / YMCA on Webster Street to serve as a youth center.

In the mid-1990s, the original rectory that was constructed in 1902 was renovated to provide office space for *The Observer*, the official diocesan newspaper, as well as for parish ministries. A gift shop was also added. The second parish rectory that had been constructed in 1956 was also renovated.

In 1998, at the conclusion of a three-year study by the National Center for Preservation Technology and Training, it had become apparent that a $1 million project was required to conserve the parish church. In December of 2004, a fundraising campaign was announced to repair the cathedral at a cost of more than $1 million. Projects would include a new tile roof, a seismic retrofit, refinishing the stones in the walls, a new drainage system, and historically accurate repainting. In addition the plan called for establishing an historic museum, a gift shop, and a docent program. In May of 2005, the formation of a Heritage Team ministry was announced to spearhead fundraising efforts for the restoration of the cathedral. Volunteer docents were trained to conduct historical tours of the cathedral, and the opening of a museum was planned for early July.

On October 14, 2005, Dr. Rubén G. Mendoza of California State University, Monterey Bay (CSUMB) gave a presentation on "Hispanic Art, Architecture and Culture in Early California" as part of Monterey's Historic Fest 2005. On October 18, preservation architect Tony Crosby led a walking tour of the cathedral church. He served as the historical architect of the conservation project.

In January of 2006, all plants on the east and west sides of the cathedral were removed in order to forestall further absorption of moisture into its sandstone walls. In September of 2006, Dr. Rubén G. Mendoza of California State University, Monterey Bay (CSUMB), began excavations along the outer walls in order to determine their exact materials and the present state of the foundation.

The restoration project began in April of 2007 with the removal of the redwood trees located on the east side of the cathedral church. Roots had penetrated the foundation. The lumber was set aside for future landscaping use. On September 2, the cathedral church was closed to the public and the parish hall was used as a temporary worship space.

The Royal Presidio Chapel Annual Conservation Conference was held on October 10, 2007. Speakers included Mr. Anthony Crosby, historical architect, Dr. Rubén G. Mendoza of California State University, Monterey Bay (CSUMB), Dr. Fred Webster, seismic expert, and Mr. John Griswold, conservator for the exterior stonework. Dr. Webster reported that the foundations go down to bedrock with footings 4 to 6 feet deep. The stonework had suffered damage from tree roots. Seismic safety would require bracing with a number of steel beams. Dr. Mendoza reported that many interesting specimens had been recovered from diggings around the church dating from a Paleolithic flint knife up to 19th Century shovels, shards and coins.

In November of 2007, the interior walls were randomly inspected to confirm that their original decoration was austere whitewash. To the contrary it was established that the walls were highly decorated with designs of vibrant color. More research was indicated. Removal of interior plaster revealed that the church windows had been rectangular originally and then modified with gothic arches, but finally restored to the original shapes. About the same time it was discovered that the walls of the transept and apse from 1858 were much more fragile than those of the original church. They would require replacement with new stone, as would part of the bell tower. These changes would increase the cost of the entire project by about 25%, bringing it to more than $7 million. About 100 tons of new stone, quarried near King City, would be required.

In January of 2008, the fragile rear walls were rebuilt, and the wood-frame cupola on the bell tower was temporarily removed for repairs while rebuilding the tower was also in progress. While reconstruction of the interior was in progress the statues of the Immaculate Conception, St. Joseph, Our Lady of Sorrows, and St. Anthony were moved to the new **Heritage Center Museum** (formerly the gift shop) for safe-keeping.

The renovated cathedral church was re-dedicated with a solemn consecration by the Most Rev. Richard J. Garcia, 4th Bishop of Monterey in California, on June 3, 2009, the anniversary of which is celebrated each year as a liturgical solemnity in the cathedral church, and as a feast in all other churches of the diocese.

The parish celebrated the canonization of its founder, Saint Junípero Serra, on September 23, 2015, with a special evening Mass of Thanksgiving. On September 26, a walking pilgrimage took place, departing the cathedral at 8am and arriving at Carmel Mission Basilica for Mass at 11am.

Parish Mission Station of
The Annunciation
1954 – 1992

In 1954, the Annunciation Mission Station was constructed on Stephen Place and the first Mass was celebrated there on May 30. The mission station was closed around 1992.

The **Pacheco Crypt,** located just outside of the sanctuary, is named for Francisco P. Pacheco, a parishioner who financed the 1858 enlargement of the church; the transepts and the apse were added, as well as a new altar, and the windows were remodeled to a lancet or gothic style. Pacheco was buried in the crypt. The Very Rev. Ángel D. Casanova, 14th pastor of the parish, was entombed in the Pacheco Crypt upon his death in 1893. On February 18, 1942, the Pacheco Crypt was permanently sealed in concrete.

> A rare look of the interior of the Pacheco Crypt.
> *Photo courtesy of the parish.*

> A vacant niche in the Pacheco Crypt.
> *Photo courtesy of the parish.*

FRANCISCO P. PACHECO.
y Familia.
1858.

IN GRATEFUL MEMORY OF
VERY REVEREND ANGELO CASANOVA
VICAR FORANE AND PASTOR
SAN CARLOS MONTEREY
PLACED IN THE PACHECO CRYPT
MARCH 15, 1893
REST IN PEACE

> The statue of Saint Rosalia († 1166) was installed in 1935 and is carried in procession through Monterey to the harbor for the annual blessing of the fishing fleet every September.
> *Photo courtesy of Agnieszka A. Klasa, 2016.*

> The statue of Saint Elizabeth, Queen of Portugal († 1336), was installed in 1890 by local Portuguese whalers and dairymen. *Photo courtesy of Agnieszka A. Klasa, 2016.*

> The cathedra of the Bishop of Monterey in California is a symbol of the bishop's teaching authority as a successor of the apostles. *Photo courtesy of Agnieszka A. Klasa, 2016.*

> In the spring of 2008, the original artwork (1795-1815) on the interior walls was uncovered. This pattern of linear diamonds was to be reproduced in the final restoration project.

Photo courtesy of John Glover, 2015.

> In July of 2006, the Conservation Project Team announced that Griswold Conservation Associates had been hired to conduct a study of the Our Lady of Guadalupe bas-relief at the top of the façade of the cathedral. The history of the sculpture was explored along with an investigation of the most appropriate techniques required in its conservation. After a prayer service on May 2, the bas-relief statue of Our Lady of Guadalupe was removed and taken to a conservation studio in Los Angeles. This occasion marked the official launching of the "Cornerstone Campaign" intended to raise approximately $5.5 million for the conservation project.

Photo courtesy of John Glover, 2015.

> This statue of Our Lady of Solitude was originally at Mission Soledad when it was brought to the Royal Presidio Chapel by H. Downie.

Photo courtesy of John Glover, 2015.

Madonna del Sasso

320 E. Laurel Drive, Salinas - Monterey County - www.mdsChurch.org

Succession of Pastors

1.	Rev. Msgr. Silvano Baquedano	1960 – 1961
2.	Rev. Msgr. Thomas J. Neary	1961 – 1974
3.	Rev. Daniel C. Cronin	1974 – 1983
4.	Rev. Michael L. Cross	1983 – 1996
5.	Rev. Ronald Shirley	1996 – 2001
6.	Rev. Larry Kambitsch	2001 – 2005
7.	Rev. Edward Fitz-Henry	2005 – 2007
8.	Rev. James Henry	2007 – 2010
9.	Rev. Greg Sandman	2010 –

The parish of *Madonna del Sasso*, Italian for "Our Lady of the Stone", in the City of Salinas, can trace its roots to 1951, when a replica of the statue of Our Lady of the Stone from Ticino in Switzerland was donated and enshrined in the parish church of Holy Trinity in Greenfield. On March 23, 1955, the Most Rev. Aloysius J. Willinger, 3rd and last Bishop of Monterey-Fresno, announced that a new parish under the patronage of Madonna del Sasso would be located in Salinas.

In 1957, Msgr. Thomas J. Earley, 8th pastor of Sacred Heart in Salinas, launched a fundraising campaign for the new parish in the northern area of Salinas. 9.35 acres of land at Laurel Avenue and Maryal Street were purchased in part by the Madonna del Sasso Society of Italian-Swiss Catholics. The cost of the property was $25,000. In 1959, a parish hall was constructed and utilized as a place for divine worship. On September 27, the Society of Madonna del Sasso made the final payment for the property to the Diocese of Monterey-Fresno.

Madonna del Sasso was canonically established as a parish in its own right by decree of the Most Rev. Aloysius J. Willinger, 3rd and last Bishop of Monterey-Fresno, on August 18, 1960. In 1961, the statue of Madonna del Sasso was moved from Holy Trinity in Greenfield to the temporary sanctuary in the parish hall.

In 1968, a fundraising campaign for a new church structure and a rectory was initiated. The parish included 1,000 families and $400,000 was the estimated cost. The Society of Madonna del Sasso contributed $15,000.

In 1970, work on the construction project was in progress. P.J. Holewinski and M.L. Blevans were the architects. An innovative modern design was used. The builder was Geyer Construction Co. The original church was intended to be remodeled to become the parish hall.

The sacred liturgy had been celebrated in the parish hall from 1959 until Easter Sunday, April 9, 1971, when the first Mass in the new

ST. FRANCIS OF ASSISI   ST. THÉRÈSE OF LISIEUX   ST. MATTHEW

MADONNA DEL SASSO CATHOLIC CHURCH

parish church was celebrated. On October 24, 1971, the new parish church, offices, and rectory on East Laurel Drive were blessed by the Most Rev. Harry A. Clinch, 1st Bishop of Monterey in California, who said: "We congratulate you on this church as a symbol of the internal faith that prevails in this parish of Madonna del Sasso."[1]

The conversion of the original church into a parish hall was completed in 1979. In 1980, to mark the 400th anniversary of the apparition of Madonna del Sasso, Msgr. Arnoldo Giovannini († 2013) from Ticino, Switzerland, visited the parish. That same year, the parish religious education program (CCD) counted 1,050 children enrolled.

In 1980, a dedication concert for the new Allen organ was presented the evening of September 27. The organist was Dr. John Walker from the Riverside Church in New York City. He also presented a workshop for diocesan organists earlier that day.

On May 30, 1981, the parish sponsored a Festival of Liturgical Arts. Artists, craftsmen, musicians,

and all interested parties were invited to participate and share their ideas. Around 1983, the original convent was converted into offices and named the Cronin Center. 2,300 families were registered in the parish at that time.

The silver anniversary of Madonna del Sasso was celebrated with the solemnly dedication or consecration of the parish church on August 17, 1986, the anniversary of which is celebrated each year in the parish church as a liturgical solemnity.

In 1998, plans for the new parish hall/multi-purpose facility were approved by City of Salinas. Construction was in progress by the middle of the year. The new facility was twice the size of the previous structure. 2,800 families are registered in the parish at this time. In 1999, the construction of a new parish hall was completed by the beginning of the year, but special fundraising activities continued through the fall. The new hall was used for various diocesan activities because of its size.

1 • *The Observer*, October 27, 1971, vol. 3, no. 29, p. 5.

> The original parish church of Madonna del Sasso, circa 1959, later the parish hall.
Photo courtesy of the diocesan archives.

The Blessed Virgin Mary is the titular patron of the parish in the City of Salinas under the title of **Madonna del Sasso**, Italian for "Our Lady of the Stone."

Also known as Our Lady of Sosopoli, "the title was established at Pisidia (very likely the same as Pamphylia), an ancient region of southern Asia Minor, located north of Lycia, inland from the island of Rhodes. Numerous miracles have been attributed to the image of Our Lady painted on wood that legend says gave off a miraculous oil that was referred to at the Council of Nice in 325 AD.

"At Messina (Sicily), Italy, the title Our Lady of the Holy Letter (of Sasopoli, Sosopoli) dates from the 14th century. At a small shrine on a hill about twelve miles northwest of Florence, Italy, she is venerated at Our Lady of the Stone following the reported apparition of Our Lady to two young shepherdesses on July 2, 1490. The church of Our Lady of the Stone was built over the spot where the Virgin is said to have appeared" (*Mary In Our Life: Atlas of the Names and Titles of Mary, the Mother of Jesus, and Their Place In Marian Devotion*, by Nicholas J. Santoro (2011), pp. 506-507).

The liturgical feast day of Our Lady of the Stone is June 3. Though it is not included on the General Roman Calendar, it is celebrated as a solemnity in the parish church.

Parish Mission Station

Santa Rita Chapel

2217 North Main Street, Salinas - Monterey County

The mission station of Our Lady of Guadalupe or Santa Rita can trace its origins to 1867, when Jose Manuel Soto († 1917) established a town on part of his *Rancho Los Gatos*, also known as *Rancho Santa Rita*. The town was known as Penacart, New Republic, Sotoville, and finally as Santa Rita. A one acre plot of land for the construction of a church was set aside as part of Soto's overall plan and by the late 1870s, a small chapel was built. It was first a mission station of the parish of the Immaculate Heart of Mary in Pajaro before being transferred to the parish of Our Lady of Refuge in Castroville in 1871. The property was deeded to the Diocese of Monterey-Los Angeles in 1872. This first chapel was destroyed by fire in 1878.

In 1880, a parcel of land in Santa Rita, now 2217 North Main Street in the City of Salinas, was purchased in a tax sale for $8.63. It included a cemetery as well as the site of a new wooden chapel named in honor of Our Lady of Guadalupe. This second chapel was a mission station of the parish of Sacred Heart in Salinas. The chapel was blessed in 1911 by the Rt. Rev. Thomas James Conaty, 4th Bishop of Monterey-Los Angeles.

For over 100 years, the chapel was the center of community life for many of the pioneer families who settled in the area until around 1948 when regular liturgical services were suspended, as transportation to downtown Salinas had become more convenient and the chapel was too small to become a parish in its own right. The last sacrament to be celebrated there was First Holy Communion in 1949. [***Nota bene:*** According to an alternative account, services were suspended later in the 1960s.] In 1960, the chapel became a mission station of the new parish of Madonna del Sasso. The chapel was permanently closed and boarded up. Considerable vandalism to the exterior of the chapel followed.

In 1972, the volunteers from the local community raised $8,000 to restore the chapel, repairing the damage done by vandals, repainting the chapel, and bringing the plumbing and electrical work up to code. Sidewalks and steps were also constructed, and restoration work on the interior of the chapel was accomplished. The chapel was re-dedicated on May 21, though no regular liturgical celebrations were regularly scheduled due to a lack of available clergy.

In 2004, donations were sought to restore both the chapel and the grounds for use on special occasions. The goal was $100,000. Central Coast Roofing Co. replaced the old roof and new doors and an organ were donated. In 2005, plans for the chapel included fumigation, re-roofing, carpentry work, and repainting. In 2007, the Monterey County Historic Society involved itself in the chapel restoration project by raising $75,000 to complete new foundations, applying fresh paint, and installing new wood sash.

> Circa 1942.
Photo courtesy of the diocesan archives.

Mission San Luis Obispo de Tolosa

751 Palm Street, San Luis Obispo – San Luis Obispo County – www.MissionSanLuisObispo.org

Mission San Luis Obispo de Tolsa, the fifth California Mission, was founded by Saint Junípero Serra on September 1, 1773. The Apostle of California departed the very next day, leaving behind Fray José Cavalier, five soldiers, and two neophytes. Also known as the "Prince of the Missions" and the "Mission in the Valley of Bears," the present adobe church was constructed in 1794.

In 1820, the vestibule with a belfry was added to the mission church. In 1832, the mission church structure was damaged by an earthquake. With the secularization of the missions in 1835, Mission San Luis Obispo de Tolosa experienced a swift decline in fortune through the theft and the vandalism that followed. In 1841, Fray Ramón José Abella († 1842), the last Franciscan missionary, turned over the mission church to secular (diocesan) clergy.

In 1845, all remaining mission property, other than the mission church, itself, was sold for $510 by Governor Pio Pico. The Rev. José Miguel Gomez, 26th pastor of the mission, refused to vacate. In 1859, the mission compound, orchard, and vineyard were officially returned to the legal ownership of Church (by the U.S. government.

In 1868, the mission church was again damaged by an earthquake. In 1872, a fundraising campaign for a convent and school was initiated and in 1875, the contract for school construction was awarded to Mr. Mallet. Between 1875 and 1880, wooden siding was added to the building to hide its humble construction. The portico was removed, and a New England-style wooden steeple was built above the rectory.

In 1876, the same year that San Luis Obispo was incorporated as a city, the interior of the mission church was modernized with wooden sheathing and a board floor. New side altars were also added. In 1877, the vestibule and old belfry were torn down and ceremonies marking the end of the first scholastic year were attended by José Antonio Romualdo Pacheco († 1899), who had served as the 12th Governor of California. In 1878, the original bells that had been made in Peru in 1818 were re-cast. In 1893, the right transept of the mission church was added over a portion of the original cemetery, doubling the seating capacity.

Parish Mission Statement

*A Eucharistic Community
striving to live out the Gospel of Jesus Christ
guided by the power of the Holy Spirit.
Loving and open, faith-filled and prayerful,
gracious stewards,
passionate about the needs of others.*

> The sanctuary of the pro-cathedral church.

Saint Louis of Toulouse (Latin: *Sanctus Ludovicus Tolosa;* Spanish: *San Luis de Tolosa*), 43rd Bishop of Toulouse, is the titular patron of Old Mission San Luis Obispo. Born in 1274, St. Louis was the second son of Charles II of Anjou, 2nd King of Naples. He was also a nephew of King St. Louis IX of France. The old Roman Martyrology says that he was "of the Order of Friars Minors, renowned for holiness of life and miracles" and that he died "in Provence, at the village of Brignoles" on 19 August 1297. "His body was taken to Marseilles, and buried with due honors in the Church of the Friars Minor, but afterwards it was taken to Valencia in Spain, and enshrined in the cathedral."

St. Louis of Toulouse was canonized by Pope John XXII in 1317. His liturgical feast day is August 19. Though it is not included on the General Roman Calendar, it is celebrated as a solemnity in the mission church. While in Rome attending the Second Vatican Council (1962-1965), Bishop Clinch obtained a relic of St. Louis of Toulouse from the Holy See on behalf of the parish.

The boundaries of the parish were defined by decree of the Most Rev. John B. MacGinley, 1st Bishop of Monterey-Fresno, on January 1, 1927. Between 1933 and 1934, the exterior of the mission church was restored to its form after 1820. The colonnade and mission church floor were now several feet above the level of the modern street. The steeple was removed. A series of attic rooms, hidden by a false ceiling, were discovered.

A restoration of the mission church began in 1947, under the direction of Harry Downie and using a grant from the Hearst Foundation. Exterior work included the addition of a bell tower at the front door and the interior was restored to its 1819 configuration. An addition to the east transept was also made. The mission church was re-dedicated with a solemn consecration by the Most Rev. Aloysius J. Willinger, 3rd and last Bishop of Monterey-Fresno on June 12, 1948.

In November of 1948, a contract was signed to build a convent as part of the mission quadrangle. It was completed in 1950. Between 1950 and 1951, a new 12-room rectory at Chorro and Palm Streets was constructed on site of former parish gymnasium. The original sacristy of the mission church was restored and the mission church was re-roofed with new tile. In 1953, a new parish hall was built at west end of the mission at a cost of $80,000. In 1958, the first floor of the old friary or rectory was converted into a museum of art and literature, under the supervision of Harry Downie.

In 1960, the Lewin property adjacent to the mission church was purchased through a $15,000 donation from J.J. Donovan. A restored mission plaza was envisioned. In 1966, Mission San Luis Obispo was officially declared California Historical Landmark (no. 325). On September 11, 1971, the newly re-furbished Mission Plaza was dedicated as part of the bicentennial celebrations of the Old Mission's founding.

In June of 1976, the first annual *San Blas* Breakfast was held to raise funds to assist the church in San Luis Obispo's sister city in Mexico. It was sponsored by the Knights of Columbus. In September of 1977, the mission parish hired its first full-time youth minister. In 1978, as part of the work of the new ministry of extraordinary ministers of Holy Communion, a Ministry to the Elderly was initiated in the parish, the particular tasks of which were to bring Holy Communion to those confined to their homes. On November 3, 1979, the **Old Mission School Thrift Shop** was opened at the corner of Peach and Broad Streets.

In 1993, a retrofit study of the Old Mission complex was performed to provide seismic safety in unreinforced masonry areas. In 1996, a renovation project with estimated cost of $2 million was approved by Bishop Ryan. Termite damage repairs to front porch area were already in progress. One main purpose of the project was to bring all structures up to modem earthquake safety standards. Interior remodeling to add baptistery and entry areas was also contemplated. This would involve exterior changes to the structure. Moving the candle room and the main altar was also in the tentative plan. Restoration and relocation of certain works of art were also contemplated. Architectural adviser was Robert Rambusch Associates of New York City, experts in liturgical design. The RRM Design Group of San Luis Obispo was also consulted. Issues concerning the historicity of certain proposed alterations were raised by the California Mission Studies Association and the Southwestern Mission Research Center.

On April 30, 2005, five new mission bells were blessed by Bishop Ryan. The new five-bell peal was cast at a cost of $50,000 by the firm of Petit and Fritsen in Aarle-Rixtel, Netherlands. They were named *Diego* (748 lbs.), *Carlos* (429 lbs.), *Antonio* (297 lbs.), *Gabriel* (224 lbs.) and *Luis* (158 lbs.). A smaller sixth new bell, *Ave Virgo Maria*, will hang in the mission's patio. The three historic *San Luis* bells were to be hung in a new monument also in the patio.

During the spring and summer of 2007, the second phase of the seismic safety campaign was carried out on the *convento* wing, museum, and gift shop on the campus. On April 2, 2007, Old Mission San Luis Obispo was named a pro-Cathedral of the diocese by Bishop Garcia. On August 5, at a "Festival of the Bells" the five new bells were rung as part of a celebration of Native American and Hispanic culture. An image of Bishop Garcia's coat-of-arms was installed and blessed on Heritage Day, 19 August.

In 2008, seismic reconstruction of the mission church as part of a third phase was expected to begin at the end of the rainy season.

The parish celebrated the canonization of its founder, Saint Junípero Serra, with a Mass on the morning of November 1, 2015.

Carmel Mission Basilica

(Mission Basilica San Carlos Borromeo del Rio Carmelo)

3080 Rio Road, Carmel - Monterey County - www.CarmelMission.org - www.CarmelMissionFoundation.org

Mission San Carlos Borromeo de Monterey, the second California Mission that had been founded by Saint Junípero Serra in 1770, was severed from the *presidio* in Monterey and moved to the mouth of the Carmel River and renamed Mission San Carlos Borromeo del Rio Carmelo.

Succession of Pastors		
1. Rev. Msgr. Michael D. O'Connell	1933 – 1958
2. Most Rev. Harry A. Clinch, D.D.	1958 – 1967
3. Rev. Msgr. James Marron	1967 – 1969
4. Rev. George McMenamin	1969 – 1973
5. Rev. Msgr. Eamon MacMahon	1973 – 1989
6. Rev. Msgr. D. Declan Murphy	1989 – 2001
7. Rev. John C. Griffin	2001 – 2013
8. Rev. Paul P. Murphy	2013 –

In 1792, the original adobe orchardist's house adjacent to the mission was constructed. The duties of the orchardist were to protect the orchards (mostly pear) and other gardens from thieves and animals. On July 4, 1793, construction began on the present stone structure. It was a built around the earlier mission church in which Saint Junípero Serra was interred. In September of 1797, the Moorish style mission church was completed under Fray Fermín de Lasuén († 1803), 3rd Father-President of the Alta California Mission System.

It was in August of 1771 that the Apostle of California chose the site, about 5 miles south of Monterey on "the banks of the Carmel River and in view of the sea… a truly delightful spot, which, thanks to its plentiful supply of both land and water, gives promise of abundant harvests."[1] On August 24, 1771, a "large cross [was] raised and [fixed] in the center of the area selected for the mission."[2] Saint Junípero Serra blessed the cross and said Mass under an "*enramada*," the mission's first temporary church. By December 24, 1771, the mission's second church, known as a "*jacal*," was built on the exact same site as the first.

On June 3, 1784, Saint Junípero Serra celebrated the mission's 1,000th baptism, giving an adult native man the Christian name Millán Deogracias. *Millán* was in honor of *San Millán de la Cogolla* (Saint Emilian of Cogolla), a fourth century Spanish saint. *Millán* is very close to *millar*, Spanish for "one thousand". When combined with *Deogracias*, the play on words creates "A thousand, thank God."[3]

"The lands surrounding the Carmel Mission were fertilized by a perennial stream of pure water, and this offered advantages, which the fathers were not slow to avail themselves of, for the cultivation of many kinds of vegetables and fruits. It was on the lands of this mission that the first potatoes grown in California were raised, in 1826. The privilege of planting this esculent was given to the natives without limit, and they so improved their opportunities that the whalers, which made a regular stopping-place of Monterey, supplied themselves with great quantities. The temporal welfare of the estate had reached a great development in the year 1825, when the fathers possessed ninety thousand cattle, fifty thousand sheep, two thousand horses, two thousand calves, three hundred and seventy yoke of oxen, with merchandise to the value of $50,000, and over $40,000 in silver."[4]

1 • SAINT JUNÍPERO SERRA (1713-1784): ANTONINE TIBESAR, ed., *Writings of Junípero Serra* (1955-1966), vol. 1, p. 171; vol. 4, p. 259: MARTIN J. MORGADO, *Junípero Serra: A Pictorial Biography* (1991), p. 43.
2 • MAYNARD GEIGER, *Palóu's Life of Fray Junípero Serra* (1955), p. 116: MARTIN J. MORGADO, *Junípero Serra: A Pictorial Biography* (1991), p. 43.
3 • Cf. MARTIN J. MORGADO, *Junípero Serra: A Pictorial Biography* (1991), p. 49.
4 • ELLIOTT & MOORE, *History of Monterey County, California, With Illustrations* (1881); reprinted by Valley Publishers, 1979, p. 119.

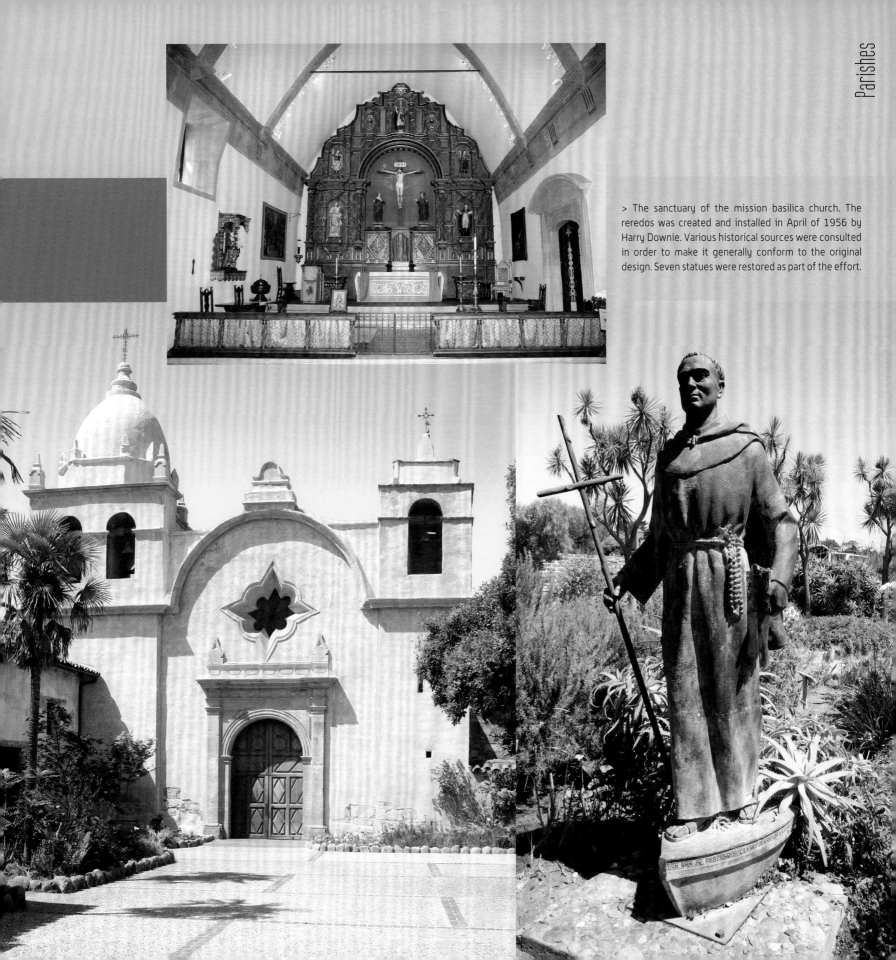

> The sanctuary of the mission basilica church. The reredos was created and installed in April of 1956 by Harry Downie. Various historical sources were consulted in order to make it generally conform to the original design. Seven statues were restored as part of the effort.

Secularization and Ruin

Between 1834 and 1836, Mission San Carlos Borromeo de Carmelo was secularized and subsequently fell into ruins, though Mass continued to be celebrated monthly in the undamaged sacristy. By 1847, the entire south and west sides of the quadrangle were in ruins. Between 1849 and 1851, various objects were transferred to the former Royal Presidio Chapel in Monterey for safekeeping. In 1852, the ceiling of the mission church collapsed. In 1859, the property in the immediate area of the old mission was returned to the Church by the U.S. Lands Commission.

Robert Louis Stevenson († 1894), Scottish novelist, poet, essayist, and travel writer, described Carmel Mission at this time in these words:

> The padre drives over the hill from Monterey; the little sacristy, which is the only covered portion of the church, is filled with seats and decorated for the service; the Indians troop together, their bright dresses contrasting with their dark and melancholy faces; and there, among a crowd of somewhat unsympathetic holiday makers, you may hear God served with perhaps more touching circumstances than in any other temple under heaven. An Indian, stone blind and about eighty years of age, conducts the singing; other Indians compose their choir; yet they have the Gregorian music at their finger ends and pronounce the Latin so correctly that I could follow the meaning as they sang… I have never seen faces more vividly lit up with joy than the faces of these Indian singers. [1]

A Visit to the Ruins

"As you sit upon one of the fallen roof-beams, and gaze upon the shattered font, the broken-down crosses, the ruined altar, and the general scene of devastation and desolation around, and remember that this is one of the most ancient and important historical monuments of California, the home and the grave of the moral hero of the age, the true pioneer of California progress—Junípero Serra, and the tomb of no less than fifteen Governors of this State, a painful feeling arises…

"Carmel Mission is the old Westminster Abbey of the State, the mausoleum of the great and the good, and the nation rewards the services of the past by giving up the dust of the good and brave to the guardianship of gophers and squirrels. Thorns and briars, nettles and loathsome weeds, adorn their graves. A few short years, and naught will remain of this holy edifice save an undistinguishable mass of debris. A few more years, and it will be too late—even now it will be somewhat difficult—to restore it. Whatever is done should be done quickly, nobly, and generously, for the present state of the mission is a standing reproach to the church which owns it, and a disgrace to the whole State of California."

ELLIOTT & MOORE, *History of Monterey County, California, With Illustrations* (1881); reprinted by Valley Publishers, 1979, pp. 118-119

> The interior of Carmel Mission, circa 1860-1870.
> *Photo courtesy of the Carmel Mission Docent Association.*

< The exterior of Carmel Mission, circa 1860s.
Photo courtesy of the Carmel Mission Docent Association.

1 • ROBERT LOUIS STEVENSON, *Across the Plains* (1880), p. 31.

144

The First Restoration

In 1882, the graves of Saint Junípero Serra and Frays Crespi, Lasuén, and Lopez were discovered, enabling the Rev. Ángel D. Casanova, 14th pastor of the Royal Presidio Chapel in Monterey, to raise interest in restoring the mission. Restoration efforts officially began in 1884, when Fr. Casanova saw the approaching centennial of the death of St. Junípero Serra as the perfect opportunity to begin what would be the first major restoration effort of the mission.

A pitched, shingle roof, 76 feet higher than the original, was installed. A window was cut into the apse behind the altar and a wall plaque marked Saint Junípero Serra's grave. The original crucifix from the 1834 inventory was installed in a niche behind a new white marble altar. For many years to come, an annual Mass was celebrated on the Sunday nearest the feast of Saint Charles Borromeo, which was followed by a barbecue.

Upon the death of Fr. Casanova in 1893, the Rev. Ramon M. Mestres, the 15th pastor of the San Carlos in Monterey, continued the restoration efforts by having a new floor installed. In 1911, Fr. Mestres constructed a rectory near the entrance to the mission church (which would later become the "Harry Downie Museum").

The interior of Carmel Mission, circa 1915.
Photo courtesy of the Carmel Mission Docent Association.

<
Archeological excavations, circa 1920-1921.
Photo courtesy of the Carmel Mission Docent Association.

The Second Restoration

In 1924, the first room of the quadrangle was restored as a memorial to the *padres* buried in the mission church. On August 28, 1931, Harry Downie, a cabinet maker from San Francisco, arrived at Carmel Mission. The second restoration of Carmel Mission was now fully underway. .

> In 1921, work on the "Cenotaph Room" at the side of the mission church began. Sculptor Joseph Jacinto "Jo" Mora († 1947) erected a temporary studio on the mission property. Jo Mora, known as the "Renaissance Man of the West," was an artist-historian, sculptor, painter, photographer, illustrator, muralist, and author. The Serra Memorial Cenotaph was dedicated on October 12, 1924, and resides in what is now known as the **Mora Chapel Museum**. *Photo courtesy of the Carmel Mission Docent Association.*

> The exterior of Carmel Mission with the new convento, circa 1925. The modern pitched, shingle roof, is also evident.
Photo courtesy of the Carmel Mission Docent Association.

In 1931, **Crespi Hall** was constructed inside the quadrangle near the west side. The new parish hall was named in honor of Fray Juan Crespi († 1782) who was the first to be buried in the sanctuary of the mission church. In 1932, the altar was restored. Harry Downie also discovered the bowl of the original baptismal font during an excavation in the cemetery. After realizing its importance, Downie refurbished it and installed it as a holy water font at the entrance to the mission church.

In 1933, plans for a complete reconstruction of the mission church and the quadrangle were made. Old documents and photographs were studied and some excavations took place. Various items were returned from San Carlos in Monterey, where they had been kept for safekeeping. Signs were detected that the mission church roof was about to collapse. Permission to reconstruct the original roof was granted, and a temporary fix was installed. It involved cutting back the front peak into a pyramidal configuration.

On October 26, 1933, Mission San Carlos Borromeo de Carmelo, popularly known as Carmel Mission, was canonically established as a parish in its own right by decree of the Most Rev. Philip G. Scher, 2nd Bishop of Monterey-Fresno.

In 1934, the sesquicentennial of the death of Saint Junípero Serra was the occasion of a fundraising dramatic pageant (August 24-28) to further reconstruction efforts. Wood from the grandstand was later used into reconstructing the roof of the mission church. The California State Senate designated August 28 as *"Junípero Serra Day."*

> "Downie Reconstruction", circa 1932-1933.
Photo courtesy of the Carmel Mission Docent Association.

> Replacement Roof Construction", 1936.
Photo courtesy of the Carmel Mission Docent Association.

In 1935, the mission garden was replanted and one side of the *convento* along the north side of the quadrangle was restored. It extended eastward from the "cenotaph room" and was temporarily used as a Blessed Sacrament chapel. In October of 1935, Bishop Scher authorized the creation of "The Carmel Mission Restoration Committee," which was allowed to raise funds from the general public.

In January of 1936, highway work near Rio Road by the Works Progress Administration uncovered archeological remnants of the original mission. That same year, Harry Downie began an extensive and authentic restoration of the entire mission which included rebuilding the quadrangle, constructing a new roof based on an outline of the original roofline that was discovered by Downie and architect Milton Latham. The old roof was removed in May. A new choir loft was also installed and the building's facade was refurbished. More restoration work was done on the *convento* south wing. The renovated mission church was blessed on July 5, 1936.

Saint Junípero Serra's restored cell was blessed on August 29, 1937, the same day that his cause of beatification and canonization was formally opened. The mission museum opened that same year. In 1938, Harry Downie constructed two massive redwood doors for the main entrance of the mission church.

In 1940, a wooden *mensa* was built for the marble altar and the restoration of the refectory and dispensary areas within the museum was completed, and work on the modern rectory, which was originally the guards' quarters, began. In 1941, the north wing of the quadrangle was completed. It included a tourist entrance, gift shop, and artifact rooms.

On June 2, 1942, the new rectory was blessed. It was built on the site of the old soldiers' quarters. This completed restoration of the southeastern section of the quadrangle. In December of 1943, the sanctuary floor was lowered to the original level, reversing an 1884 alteration. A new wooden *mensa* and marble *gradin* were installed.

In 1950, a $100,000 fundraising drive was launched to complete the west side of the quadrangle. A contribution of $5,000 was received from the Bing Crosby Golf Tournament at Pebble Beach. In 1951, Crespi Hall was moved to the northwestern corner of the property. At that time it was called the "Serra-Lasuén Hall." A long Spanish-style convent was built parallel to the west wing. It was blessed the following year on December 21, and would later become the official residence of the bishops of Monterey in California.

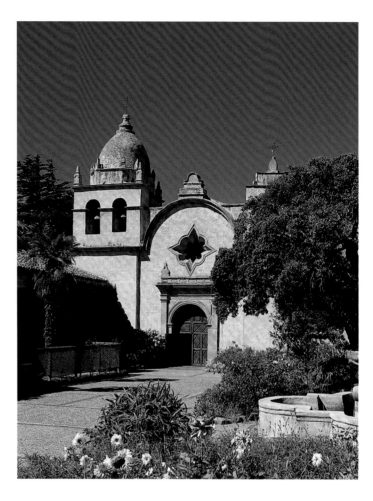

In July of 1951, Carmel Mission hosted the Jubilee Mass that celebrated the 40th anniversary of the ordination to the priesthood of the Most Rev. Aloysius J. Willinger, 3rd and last Bishop of Monterey-Fresno. "More than 100 priests of the diocese, in addition to a number of visiting clerics, assisted at the Mass". The procession is shown crossing the courtyard from the rectory to the mission church.

Photo courtesy of the diocesan archives.

According to correspondence between the Most Rev. Aloysius J. Willinger, 3rd Bishop of Monterey-Fresno and the Rev. Msgr. Harry A. Clinch, Auxiliary Bishop of Monterey-Fresno and 2nd pastor of the parish, both the church and high altar of the mission church were dedicated with a solemn consecration by Bishop Clinch, on January 6 and 7, 1960, the anniversary of which is celebrated each year in the basilica on January 5 as a liturgical solemnity. [**Nota bene:** The wall of the sacristy records the date of dedication as January 5, 1961.]

The Title of Minor Basilica

On February 5, 1960, Pope St. John XXIII († 1963) promulgated the Apostolic Letter *Caeruleum mare*, Latin for "the blue sea", granting the title and privileges of minor basilica to Mission San Carlos Borromeo de Carmelo.[1]

Where the blue sea washes the California shore there is a church consecrated to Saint Charles Borromeo. It draws to itself the souls of men not only because of the pleasant surroundings but more especially because it is a center famous for holiness…

We have consulted the Sacred Congregation of Rites, and, hereby with assurance and after mature deliberation, with the fullness of our apostolic power and by virtue of this document, we raise this Church, dedicated to Saint Charles Borromeo, in the Diocese of Monterey-Fresno, to the honor and dignity of a minor basilica with all the rights and privileges which belong to such sacred churches, all things to the contrary notwithstanding. We decree and declare that this document is to hold and endure validly and effectively forever, and its full and complete effects prevail, and whatever pertains to it in the future will be approved.

A basilica is "a title assigned by formal concession or immemorial custom to certain more important churches, in virtue of which they enjoy privileges of an honorific character which are not always very clearly defined"[2] Basilicas are divided into two classes: major and minor. There are only four major basilicas (Latin: *basilicae maiores*), also called papal basilicas, and they are to be found in Rome. A minor basilica (Latin: *basilica minor*) is a church that has been specially honored by His Holiness the Pope, "thereby signifying their particular link with the Roman Church and the Supreme Pontiff."[3]

The concession of the title of basilica to Carmel Mission was publicly celebrated on April 27, 1961, which coincided with the celebration of the fiftieth anniversary to the priesthood of Bishop Willinger.[4] Following the Second Vatican Council (1962-1965), norms concerning minor basilicas were established in the decree *Domus Dei* (July 6, 1968) and in the instruction *Domus ecclesiae* (November 9, 1989).

Pope St. John XXIII's Apostolic Letter Caeruleum mare elevating the mission church of San Carlos Borromeo in Carmel to the honor of minor basilica.
Photo courtesy of the diocesan archive.

1 • Cf. *Acta Apostolicæ Sedis*, vol. 52 (1960), pp. 555-556.
2 • GERHARD GIETMANN and HERBERT THURSTON, *The Catholic Encyclopedia* (1907), vol. 2.
3 • CONGREGATION FOR DIVINE WORSHIP AND THE DISCIPLINE OF THE SACRAMENTS, Instruction *Domus ecclesiae* (9 November 1989), n. 4.

4 • Cf. *Central California Register* (April 7, 1961), vol. 37, no. 15, pp. 1 and 3.

The Privileges of a Minor Basilica

- Precedence before other churches, except for the diocesan cathedral.
- The right to include the papal symbol of the crossed keys on a basilica's banners, furnishings, and coat of arms.
- The right of the rector (pastor) of the basilica to wear a distinctive mozzetta over his surplice.
- The granting of a plenary indulgence on certain days to those who pray in the basilica:

> The faithful who devoutly visit the basilica and within it participate in any sacred rite or at least recite the Lord's Prayer and the profession of faith may obtain a plenary indulgence under the usual conditions (sacramental confession, eucharistic Communion, and prayer for the intention of the Supreme Pontiff):
>
> 1. on the anniversary of the dedication of the same basilica **[January 5]**;
> 2. on the day of the liturgical celebration of the title **[November 4, the feast of St. Charles Borromeo]**;
> 3. on the Solemnity of the Holy Apostles Peter and Paul **[June 29]**;
> 4. on the anniversary of the granting of the title of basilica **[February 5]**;
> 5. once a year on a day to be determined by the local Ordinary **[July 1, the feast of St. Junípero Serra]**;
> 6. once a year on a day freely chosen by the each of the faithful.
>
> CONGREGATION FOR DIVINE WORSHIP AND THE DISCIPLINE OF THE SACRAMENTS
> Instruction *Domus ecclesiae* (9 November 1989), n. 17

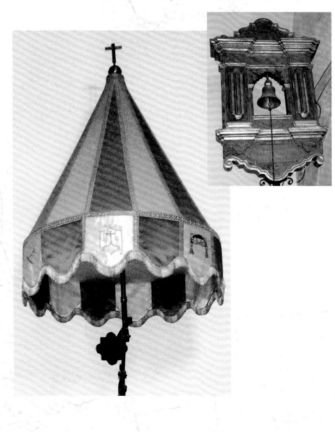

The *umbraculum*, Latin for "umbrella" (Italian: *ombrellino*), is one of the symbols bestowed by His Holiness the Pope when he elevates a church to the rank of minor basilica. The *umbraculum* of a major basilica is made of gold cloth and red velvet, while that of a minor basilica is made of yellow and red silk. The *umbraculum* is also represented behind the shield in the coat of arms of a basilica. Traditionally, an *umbraculum* is placed prominently at the right of +the main altar and is opened whenever the His Holiness the Pope visits the basilica.

Memorial Museum was added between the parish convent and Crespi Hall through the generosity of Doña Maria Antonia Field née Munras († 1962). It was blessed on September 20 by the Most Rev. Harry A. Clinch, Auxiliary Bishop of Monterey-Fresno and pastor of the parish. In 1963, the sacristy was re-plastered and a new ceiling and vestment cases were added. In 1964, the annual fiesta was revived. In 1965, the ceiling of the basilica was re-plastered to emulate its original 1797 appearance. Between 1965 and 1966, the marble *gradin* was removed to allow Mass to be celebrated *versus populum* or "facing the people."

Henry J. Downie
Knight of the Order of Saint Gregory the Great
Curator and Diocesan Mission Consultant

Henry John "Harry" Downie was born in San Francisco on August 25, 1903, and baptized at Mission San Francisco de Asís (Mission Dolores) on September 20. Of Scotch-Irish parentage, Downie was a third generation San Franciscan and in his youth had spent many holidays at Carmel. An expert in California mission lore and a cabinetmaker "with a special reputation for the restoration of Spanish antiques," Downie arrived at Carmel Mission on August 28, 1931, at the request of Msgr. Philip Scherer, pastor of San Carlos Borromeo in Monterey. Msgr. Scherer had asked Downie "to restore some statues… but his job quickly expanded to mission restorer" and he was subsequently appointed curator.

Between 1931 and 1932, Downie restored various historic statues and paintings at **San Carlos Borromeo in Monterey** before overseeing an extensive restoration of its interior in 1942. Downie supervised renovations at **Mission San Luis Obispo** between 1947 and 1948 and at **Mission San Antonio** in Jolon between 1948 and 1949, as well as the construction of the parish church and rectory of **Our Lady of Mount Carmel** in Carmel Valley. Between 1953 and 1959, Downie oversaw restoration work at **Mission San Juan Bautista**.

In 1954, Downie assisted the Native Daughters of the Golden West in the rebuilding of **Mission *Nuestra Señora de la Soledad***, carving a replica statue of Our Lady of Solitude to stand behind the restored altar (the original statue had been moved to San Carlos Borromeo in Monterey). Further restoration work began in 1960 at **Old Mission San Juan Bautista**, which was overseen by Downie.

"Known for his meticulous research and his use of original Spanish sources to help guide him in his restoration work," Harry J. Downie died on March 10, 1980. The funeral Mass was celebrated on March 13 by Bishop Harry A. Clinch, and the homilist was the Rev. Larry Farrell. *The Observer* printed a special supplement dedicated to the life and work of Harry Downie (March 12, 1980, vol. 11, no. 45). Downie, "whose life centered around the restoration of the California Missions" was buried in the Carmel Mission cemetery (*The Observer*, March 12, 1980, vol. 11, no. 45, p. 1). His wife, Mabel Francis Downie née McEldowney, was buried beside him in 1981.

On October 11, 1980, the **Harry Downie Museum** was dedicated at Carmel Mission Basilica. Housed in three rooms in what was once the old mission rectory, the museum commemorates Downie's work of restoring Carmel Mission.

In 1982, the **MacMahon Center** was constructed as an additional parish hall and meeting facility, named in honor of Msgr. Eamon MacMahon, 5th pastor of the parish. In 1986, Msgr. MacMahon and Mr. Ed Soberanes, the parish organist, consulted with members of the Carmel Bach Festival and the American Guild of Organists to find a suitable pipe organ for the loft that would not block the mission basilica's distinctive star-shaped window. Casavant Freres of Quebec was hired to construct an organ with two consoles and 1,922 silver pipes, at a cost of $350,000. Installation took three months. Sir Richard J. Menn, G.C. St.G.G., diocesan curator and mission historian, carved and painted the woodwork casings that hold the 34 ranks of pipes, using a cherub from an old mission altarpiece in his design. The organ was officially dedicated in September 1986. Virtuoso organ recitalist James Welch from the University of California, Santa Barbara, performed a Bach concert on the organ that New Year's Eve.

Around 1999, the **Murphy Center**, an additional parish hall and gymnasium was constructed and named in honor of the Rev. Msgr. D. Declan Murphy, 6th pastor of the parish. In 1998, the old **Orchard House**, an adjacent property at 3100 Rio Road, was sold to the diocese, subject to life tenancies of Sir H. Lewis C. Scott († 2011) and Sir Richard J. Menn, G.C. St.G.G., diocesan curator. Surrounding buildings and gardens were included. Around 2009, this property was traded with the parish for the former convent and current residence of the Bishops of Monterey in California. Orchard House is anticipated to become the new residence for the parish clergy.

In 2004, the first annual **Founder's Day** celebration was held. Also around 2004, the parish established its **Bereavement Ministry**, which "provides caring consolation and spiritual support to parish families who are grieving the death of a loved one." Its popular planning handbook is shared with parishes throughout the country via CD, and is also available in Spanish.

In 2007, the California Missions Foundation provided a $10,000 grant partially to finance a buildings survey of mission property and a plan for future conservation projects. By March of 2007, the Munras Museum was in the process of renovation under the direction of Dr. Julianne Burton-Carvajal, a scholar of California social history. In 2008, the **Carmel Mission Foundation, Inc.** was formed to fund the restoration and preservation of the historic properties and artifacts of Carmel Mission Basilica.

The final resting place of St. Junípero Serra on the "Gospel side" of the sanctuary of the mission church, marked by this standard image of the saint since May 2015.
Photo courtesy of Agnieszka A. Klasa, 2016..

> In 2011, the parish published a book titled *Art from the Carmel Mission*, in both hard cover and soft cover editions, in honor of the 300th anniversary of the birth of St. Junípero Serra. The book was prepared by Gail Sheridan and Mary Pat McCormick, both members of the Carmel Mission Docent Association. The book was edited by Sandra E. Berris, with photography by Dennis Wyszynski.

The Third Restoration

In August 2012, the third major restoration of Carmel Mission began with the erecting of scaffolding and the installation of a weather protection structure over the basilica. The roof tiles were removed and the roof trusses were strengthened by the installation of additional wood beams and metal collectors. Cement bond beams and steel I-beams were inserted to reinforce and tie the structure together. The basilica's 220-year-old-walls were also stabilized and new electrical and fire suppression systems installed, along with new interior lighting and custom-made chandeliers. The radiant heating system was upgraded and a new restroom building constructed. Repairs were also made to the exterior walls, buttresses, towers, and dome. Special restoration techniques and materials had to be developed that were compatible with existing historic materials. This $5.5 million phase of the third major restoration was completed in June of 2013, making the basilica three times stronger than before. Funds are currently being raised funds for the second phase of this third major restoration, a multi-million dollar effort to restore and upgrade the mission's five museums (Downie, Mora, Convento, Munras, and South Addition), as well as the Basilica forecourt; the Quadrangle courtyard; the Orchard House complex; and other remaining historic structures.

With its historic structures and 3,400 pieces of art and artifacts, the Carmel Mission complex contains a treasure-trove of California history, including California's first library, oldest continuously occupied residence, and Saint Junípero Serra's 400-year-old Bible, used by Ronald Reagan when first sworn in as governor of California.

> On November 13, 2013, His Royal Highness, Felipe Juan Pablo Alfonso de Todos los Santos de Borbón y Grecia, the Prince of Asturias, visited Carmel Mission Basilica in honor of the 300th birthday of Saint Junípero Serra. The heir to the Crown of Spain was accompanied by his consort, HRH Doña Letizia, the Princess of Asturias, as well as Ramón Gil-Casares, Ambassador of Spain to the United States, and José Ramón Bauzà Díaz, 9th President of the Balearic Islands. The Prince and Princess of Asturias were briefed on the history of the basilica by Deacon Nicholas Pasculli. Their Royal Highnesses placed a wreath on the grave of Saint Junípero Serra and, after touring the Convento Museum, joined about 90 guests for a private reception in the mission's main courtyard.

Photos courtesy of Paul Desmond and TMD (The Marketing Department, Inc.).

The Canonization of Saint Junípero Serra

The parish prepared for the canonization of its founder, Saint Junípero Serra, by praying a novena in thanksgiving. Beginning on September 14, 2015, the novena was prayed in the Blessed Sacrament Chapel for nine evenings leading up to the canonization on September 23. On the day of canonization, a special liturgy was celebrated at noon by the Rev. Miguel Rodriguez, the parochial vicar of the parish. From the high altar of the basilica, Fr. Rodriguez, said that "we can now say 'Saint Junípero Serra.'" This prompted the packed basilica "to erupt in cheers and thunderous applause". After Mass, "more than 400 people crowded" the mission's central courtyard to watch the live broadcast of the papal Mass (cf. *Monterey Herald*, September 24, 2015, p. 1).

The Rev. Miguel Rodriguez and Deacon Bill Reichmuth process in for Mass, with a first class relic of Saint Junípero Serra. Fr. Rodriguez recited the three presidential prayers in Spanish.

Photo courtesy of the *Monterey Herald*, September 24, 2015.

Photo courtesy of Geoffrey Lopes da Silva, 23 September 2015

The parish celebrations concluded with a solemn Mass on Sunday, 27 September, at which premiered the hymn *Always Forward, Never Back*, composed especially for the parish by Christopher Walker for the occasion of the canonization.

"Always forward, never back!
Christ, companion, guide and goal;
where You lead our steps will follow,
...love in heart and mind and soul."

> Statue of Saint Francis of Assisi († 1226) that is located on the "Gospel Side" of the basilica dates from late 17th century Mexico.

> The altar of the basilica's Blessed Sacrament Chapel.

This statue of Christ the King was carved by Harry Downie, utilizing a technique that natives would have used. It rests on a 17th century altar from Italy.

The Blessed Sacrament Chapel - 1945

In November of 1945, work began on the **Blessed Sacrament Chapel**, located between the museum and the rectory. Besides serving as the site for the celebration of daily Mass, the chapel is also a memorial chapel for the late Anne Sutter († 0000) who is interred there. In March of 1947, construction of the Blessed Sacrament Chapel was completed and it was blessed on June 11. It filled out the east wing. Part of its wall is a fragment surviving from the original black-smith and carpentry shop from 1774.

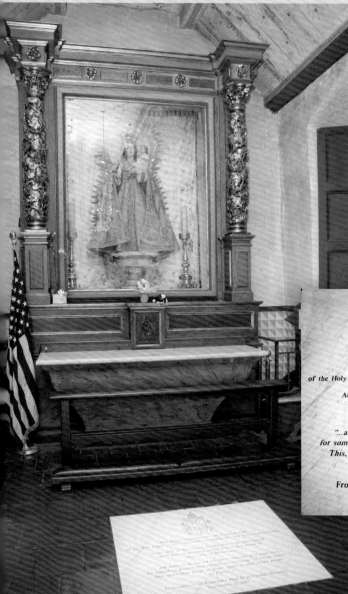

The Our Lady of Bethlehem Chapel - 1948

The **Our Lady of Bethlehem Chapel** was originally built between 1811 and 1817 and used as a mortuary chapel, utilizing stones from earlier constructions. In 1948, Harry Downie retrieved the statue of Our Lady of Bethlehem from the Westfall family and restored it from its dilapidated state. He brought back its crown and figure of the Child Jesus from the Royal Presidio Chapel in Monterey. The Bethlehem Chapel contains a floor marker commemorating the 1987 visit of Pope St. John Paul II, who referred to Carmel Mission Basilica as "the historical and spiritual heart of California."

This plaque commemorates the Pastoral Visit of the Holy Father to the Carmel Mission during his visit to the United States.

At the altar of this chapel, His Holiness Pope John Paul II spent time in personal prayer before this image of Our Lady of Bethlehem.

"...and much to be envied are those who can give their lives for something greater than themselves in loving service to others. This, more than words or deeds alone, is what draws people to Christ...."

From address of Pope John Paul II at Carmel Mission September 17, 1987

*All of the sanctity,
all of the history,
all of the glory of our California
Church and State
is interred here in this holy soil.*

TIMOTHY CARDINAL MANNING
3rd Archbishop of Los Angeles
The Observer, July 7, 1982, vol. 14, no. 14, p. 1

Parish Mission Station of
Saint Francis of the Redwoods
Highway #1, Big Sur - Monterey County

The parish mission station of Saint Francis of the Redwoods in Big Sur can trace its origins to the early 1950s, when the Rev. Francis Franchi, SJ, of Santa Clara would regularly celebrate Mass in a small chapel for Camp Pico Blanco, a Boy Scout camp on land donated to the Boy Scouts in 1948 by William Randolph Hearst († 1951).

In 1955, Miss Frances M. Molera († 1968) donated 160 acres known as the Hopkins Ranch between her property in the *Rancho El Sur* and the Big Sur Post Office to the Bishop of Monterey-Fresno for a much-needed chapel to serve the neighboring population, which at the time was quite large in the summer when vacationers were visiting Big Sur Park.

In May of 1958, the Crosby Golf Tournament, precursor of the modern-day AT&T Pebble Beach Pro-Am, donated $2,000 to help pay for the construction of the chapel, which was added to the $1,300 contributed from various sources. A crucifix for the chapel had already been made by Wid Dayton, who carved it out of Big Sur rhodonite (cf. *Monterey Peninsula Herald*, May 7, 1958). The chapel was to be constructed of non-local redwood lumber and rocks from the Big Sur River. Construction was completed by January of 1959.

Christ Child

23230 Summit Road, Los Gatos – Santa Cruz County – www.ChristChild.org

The parish of Christ Child in the Town of Los Gatos can trace its origins to around 1964, when it began as a mission station of the parish of Saint Joseph in Capitola. Property on Summit Road had been purchased and a simple, wood-frame church was built. In 1969, the mission station of Christ Child was transferred to the jurisdiction of the parish of Saint Michael in Boulder Creek, and then to the parish of San Agustín in Scotts Valley. In 1977, the decision was made to work toward establishing the community as a separate parish.

In 1980, a resident chaplain was appointed and the mission station of Christ Child began to operate independently, with "Parish Beginnings" seminars held during Advent. In 1981, the resident chaplain moved into a purchased mobile home. In 1982, the new multipurpose building (rectory, community center, and parish offices) was built at a cost of $225,000. It was dedicated with a simple blessing on July 11.

On May 1, 1983, the parish of Christ Child was canonically established by decree of the Most Rev. Thaddeus A. Shubsda, 2nd Bishop of Monterey in California. In 1993, the parish church was remodeled and stained glass installed at a cost of $64,000.

The parish in Los Gatos is named in honor of the **Christ Child** or the Child Jesus (Spanish: *El Niño Jesús*), referring to the Lord Jesus Christ from His Nativity to the age of 12.

The four evangelists say nothing about the childhood of Jesus between His infancy and the finding in the temple at the age of 12. Devotion to the Christ Child has been popular under the title of the Infant of Prague (Spanish: *Niño Jesús de Praga*).

The Christ Child is celebrated liturgically on 25 December, the Nativity of the Lord. The month of December has been traditionally dedicated to the Divine Infancy. The principal feast of the Infant of Prague is the Holy Name of Jesus, an optional memorial on January 3 in the Ordinary Form of the Roman Rite, the second Sunday after Epiphany in the Extraordinary Form.

Cristo Rey

240 Calle Cebu, Salinas - Monterey County

> Circa 1952. *Photo courtesy of the diocesan archives.*

Succession of Pastors

Rev. Humbero Hemosa	
administrator	1958 – 1985
1. Very Rev. Manuel Canal, V.F.	
administrator	1985 – 1995
pastor	1995 – 1998 and 1999 – 2002
Rev. Geronimo E. Cuevas	
administrator	1998 – 1999
2. Rev. Miguel Grajeda	2002 – 2005
3. Rev. José Chavez	2005 – 2008
4. Rev. Antonio Sanchez	2008 –

The parish of *Cristo Rey* in Salinas, Spanish for "Christ the King," can trace its roots to 1951 when it began as a mission station of the parish of Sacred Heart in Salinas. The original chapel was constructed at Front Street and Sherwood Drive (later renamed Calle Cebu), on land donated by the Klute family. The mission station was intended to serve the needs of Spanish-speaking faithful. A large proportion of attendees were migrant farm workers. The *Cristo Rey* chapel was blessed on the morning of December 12 by the Most Rev. Aloysius J. Willinger, 3rd Bishop of Monterey-Fresno. By 1957, the number of families belonging to the mission station community of *Cristo Rey* had grown to 400. In 1961, the sacrament of Confirmation was celebrated for the first time by Bishop Willinger.

The chapel was completely refurbished in 1986. On December 31, 1990, adjacent land for parking was acquired (*Rancho el Sausal* property) and in 1992, this parking lot was paved. In 1994, the diocese considered establishing a separate "personal parish" for Spanish-speaking faithful. In 1995, the old parish hall and miscellaneous temporary buildings were demolished.

Cristo Rey in Salinas was canonically established as a parish in its own right by decree of the Most Rev. Sylvester D. Ryan, 3rd Bishop of Monterey in California, on January 16, 1996. Later that same year, on December 15, Bishop Ryan blessed a newly-constructed community center building.

The parish of *Cristo Rey* is named in honor of **our Lord Jesus Christ, the Universal King** (Latin: *Domini nostri Iesu Christi universorum Regis*; Spanish: *Nuestro Señor Jesucristo, Rey del Universo*). The title *king* is used in reference to Christ throughout Sacred Scripture (cf. *Matthew* 2:2, 27:11, and 27:42, *Mark* 15:32, *John* 1:49 and 18:36-37, *1 Timothy* 1:17 and 6:15, *Revelation* (*Apocalypse*) 1:5, 15:3, and 19:16). The liturgical feast of Christ the King was "established by Pope Pius XI in 1925 to be celebrated… by the Western church." The purpose was "to reassert the authority of our Lord to rule all nations and of His Church to teach the human race, to bring men back to Him, and so to establish 'the peace of Christ in the Kingdom of Christ'" (Donald Attwater, *A Catholic Dictionary* (1958), p. 94).

Christ the King (Latin: *Christus Rex*) is celebrated liturgically on the last Sunday in Ordinary Time as the Solemnity of Our Lord Jesus Christ, King of the Universe. In the Extraordinary Form of the Roman Rite, the feast is celebrated as a first class feast of Our Lord Jesus Christ the King (*Domini nostri Iesu Christi Regis*) on the last Sunday in October (Sunday before All Saints).

Holy Cross

Succession of Pastors

1.	Rev. Filomeno Ursua	1850 – 1851
2.	Rev. Juan Francisco Llebaria	1851 – 1854
3.	Rev. Juan B. Comellas	1854 – 1856
4.	Rev. Benito Capdevila	1856 – 1860
5.	Rev. Apollinarius Rousell	1860 – 1863
6.	Rev. Ángel Delfino Casanova	1863 – 1868
7.	Rev. Joachim Adam	1868 – 1883
8.	Rev. Hugh McNamee	1883 – 1902
9.	Rev. Msgr. P.J. Fisher, V.F.	1902 – 1918
10.	Rev. Patrick J. O'Reilly	1918 – 1927
11.	Rev. Patrick J. McGrath	1927 – 1933
12.	Rev. John Galvin	1933 – 1944
13.	Very Rev. Philip F. Kennedy	1944 – 1948
14.	Rev. Leo J. Beacom	1948 – 1950
15.	Rev. Msgr. William MacLoughlin	1950 – 1969
16.	Rev. William Scully	1969 – 1974
17.	Rev. Msgr. Michael J. Buckley	1974 – 1981
18.	Very Rev. James Henry, V.F.	1981 – 1991
19.	Rev. Michael A. Marini	1991 – 2000
20.	Rev. Mark Stetz	2001 – 2009
21.	Rev. Joseph L. Occhiuto	2009 – 2016
	Rev. Martin Cain, *administrator*	2016

Mission Santa Cruz

The parish of Holy Cross in the City of Santa Cruz can trace its roots to August 28, 1791, when Fray Fermín de Lasuén, 3rd Father-President of the Alta California Mission System, planted a cross on a site about a mile from the San Lorenzo River, founding the twelfth California mission named *La Misión de la Exaltación de la Santa Cruz,* Spanish for "The Mission of the Exaltation of the Holy Cross," popularly known as Mission Santa Cruz. [*Nota bene:* According to Msgr. J. Culleton, the actual founding was on September 25, 1791, by Fray Alonzo Salazar and Fray Baldmero Lopez.]

In 1792, the first two log-palisade churches on the flat lands were washed away by flood waters. In 1793, a permanent rock and adobe church on Mission Hill was begun and completed the following year. The mission church was blessed on May 10, 1794.

In 1795, the mission quadrangle of workshops was completed; it included a two-story granary. In 1796, a gristmill was built near the mission. It incorporated ironwork donated by Captain George Vancouver († 1798) at the time of his visit in 1794. In 1798, 138 (about 80%) of the neophytes deserted from the mission.

In 1812, Fray Andrés Quintana, OFM, was suffocated by some Christian American Indians of Mission Santa Cruz and Mission Santa Clara. Fr. Quintana is considered one of several martyred Franciscan missionaries of California.

With the secularization of the California missions in 1834, the land and possessions of Mission Santa Cruz were taken by settlers and the natives dispersed. The buildings were left to deteriorate. It supported about 250 natives at the time of secularization.

In 1840, the bell tower collapsed as a result either of an earthquake and/or heavy rains. At that time about 70 natives remained in the neighborhood. The nave of the mission church was still used for the celebration of Mass. In 1844, the last Franciscan pastor, Fray Antonio Real, left the mission. In all likelihood, Mission Santa Cruz then became a mission station of Mission San Juan Bautista.

The **Holy Cross** (Latin: *Sancta Crucis*; Spanish: *Santa Cruz*) "to which Christ had been nailed, and on which He had died, became for Christians, quite naturally and logically, the object of a special respect and worship" (*The Catholic Encyclopedia* (1908), vol. 4), and is referred to several times in the letters of Saint Paul the Apostle (cf. *1 Corinthians* 1:17, *Galatians* 2:19 and 6:14, *Ephesians* 2:16, *Philippians* 3:18, and *Colossians* 2:14).

"For St. Paul the Cross of Christ was not only a precious remembrance of Christ's sufferings and death, but also a symbol closely associated with His sacrifice and the mystery of the Passion. It was, moreover, natural that it should be venerated and become an object of a cult with the Christians who had been saved by it" (Fernand Cabrol, *The Catholic Encyclopedia* (1908), vol. 4).

"Had there been no cross, Christ could not have been crucified. Had there been no cross, life itself could not have been nailed to the tree. And if life had not been nailed to it, there would be no streams of immortality pouring from Christ's side, blood and water for the world's cleansing" (Saint Andrew of Crete: *The Liturgy of the Hours*, 14 September, Office of Readings).

The Holy Cross is commemorated liturgically on September 14 as the feast of the Exaltation of the Holy Cross (Latin: *In Exaltatione sanctæ Crucis*). It is celebrated as a solemnity in the parish church.

Circa 1858.
Photo courtesy of the diocesan archives

Circa 1891.
Photo courtesy of the diocesan archives

Circa 1908.
Photo courtesy of the diocesan archives

In 1855, the Archdiocese of San Francisco was created with a southern boundary along the 37 degree 5 min. parallel of latitude such that remote parts of the County of Santa Cruz were in the northern jurisdiction and part of Santa Clara County including Gilroy was in the Diocese of Monterey.

Holy Cross Church

In January of 1857, two earthquakes led to the collapse of the mission church structure. On July 5, the Rt. Rev. Thaddeus Amat y Brusi, 2nd and last Bishop of Monterey, laid the cornerstone for a new church to be built west of the original mission church. In 1858, a frame church with a central belfry was constructed and-dedicated with a simple blessing on July 4. The new church has been poorly constructed, requiring major repairs in 1864 and 1869. In the 1870s, the original rectory was constructed. Between 1885 and 1886, the remains of the old mission church were torn down and removed. In 1888, a new brick church with a granite foundation was constructed on the approximate site of the original adobe mission church. The new church was dedicated with a simple blessing on September 16, 1888.

In 1891, on the occasion of the centennial of the original mission, a granite memorial archway was erected in front of the church. It was donated by the citizens of Santa Cruz. In 1903, a larger rectory was constructed at High and Potrero Streets. In 1906, buildings were damaged by the San Francisco earthquake. Bishop Conaty offered to lend funds for repair projects which were made in the following years. Ceiling paintings and a new Stations of the Cross were added.

In 1925, the lot adjacent to church was purchased for $1,500. In 1928, the parish hall and auditorium was built on High Street, using timbers from the old parish school. Cost was approximately $7,500. The old rectory located at 56 High Street was sold for $100. In 1947, a $20,000 renovation of the parish complex was accomplished. Three garages were constructed near the rectory. In 1949, the parish church, a brick structure, was painted white to protect against water damage.

In 1964, the old wooden rectory from 1903 was torn down and a new rectory at 126 High Street was constructed, immediately west of the parish church. In 1966, major repairs to the rectory were required because of severe design flaws. In 1977, major water and termite damage in the roof of the parish church was discovered. An extensive project involving major engineering changes was accomplished. The entire structure was fumigated. Over the following years, new steel beams were installed along with new heating and electrical systems.

In 1981, a major renovation project for the entire parish church was completed, which included updating the electrical system, redesign of the sanctuary, and the installation of new pews. New interior arrangements included a baptismal font installation near the altar. On October 2, 1982, an historical plaque was placed in Plaza Park to commemorate designation of the site of the old mission as California Registered Historical Landmark (no. 342).

The renovated parish church was re-dedicated with a solemn consecration on the occasion of its centenary on September 17, 1989, by the Most Rev. Thaddeus A. Shubsda, 2nd Bishop of

B etween 1931 and 1932, a one-third or one-half size *replica* of the original mission church was built at Emmett and School Streets. Few efforts to duplicate the actual interior features were attempted, but some remaining furnishings from the original church were incorporated. Cost was about $15,000 and a donation by Mrs. Richard Doyle, niece of Senator James Phelan, was instrumental to the project. The replica of Mission Santa Cruz was dedicated with a simple blessing by the Most Rev. Thomas K. Gorman († 1980), 1st Bishop of Reno, on May 1, 1932.

Monterey, the anniversary of which is celebrated each year in the parish church as a liturgical solemnity. A restored 100-year old Felgemaker pipe organ was installed. Exactly one month later, on October 17, the Loma Prieta earthquake damaged the parish church so severely that liturgical celebrations were transferred to the parish hall. On June 30, 1990, the parish hall was destroyed by fire, requiring the parish to use an outdoor inflatable tent-pavilion.

In December of 1993, church repairs and retrofitting for earthquake protection were completed at a cost of $1.5 million. It was facilitated by a loan from the U.S. Small Business Administration. In 1994, master planning for the future of the parish complex was initiated.

In 1998, the Diocese of Monterey and the City of Santa Cruz entered into an agreement which allowed the parish to use part of a city right-of-way for its parking lot and the city to use church property between Potrero and High Streets for a public bike path. That same year, the construction of an assembly hall and a gymnasium / sports center was planned. The old high school building was to be reconfigured into an educational center. Total cost was estimated at $3.4 million. Charles Franks & Associates of Capitola were the architects.

The parish celebrated the canonization of Saint Junípero Serra on the morning of November 1, 2015, with Mass, followed by a reception.

Holy Eucharist

Succession of Pastors		
1. Rev. Harry Freiermuth	1969 – 1971
2. Rev. Michael G. O'Sullivan	1971 – 1974
3. Rev. Joseph Watt	1974 – 1983
4. Rev. Ron Shirley	1983 – 1989
5. Rev. John C. Griffin	1989 – 2001
6. Rev. Paul P. Murphy	2001 – 2008
7. Rev. Joe Grimaldi	2008 – 2011
8. Rev. Derek Hughes	2011 –

The parish of Holy Eucharist in Corralitos can trace its origins to 1960, when "a released time religious education program" for local children was set up in the Corralitos Youth Center by the parish of Our Lady, Help of Christians in Watsonville. In 1965, as a mission station of Valley Church, weekly Masses began to be celebrated in Corralitos Grange Hall and the St. Pius X Guild was set up as a center for the faithful in Corralitos.

In 1968, a 40-acre property was purchased on Buena Vista Road. It included an old farmhouse (c. 1900) at 527 Corralitos Road. In February of 1969, a newly-assigned resident pastor moved into the remodeled building which served as a rectory, chapel, classroom, and office. Initial plans to build a church on a 40-acre site in Freedom were abandoned.

Holy Eucharist in Corralitos was canonically established as a parish in its own right on December 15, 1969, by decree of the Most Rev. Harry A. Clinch, 1st Bishop of Monterey in California. Sunday Mass continued to be celebrated in the Grange Hall.

By 1970, the parish's religious education program included about 80 children. In 1973, the Butler building was purchased as the center of another multi-use structure on parish property. In 1974, the groundbreaking for a new parish center took place. Fundraising activities included a marathon run by the pastor on March 2. The first Mass in the incomplete structure was celebrated on September 9.

> Pope Benedict XVI distributing Holy Communion

> Circa 1970. *Photo courtesy of the diocesan archives*

The parish in Corralitos is named in honor of the **Most Blessed Sacrament of the Eucharist** (Latin: *Sanctissimo eucharistiæ sacramento;* Spanish: *Santísimo Sacramento de la Eucaristía*), which is "a sacrament of the New Law in which, under the appearances of bread and wine, the body and blood of Christ are truly, really, and substantially present, as the grace-producing food of our souls... The holy Eucharist is the *living* Christ; as a living body is not without its blood, or living blood without a body, so Christ is received whole and entire under either form of bread or wine. The use of the word 'eucharist' has its origin in our Lord's giving thanks at the Last Supper" (Donald Attwater, *A Catholic Dictionary* (1958), p. 177).

The institution of the Most Blessed Sacrament of the Eucharist is remembered liturgically at the Solemn Evening Mass of the Lord's Supper on Holy Thursday, and on the Solemnity of the Most Holy Body and Blood of the Lord (*Sanctissimi Corporis et Sanguinis Christi*), popularly known as "*Corpus Christi*".

The new parish church was dedicated with a simple blessing on June 11, 1977, by Bishop Clinch. On September 23, 1979, Bishop Clinch blessed a new patio area and a bell tower. On October 7, 1979, the parish sponsored a 100-mile and a 50-mile bicycle rally. In the fall of 1982, an addition to the kitchen facilities was undertaken.

A newly renovated parish church following the Loma Prieta earthquake in 1989 was dedicated with a simple blessing on November 1, 1992, by the Most Rev. Sylvester D. Ryan, 3rd Bishop of Monterey in California.

> This statue of Saint Francis of Assisi was donated in 2011 by Judy Siri, in memory of her late husband, Frank J. Siri, Jr. († 2010).

167

Holy Trinity

27 S. El Camino Real, Greenfield - Monterey County

> The exterior of the first parish church, c. 1935
. *Photo courtesy of the diocesan archives*

The parish of Holy Trinity in the City of Greenfield can trace its origins to 1933, when it began as a mission station of the parish of Our Lady of Solitude in Soledad, with Mass being celebrated in a rented hall. In 1934, a small chapel was constructed, financed partly by a $1,250 grant from the Catholic Church Extension Society (Catholic Extension). The site was a 30-acre property donated in 1919 by the Espinosa family at Elm Avenue and Highway 101.

In 1935, Holy Trinity chapel was dedicated on June 28; the name being chosen by the Catholic Church Extension Society (Catholic Extension). In 1949, a $20,000 parish hall was built west of chapel. Holy Trinity was canonically established as a parish in its own right by decree of the Most Rev. Aloysius J. Willinger, Coadjutor Bishop of Monterey-Fresno, on November 3, 1952. In 1952, the rectory was built south of the parish church.

In 1985, the ground-breaking for a new parish church on a site south of the old parish church took place, with the first Mass being celebrated in the new parish church on July 13, 1986. The new parish church was dedicated with a solemn consecration by the Most Rev. Thaddeus A. Shubsda, 2nd Bishop of Monterey, on May 22, 1988, the anniversary of which is celebrated each year in the parish church as a liturgical solemnity. The old chapel became an education center.

The parish in Greenfield is named in honor of the **Most Holy and Undivided Trinity**, "three Persons in one God. God is one in nature but in that one God there are three distinct persons, the Father, the Son who proceeds from the Father by generation, and the Holy Spirit who proceeds from the Father and the Son" (Donald Attwater, *A Catholic Dictionary* (1958), p. 500).

The Most Holy Trinity is celebrated liturgically as the Solemnity of the Most Holy Trinity (Latin: *Sanctissimæ Trinitatis*; Spanish: *Santísima Trinidad*) on the first Sunday after Pentecost popularly known as "Trinity Sunday."

> Original parish church and current parish hall.

Immaculate Conception

> An undated aerial view of the parish.
Photo courtesy of the diocesan archives.

Succession of Pastors

1.	Rev. Emile Cole	1904
2.	Rev. John Reynolds	1904 – 1909
3.	Rev. J.P. Dubbel	1909 – 1910
4.	Rev. W.J. Slattery	1910 – 1911
5.	Rev. Gregory Ashe	1911
6.	Rev. Francis Woodcutter	1911 – 1913
7.	Rev. A. Bucci	1913 – 1919
8.	Rev. Austin Fleming	1919 – 1920
9.	Rev. M.C. Murphy	1920 – 1923
10.	Rev. M. Hentz	1924 – 1925
11.	Rev. Cornelius Casey	1935 – 1938
12.	Rev. Walter Burke	1938 – 1945
13.	Rev. William Stuhlmann	1945 – 1958
14.	Rev. John McKee	1958 – 1961
15.	Rev. John McSweeney	1961 – 1969
16.	Rev. Msgr. Thomas Morgan	1969 – 1983
17.	Rev. Laurence J. McHugh	1983 – 1988
18.	Rev. Michael Miller	1988 – 1989
19.	Rev. Kenneth J. Laverone	1989 – 1992
20.	Rev. Gary Bryne	1992 – 1997
21.	Rev. Larry Betrozoff	1997 – 2003
22.	Rev. Richard D. Clark	2003 – 2005
23.	Rev. Larry Kambitsch	2005 – 2012
24.	Very Rev. Heibar Castañeda, V.F.	
	administrator	2012 – 2014
	pastor	2014

The parish of Immaculate Conception in *Tres Piños* can trace its origins to 1877, when it began as a mission station of the parish of Sacred Heart in Hollister. The first Mass was celebrated on December 8. Subsequently, one Mass was celebrated each Sunday. In 1892, land on *Quien Sabe* Road was purchased for $75 and a chapel named in honor of the Immaculate Heart of the Blessed Virgin Mary was constructed.

On April 12, 1904, Immaculate Heart was canonically established as a parish in its own right by the Rt. Rev. Thomas J. Conaty, 4th Bishop of Monterey-Los Angeles. The boundaries of the new parish named in honor of the Immaculate Conception of the Blessed Virgin Mary included the unincorporated towns of Panoche and New Idria.

Between 1908 and 1909, two side altars and four new statues were added to the original five at a cost of $2,000. In 1912, stained glass windows were installed in the parish church, but the parish was not able to pay for them in a timely manner.

The boundaries of the parish were defined by decree of the Most Rev. John B. MacGinley, 1st Bishop of Monterey-Fresno, on January 1, 1927. They were later modified by the Most Rev. Philip G. Scher, 2nd Bishop of Monterey-Fresno, on December 2, 1935.

In 1925, Immaculate Conception once again became a mission station of Sacred Heart parish in Hollister until November 15, 1935, when it was again canonically established as a parish in its

The parish in Tres Piños is named in honor of the **Immaculate Conception**, the dogma that the Blessed Virgin Mary, "in the first instant of her conception was, by a singular grace and privilege of Almighty God in view of the merits of Jesus Christ the Saviour of the human race, preserved exempt from all stain of original sin...

"It was altogether becoming that as the Only Begotten had a Father in Heaven whom the seraphim extol as thrice holy, so He should have a mother on earth who should never lack the splendor of holiness" (Pope Blessed Pius IX, *Ineffabilis Deus*).

The Immaculate Conception of the Blessed Virgin Mary (Latin: *In Conceptione Immaculata Beatæ Mariæ Virginis*; Spanish: *Inmaculada Concepción de María*) is celebrated liturgically as a solemnity on December 8. It is a holy day of obligation, as well as the patronal feast of the United States.

own right. Between 1937 and 1938, the parish rectory and the sacristy were renovated and improved.

On December 15, 1939, John F. Etcheverry deeded four acres of land on the main highway through *Tres Piños* and the Somavia family donated $12,000, for the construct a parish hall on the land. [**Nota bene:** This gift was in thanksgiving for their daughter's recovery from a serious illness.] The contractor was the L.G. and V.G. Young Co. The parish church and rectory were also moved two blocks to the new site and a well was drilled. Mr. W.P. Murphy contributed $2,000 to the project. The new parish church was dedicated with a simple blessing on June 2 by the Most Rev. Philip G. Scher, 2nd Bishop of Monterey-Fresno. [**Nota bene:** That same day, Bishop Scher also blessed a private chapel in the Somavia family's residence.]

In 1941, the lots previously occupied by the parish church and rectory were sold for $300. Between 1942 and 1943, an outdoor Lourdes grotto and statue were donated. In 1945, a war memorial with Winged Victory statue was erected on the parish grounds, while a steel tabernacle and an organ were purchased for the parish church. In 1948, the rectory was renovated.

In 1950, the exteriors of all parish complex buildings were repainted at the expense of the Somavia family and the outdoor Stations of the Cross and replica of Michelangelo's *Pietà* were erected.

In 1958, a furnace explosion and fire and at the parish rectory caused major damage. Renovation of the rectory took place in 1973. Between 1988 and 1997, the parish of Immaculate Conception in *Tres Piños* was administrated from the parish of Sacred Heart in Hollister, but remained a separate parish.

Mission San Antonio de Padua

End of Mission Road, Jolon - Monterey County - MissionSanAntonio.net

Succession of Pastors

1.	Fray Miguel Pieras	1771 – 1994
2.	Fray Buenaventura Sitjar	1794 – 1795
3.	Fray Marcelino Cipres	1795-1804
4.	Fray Juan B. Sancho	1804 – 1829
5.	Fray Pedro Cabot	1829 – 1834
6.	Fray José M. Vasquez del Mercado	1834 – 1839
7.	Fray José de Jesus M. Gutierrez	1840 – 1844
8.	Rev. José Miguel Gomez	1845
9.	Rev. Doroteo Ambris	1846 – 1882
	Mission Station of various parishes	1883 – 1951
10.	Very Rev. Gregory Wooler	1951
11.	Rev. Timothy Noonan, OFM	1951
12.	Rev Bartholomew Welsh, OFM	1951 – 1955
13.	Rev. Julian Girardot, OFM	1955 – 1957
14.	Rev. Erwin Schoenstein, OFM	1957 – 1958
15.	Rev. Philip Colloty, OFM	1958
16.	Rev. Edgar Sever, OFM	1958 – 1961
17.	Rev. Celestine Chinn, OFM	1961 – 1964
18.	Rev. Matthew Poetzel, OFM	1964 – 1970
19.	Rev. Mathias Tumulty	1970 – 1971
20.	Rev. Joseph LaRue, OFM	1978 – 1988
21.	Rev. Leo Spietsma, OFM	1988 – 1994
22.	Rev. Salvador Parisi, OFM	1994 – 1997
23.	Rev. John Gini, OFM	1997 – 2005
	Lay administrator	2005 – 2006
24.	Rev. Dominic J. Castro	2006
25.	Rev. Dennis Peterson	2009
	Lay administrator	2009 –

> *Photo courtesy of Joan Steele.*

Mission San Antonio de Padua, the third California Mission, was founded on the San Antonio River by Saint Junípero Serra on July 14, 1771. In 1773, the mission was moved to its current site on Mission Creek, farther up the Valley of the Oaks, to a more dependable water supply. The construction of the adobe mission church was completed in 1782.

In 1804, Fray Juan Bautista Sanchó († 1830) settled at Mission San Antonio de Padua where he remained until his death. He co-wrote an *Interrogatorio* which recorded the conditions of the natives, their customs, use of local flora, and their music. He also compiled vocabularies of several of their languages and composed two Mass settings: *Misa en Sol* and *Misa de los Angeles*. Construction of the third and current mission church began between 1809 and 1810. Measuring 40 by 120 feet in size, the large ceiling timbers were floated down the river from a mountain area. In 1813, the third mission church was completed and blessed. In 1821, the arched facade was added to the portico of the "Great Church." In 1827, a water system including dams and aqueducts were built.

On November 14, 1834, the mission was secularized by General José Figueroa († 1835), 19th Governor of Alta California, and the mission property began its long decline into ruin: "This mission on its secularization fell into the hands of an administrator who neglected its farms, drove off its cattle, and left its poor Indians to starve."[1]

---

1 • ELLIOTT & MOORE, *History of Monterey County, California, With Illustrations* (1881); reprinted by Valley Publishers, 1979, p. 16.

Saint Anthony of Lisbon and Padua (Latin: *Sanctus Antonius Olisiponensis de Padua*; Portuguese: *San Antonio de Lisboa e Padua*) is the titular patron of Old Mission *San Antonio de Padua* in Jolon. Born Fernando Martins de Bulhões at Lisbon (Portugal) in 1195, St. Anthony "joined the Canons Regular of Saint Augustine but, shortly after ordination to the priesthood, transferred to the Friars Minor to devote himself to spreading the Faith among African peoples. He had his greatest success, however, preaching in France and Italy and converting heretics. He was the first member of this Order to teach theology to his brethren. His sermons are notable for their learning and gentleness. Saint Anthony died at Padua (Italy), in 1231" (*The Liturgy of the Hours*, June 13).

Less than a year after his death, he was canonized by Pope Gregory IX († 1241) and in 1946, Venerable Pope Pius XII proclaimed him a Doctor of the Church. His liturgical feast day is June 13, which is celebrated as a solemnity in the mission church.

> Circa 1800s. *Photo courtesy of the diocesan archives.*

> 1903. *Photo courtesy of the diocesan archives.*

> Circa 1808s. *Photo courtesy of the diocesan archives.*

> 1910. *Photo courtesy of the diocesan archives.*

"The mission grapes were very sweet; wine and aguardiente were made from them in early days, and the grapes were brought to Monterey for sale. The vineyard and garden walls are now gone, and the cattle have destroyed the vines; many of the buildings are down, and the tiles have been removed to roof houses on some of the adjoining ranches. The church is still in good repair. There was formerly a good grist-mill at the mission, but that also, like the mission, is a thing of the past."[2]

A Centenarian of Monterey

F.M. Jolly, Census Enumerator in the San Antonio District, has, it is believed, found the oldest person in the State, being an Indian named Juan Capistrano, whose age is one hundred and thirty-three years. Being interrogated in the Indian tongue, his vernacular, he says he came to San Antonio about the time of the founding of that mission, one hundred and seven years ago, and had then a wife and two children. Having been taught Latin by the priest, he was a singer in the choir there about one hundred years ago.

ELLIOTT & MOORE,
History of Monterey County, California, With Illustrations (1881); reprinted by Valley Publishers, 1979, p. 108

In 1844, the final baptism by a Franciscan missionary was celebrated. In 1845, the mission property was offered for sale after all American Indians dispersed. In 1862 and 1863, the buildings and 33 acres of land in their near vicinity were returned to the Diocese of Monterey by the U.S. government. In 1882, the last resident Franciscan died and the mission property was abandoned. Roof tiles were removed, leading to crumbling of the adobe walls.

In 1883, Mission San Antonio de Padua became a mission station of the parish of Mission San Miguel Arcángel until 1891 when it then became a mission station of Saint John the Baptist in King City. In 1900, the Rev. Andrew Garriga, 3rd pastor of Saint Theodore in Gonzales and 6th pastor Saint John the Baptist in King City, re-instituted the annual solemn feast of Saint Anthony of Padua at the ruins of the mission. Mass was celebrated in the vestibule of the chapel for the few remaining mission Indians. Between 1903 and 1907, the Historic Landmarks League restored significant parts of the structure. Between 1904 and 1906, heavy rains and the 1906 earthquake set back the reconstruction project.

2 • ELLIOTT & MOORE, *History of Monterey County, California, With Illustrations* (1881); reprinted by Valley Publishers, 1979, pp. 16-17.

In 1924, William R. Hearst († 1951), American newspaper publisher and former member of the U.S. House of Representatives from New York's 11th district, offered to purchase the mission property and to restore the church. The Most Rev. John B. MacGinley, 1st Bishop of Monterey-Fresno, explained that the land was held by the Church in a sacred trust, but assistance in the restoration effort would be appreciated. Between 1926 and 1927, after a conference between the Rev. John J. Crowley, Chancellor of the Diocese of Monterey-Fresno, and William Randolph Hearst, Bishop MacGinley offered to sell the 33-acre mission property, reserving only three or four acres—including the actual buildings—for unrestricted religious purposes. A difficulty arose concerning ownership of a graveyard next to the mission church and ultimately Hearst let the entire matter lapse.

In 1928, Mission San Antonio de Padua once again became a mission station of Mission San Miguel Arcángel, with occasional celebrations of the liturgy at the ruins. In 1929, associates of Hearst renewed negotiations to purchase Mission San Antonio. Bishop MacGinley was agreeable provided that use of the mission church for Catholic worship be maintained and that Mr. Hearst committed himself to restore the mission structures to their original appearance within two years. A proposed revision of the agreement later removed the mission church and cemetery from the title transfer. Eventually negotiations again collapsed.

In 1935, a three-room adobe building was constructed for visiting priests and for a caretaker. In 1941, the U.S. Army conducted maneuvers around the mission and purchased "islands" of property embedded in the Hearst Ranch. These activities severely impacted religious use of the property. Franciscans received permission to vacate the mission and celebrate Mass at a private home in Lockwood. In 1942, the Diocese of Monterey-Fresno permitted the U.S. Forest Service (Department of Agriculture) to assign a forest-fire control officer to reside in the caretaker cottage with his family.

In 1946, Samuel F.B. Morse († 1969) of the Del Monte Properties Co., an environmental conservationist and the developer of Pebble Beach, became interested in preserving the mission. Harry Downie's estimate of immediate costs was approximately $121,000. Eventually Morse recommended selling or leasing the site to the State of California so that restoration along the lines of Mission La Purisima Concepción in Lompoc and Mission San Francisco Solano in Sonoma could take place. Bishop Scher agreed, but only subject to maintaining complete control by the Church, similar to previous negotiations with Hearst.

In 1947, the diocese submitted a claim for approximately $1,500 to the U.S. Army for damage to the mission caused during wartime maneuvers. The claim was denied the following year. That same year, a $50,000 grant from the Hearst Foundation to the Franciscans for restoration was received.

Between 1948 and 1949, thoroughgoing restoration of the mission took place under the supervision of Harry Downie. The original statute of Saint Anthony and the original bell, which was cast at Sitka around 1710, were returned.

In 1950, the U.S. government deeded a portion of Fort Hunter-Liggett to the Franciscans. This property surrounds the actual mission which is on land belonging to Diocese of Monterey. The rebuilt mission church was re-dedicated with a solemn consecration on June 4. A new bell made from metal from two San Gabriel bells. These had been cast in Boston in the 1700s by Paul Revere († 1818).

On July 25, 1951, Mission San Antonio de Padua in Jolon was canonically established as a parish by decree of the Most Rev. Aloysius J. Willinger, Coadjutor Bishop of Monterey-Fresno. Franciscan friars were to be pastors, but appointed by the diocesan bishop.

In 1972, Indian leaders threatened to take over the mission grounds and buildings to satisfy their claims under the 1834 secularization decree of the Mexican government. A group of 20 Indians camped on the Mission San Antonio de Padua grounds in March. Eventually Bishop Clinch directed the Indian group to vacate the property and indicated that the Franciscan order supported his decision. The Indians eventually complied. In June, the Most Rev. Harry A. Clinch, 1st Bishop of Monterey in California, rejected all demands for a change in the status of the mission.

In 1975, the Advisory Council on Historic Preservation requested that the U.S. Army undertake an evaluation of the historic status of the mission and how that might affect the Master Plan of 1965 for building more housing at Fort Hunter-Liggett. The Franciscan administrator, local political figures, and preservation groups lobbied the U.S. Army to move the planned construction further away from the mission than the designated quarter-mile buffer zone. Bishop Clinch disassociated the diocese from that campaign. The U.S. Army's construction plans were postponed.

In 1976, archeological work was performed by a team under the direction of Dr. Robert Hoover of the California Polytechnic State University in San Luis Obispo (Cal Poly). Among other projects they examined pollen and seed traces contained in original adobe bricks.

In 1988, the U.S. Army announced a proposal to build 180 housing units northwest of the mission over a five-year period. This project was opposed by the resident pastor, Rev. Sprietsma, OFM, and an ad-hoc group, Friends of San Antonio Mission (later, San Antonio Mission Preservation Coalition). Opposition was joined by the Most Rev. Thaddeus A. Shubsda, 2nd Bishop of Monterey in California, and the local state assemblyman. The U.S. Army decided to perform additional studies of environmental impacts.

In 1989, twenty-four housing units were built next to the mission on land that partly intruded into the previously agreed buffer zone. The U.S. Army presented various reasons to justify the precipitous nature of the project and justifications for it. Bishop Shubsda was not satisfied with their response and believed the project violated legal provisions.

On September 15, 1990, at a meeting in the offices of Congressman Leon E. Panetta, the U.S. Army agreed to accept the Infantry Road site (vice Mission Creek site) for a further 150 units of family housing. Fr. Leo, the Diocese, and the San Antonio Mission Preservation Coalition considered this a partial victory, but decisions on preserving the old mission water system sites and actual boundaries for a no-construction zone were postponed. Also, the U.S. Army did not surrender rights to build at the Mission Creek site at some future date.

In 1991, Friends of the Historic San Antonio Mission (FHSAM) was incorporated as a "grant proposal organization" to support historical and preservation projects at the Mission proper and the historical mission properties in its vicinity. Specifically it supported the concept of a "no-building" buffer zone around the Mission to discourage the U.S. Army from further disturbance of the landscape. The Franciscan pastor was a member of the Board of Directors. Eventually FHSAM decided to advocate a study directed toward giving the Mission National Historic Landmark status and establishing a 7,000-acre Historic National Park around it. It also recommended that the Diocese enter into an agreement with the National Park Service which would give the NPS a form of shared responsibility for the property allowing use of government funds for structural maintenance. Such arrangements had been in effect in the area in and around San Antonio, Texas, for some time.

In 1993, the Most Rev. Sylvester D. Ryan, 3rd Bishop of Monterey in California, by letter to the NPS and other governmental officials, officially opposed the concepts of Historic Landmark status and establishment of a National Park. In 1996, the closing and downsizing of U.S. Army activities at the Fort significantly decreased the population of the local parish. About 20 families remained.

In December of 2004, the Franciscans transferred responsibility for the mission back to the Diocese of Monterey. Most artifacts in the museum were to remain on site. The diocese announced its intention of maintaining Sunday Masses, the retreat center, and facilities for tourists and school children.

On November 13, 2005, an "Evening in the Garden" public event was introduced. A wine tasting and a candlelight tour of the mission museum with music by a baroque orchestra were featured in this new fundraising effort. Between July 30 and August 7, 2006, "Gospel Road," a weeklong service / learning retreat was held at the mission. It focused on social justice and was intended for small teams of adult / teenage workers in various areas of social service.

In 2006, the quadrangle courtyard was refurbished with volunteer labor and materials during the final months of the year. The "Gifts from the Garden" project began sale of mission-grown items, such as cuttings and fruit preserves, in the gift shop.

Photo courtesy of Joan Steele.

In August of 2007, the U.S. Army issued a document, *Programmatic Environmental Impact Statement for Army Growth and Force Structure Realignment* which called for housing an additional 3,500 to 5,000 regular troops and 12,000 dependents at Fort Hunter Liggett. Meanwhile, the National Park Service was calling for the entire 165,000-acre base to be added to its holdings. It opposed the Army's plan in alliance with the Ventana Wilderness Alliance. It appeared that neither of these plans immediately impacted Mission San Antonio de Padua.

The parish celebrated the canonization of its founder, Saint Junípero Serra, on the afternoon of October 31, 2015, with a special Mass, followed by a reception.

Mission San Juan Bautista

406 2nd Street / 2nd & Mariposa Street, San Juan Bautista - San Benito County - www.OldMissionSJB.org

Succession of Pastors

1. Fray Jose Manuel de Martiarena, OFM — 1797 – 1800
2. Fray Jacinto Lopez, OFM — 1800 – 1801
3. Fray Domingo Santiago de Iturrate, OFM — 1801 – 1809
4. Fray Felipe Arroyo de la Cuesta, OFM — 1809 – 1812
5. Fray Esteban Tapis, OFM — 1812 – 1825
6. Fray Felipe Arroyo de al Cuesta, OFM — 1825 – 1833
7. Fray José Antonio Anzar, OFM — 1833 – 1854
8. Rev. J. Mollnier — 1854 – 1856
9. Rev. Francis Mora — 1856 – 1860
10. Rev. Antonio Ubach — 1860 – 1865
11. Rev. Cipriano or Cypriano Rubio — 1865 – 1875
12. Rev. Valentin Closa — 1875 – 1909
13. Rev. John Pujol — 1909 – 1914
14. Rev. Pantaleon Triana — 1914 – 1918
15. Rev. Peter Stoetters — 1918 – 1919
16. Rev. Joseph O'Reilly — 1919 – 1928
17. Rev. Francis Caffrey, MM — 1928 – 1941
18. Rev. Reginald Markam, MM — 1941 – 1945
19. Rev. John Forde — 1945 – 1947
20. Rev. E.T. Haskins — 1947 – 1950
21. Rev. E.A. Cronin — 1950 – 1954
22. Rt. Rev. Michael Sullivan, V.G. — 1954 – 1962
23. Rev. George McManamin — 1962 – 1969
24. Rev. Msgr. Anancio Rodriguez — 1969 – 1983
25. Rev. Felix J. Migliazzo — 1983 – 1986
26. Rev. Max Santamaria — 1986 – 1994
    Rev. Richard McManus, OFM
    administrator — 1994
    Rev. Edward Fitz-Henry
    administrator — 1994 – 2005
27. Rev. Dennis M. Gilbert — 2005 – 2006
28. Rev. Barry Brunsman — 9/2006 – 2007
29. Rev. Greg Sandman — 2/2007 – 8/2007
30. Rev. Edward Fitz-Henry — 2007 – 2011
31. Very Rev. James Henry, V.F.
    administrator — 2011 – 2013
    pastor — 2013 – 2014
32. Rev. Jerry Maher — 2014 – 2016

MISSION
SAN JUAN BAUTISTA

FOUNDED JUNE 24, 1797 BY FATHER LASUEN
15TH OF THE 21 MISSIONS LARGEST AND ONLY
CHURCH WITH 3 AISLES. DEDICATED IN 1812
MONASTERY WING CONSISTED OF 36 ROOMS

THIS MISSION HAS NEVER BEEN ABANDONED
IT IS NOW THE PARISH CHURCH OF
SAN JUAN BAUTISTA

Mission San Juan Bautista, the 15th California Mission, was founded by Fray Jose Manuel de Martiarena and Fray Pedro Martinez on June 24, 1797, during the mission presidency of Fray Fermín de Lasuén († 1803). In 1798, construction of the mission was completed with granary, barracks, and monastery. The mission complex was soon extensively damaged by 20 days of earthquakes. **[Nota bene:** Mission San Juan Bautista is adjacent to the San Andreas Fault.]

The cornerstone for a new and larger mission church was laid on June 13, 1803, which was dedicated with a simple blessing on June 25, 1812. The original plan had called for a three-aisle structure. This was scaled back to the usual one-aisle pattern because of concerns about earthquakes.

William H. Hannon, a Southern California real estate developer and devout Catholic, arranged to have one hundred statues of Saint Junípero Serra erected at various locations in California that were important in the life the saint. [**Nota bene:** One statue was placed outside California, at St. Louis University.] The life-sized statues were sculpted by Dale Smith.

It is said that Hannon began the custom of rubbing the toes of the Serra statues for "good luck," often telling children "After all, he walked all across California, so those toes are lucky; maybe rubbing his toe will help on your next big test."

Photo courtesy of John Glover, 2015.

In December of 2000, the eight-foot statue of Saint John the Baptist, dressed as a California Indian, was installed in front of the mission. *Photo courtesy of John Glover, 2015.*

Saint John the Baptist (Latin: *Sanctus Ioannes Baptista*) is the titular patron of Old Mission *San Juan Bautista*. St John the Baptist was the "precursor of our Lord, son of Zachariah and Elizabeth, who, while yet in his mother's womb, was filled with the Holy Spirit" (cf. *The Roman Martyrology*, 24 June). He was "put to death by Herod about the feast of Easter. However, his solemn commemoration takes place today, when his venerable head was found for the second time. It was afterwards solemnly carried to Rome, where it is kept in the church of St. Sylvester, near the Campus Martius, and honored by the people with the greatest devotion" (*The Roman Martyrology*, 29 August).

St. John the Baptist is the only saint whose both birth and death are liturgically commemorated: June 24 (Solemnity of Nativity of Saint John the Baptist) and August 29 (Memorial of the Passion of Saint John the Baptist).

In 1814, the town of San Juan Bautista began to grow around the mission plaza. In 1818, the golden reredos was painted by a stranded Boston sailor, Thomas Doak, with his Indian assistants. In 1824, Indian enrollment at the mission was 1,248. In 1825, Fray Estevan Tapís was buried beneath the sanctuary.

> This mission looms over a rich valley ten leagues from Monterey… Its lands swept the broad interval and adjacent hills. In 1820 it owned forty-three thousand eight hundred and seventy head of cattle, one thousand three hundred and sixty tame horses, four thousand eight hundred and seventy mares, colts and fillies. It had seven sheep farms, containing sixty-nine thousand five hundred and thirty sheep; while the Indians attached to the mission drove three hundred and twenty-one yoke of working oxen. Its store-house contained $75,000 in goods and $20,000 in specie.[1]

With the secularization of the missions between 1833 and 1835, mission property remained in the care of a succession of Franciscan pastors until 1854, when Fray Jose Antonio Anzar, OFM, turned over the mission to a diocesan priest, the Rev. John Molinier. In 1859, the mission and a small portion of its land were officially returned to the Church by the U.S. government.

1 • ELLIOTT & MOORE, *History of Monterey County, California, With Illustrations* (1881); reprinted by Valley Publishers, 1979, p. 17.

In 1865, a wooden bell tower in the New England style was added, along with wooden flooring and paneling to the interior of the mission church at various times during the 1860s.

In 1906, the mission church was badly damaged by the San Francisco earthquake. Subsequently it was rebuilt and strengthened with steel reinforcing, concrete buttresses, and heavy cross bracing. In 1908, an abortive $50,000 preservation and restoration project was initiated. In 1915, the wooden bell tower was partially destroyed in a storm. Pointed roof was not replaced. In 1922, concrete buttresses were built to support inner walls of the church.

The boundaries of the parish were defined by decree of the Most Rev. John B. MacGinley, 1ˢᵗ Bishop of Monterey-Fresno, on January 1, 1927.

In 1928, Bishop MacGinley assigned administration of the parish to the Maryknoll Fathers who promised to pay interest on the parish debt of $8,000. The annual fiesta was also initiated in 1928. The annual fiesta and barbecue was suspended in 1942 due to the Second World War. In 1929, the bell tower was further remodeled to become more compatible with the mission's original architecture. In 1932, a modern rectory was constructed. In 1937, a new roof was added to the mission church.

La Casa Maria social hall was constructed in 1940 through a donation by Walter Murphy of Chicago. *La Casa Maria*, Spanish for "the house of Mary," was blessed in 1941 by the Most Rev. Philip G. Scher, 2ⁿᵈ Bishop of Monterey-Fresno. Between 1945 and 1946, jurisdiction over the parish of San Juan Bautista was returned to diocesan clergy. The new pastor inaugurated an annual rodeo. Between 1948 and 1950, a restoration project was financed in part by the Hearst Foundation. The anachronistic bell tower was dismantled in 1949. Victorian additions to the mission church's interior were removed.

In 1953, the interior of the mission church was plastered using funds raised by the rodeo. In 1954, the mission museum was enlarged and remodeled under the direction of Harry Downie. A gift shop was also added. In 1956, the roof was repaired and displays in 30 rooms on mission corridor were improved and rearranged. In 1959, thirty new redwood doors were installed, all exact replicas of the originals, many of which had been destroyed or damaged in 1906.

In 1960, further restoration work began under the direction of Harry Downie and financed by the Hearst Foundation. Between 1975 and the 1990s, almost continuous restoration projects were in progress, most of which were financed by the annual fiestas, rodeos, and Christmas events. In 1976, the side walls of the mission church, which were damaged in 1906, were restored.

Old Mission San Juan Bautista was featured prominently in the 1958 Alfred Hitchcock film *Vertigo*. Judy Lanini, daughter of Herbert Coleman, the film's associate producer, suggested the mission to Hitchcock as a filming location.

"A steeple, added sometime after the mission's original construction and secularization, had been demolished following a fire, so Hitchcock added a bell tower using scale models, matte paintings, and trick photography at the Paramount studio in Los Angeles. The tower does not resemble the original steeple. The tower's staircase was assembled inside a studio."

Theatrical poster for the film *Vertigo*. Restored by Adam Cuerden.

On December 3, 1983, a procession was held in the town to unveil a new set of 44 paintings of the saints of the California Missions. These replaced a worn-out, weathered set formerly displayed each Christmas season on the main street of the town. The Chamber of Commerce commissioned the new paintings on wood by Ursula "Tibi" Hanes Guthrie, a well-known sculptor and artist of San Juan Bautista.

In 1992, a new tile roof was put on the *convento*. In 1992, the California Department of Parks & Recreation made a proposal to ban parking on the plaza. The diocese believed this might have adverse consequences on church attendance.

Beginning in 1995, Dr. Rubén G. Mendoza of California State University, Monterey Bay (CSUMB), and his archaeology students, began a series of archeological digs on the grounds of the mission. Discovery of large numbers of artifacts led to enlargement of the mission museum and the addition of new display cases. Evidence of an undocumented convent wing was uncovered, which appeared to have burned down in the 1830s.

On June 24, 1997, as part of the mission's bicentennial celebration, the Most Rev. Sylvester D. Ryan, 3rd Bishop of Monterey in California, blessed the restored **Our Lady of Guadalupe Chapel** (c. 1799), located "behind the mission." On September 30, 1998, the parish regained use of its social hall and adjacent parking lot which had been leased to Cadematori's Restaurant for about 12 years.

In 2005, moisture damage to the adobe walls was detected. After removal of the bell tower (1949), plants had been introduced in that area. This promoted buildup of damaging moisture in the walls and in the contents of the museum area including books and documents.

In 2006, footings for the removed wooden bell tower and the original (unbuilt) tower were discovered in an archeological dig. A project under the supervision of Dr. Rubén G. Mendoza of California State University, Monterey Bay (CSUMB) was launched to prevent further moisture damage in the museum / archive area and to restore as many documents as possible.

On June 10, 2007, the solemnity of the Most Holy Body and Blood of Christ (*Corpus Christi*), the Most Rev. Richard J. Garcia, 4th Bishop of Monterey in California, led a solemn procession to four stations in the vicinity where hymns were sung and prayers recited to draw attention to the need for immigration reform in the United States.

The parish celebrated the canonization of Saint Junípero Serra on the morning of December 21, 2015, with a winter solstice celebration and native peoples' dance.

The Orchard of Mission San Juan Bautista

The mission orchard consisted of a well-assorted variety of apples, pears, and quince, and is situated in the fertile valley immediately under the plateau, whereon the church is built. Ten acres were devoted to this orchard, and the trees matured without irrigation... The mission vineyard, olive and peach orchards, were situated about a mile south from the church, and contained thirty acres...

ELLIOTT & MOORE, *History of Monterey County, California, With Illustrations* (1881); reprinted by Valley Publishers, 1979, p. 145

Mission San Miguel Arcãngel

775 Mission Street, San Miguel - San Luis Obispo County - www.MissionSanMiguel.org

The Mission San Miguel Arcãngel was founded on July 25, 1797 by Fray Fermín de Lasuén († 1803). Fifteen native children were baptized that same day. An initial mud-roofed church was soon built and a small village grew up around it, with a larger mission church being constructed the following year.

In 1804, a first expedition to the area east of the mission was sent out. Friendly natives were found at first, but eventually hostile villages ended hopes of founding *asistencias* or sub-missions. In 1806, fire destroyed part of the original mission church, as well as most of the workshops and granaries.

In 1816, construction of the new mission church began, with large timbers being hauled from the Cambria area 40 miles away. Interior decorations were painted by Native American artists. In 1818, the construction of the new mission church was completed. [*Nota bene:* Other accounts specify completion of the structure was in 1820.] In 1824, decoration of the mission church by Esteban C. Munras († 1850) and native apprentices was completed. No changes have been made since then.

In 1834, Mission San Miguel Arcãngel became the last mission to be secularized, even though the local Indians had expressed their desire that the *status quo* be continued.

In 1842, the last resident pastor departed and Mission San Miguel Arcãngel became a mission station of the parish of Old Mission San Luis Obispo. In 1845, the mission properties were sold after the local American Indians became demoralized and dispersed. Only the mission church and the priest's quarters remained.

> One of the many Hannon / Smith statues of St. Junípero Serra. *Photo courtesy of John Glover, 2015.*

Saint Michael the Archangel (Latin: *Sanctus Michael Archangelus*) is the titular patron of Old Mission San Miguel Arcángel and the parish of Saint Michael in Boulder Creek. Pope St. Gregory I, the Great, taught that "some angels are given proper names to denote the service they are empowered to perform... Michael means 'Who is like God?' ...Whenever some act of wondrous power must be performed, Michael is sent, so that his action and his name may make it clear that no one can do what God does by his superior power" (Hom. 34: *The Liturgy of the Hours*, 29 September).

"Christian tradition gives to St. Michael four offices: (1) to fight against Satan, (2) to rescue the souls of the faithful from the power of the enemy, especially at the hour of death, (3) to be the champion of God's people, the Jews in the Old Law, the Christians in the New Testament; therefore he was the patron of the Church, and of the orders of knights during the Middle Ages, (4) to call away from earth and bring men's souls to judgment" (Frederick Holweck, *The Catholic Encyclopedia* (1911), vol. 10).

His liturgical feast is September 29, which is celebrated as a solemnity in the parish church. There is additional liturgical commemoration in the Extraordinary Form of the Roman Rite on May 8.

In 1859, some of the mission property was returned to the Catholic Church by the U.S. government. An aged American Indian caretaker helped to maintain the buildings, part of which was used for a time as a tavern.

In 1878, the first resident pastor was assigned by the Diocese of Monterey-Los Angeles and $3,000 worth of restoration work on the roof was performed. In 1888, a new 2,500 bell was cast using parts of six old, broken ones.

In 1892, Mission San Miguel Arcángel parish established a mission station in Paso Robles in honor of Saint Rose of Lima. In 1901, the main buildings of the mission were renovated. In 1912, the new resident pastor undertook a project to mark all the graves of past Franciscan friars, some of which were in the church sanctuary. A special memorial celebration took place on November 13, with about 20 clergy in attendance, including seven Franciscans.

The boundaries of the parish were defined by decree of the Most Rev. John B. MacGinley, 1st Bishop of Monterey-Fresno, on January 1, 1927. In 1928, Mission San Miguel Arcángel parish was entrusted to the Franciscan order by the Most Rev. John B. MacGinley, 1st Bishop of Monterey-Fresno. In 1929, the Franciscan Province asked to be relieved of the responsibility for the Mission San Miguel Arcángel parish and its mission station of Mission San Antonio because of the poor economic situation locally. They declined an offer of the parish in Taft, and Bishop MacGinley postponed consideration of relieving them at Mission San Miguel Arcángel.

In 1929, noises indicated that the roof of the mission church was about to collapse. Engineers sent by the California Restoration Society confirmed that fact and recommended that the church be vacated and the interior shored up. This was done at the expense of the California Restoration Society who also pledged to raise $30,000 to restore the property. After protracted and frustrating negotiations with the Franciscan Province, the diocese, and various attorneys, the California Restoration Society withdrew its offer and removed itself from the project.

Between 1931 and 1932, approximately $12,000 worth of restoration work, including a new roof, was performed. In 1934, the Franciscan Province purchased an old burial ground adjacent to the official mission cemetery for $75. This property was later sold to the county for road purposes. In 1935, a controversy between the Chancery Office and the Franciscan Province arose concerning the precise status of Mission San Miguel Arcángel, especially regarding use of and accounting for donations from tourists and others wishing to help in restoration efforts.

On November 26, 1939, the Most Rev. Philip G. Scher, 2nd Bishop of Monterey-Fresno, blessed the rebuilt chapel (separate from the mission church). In 1944, the mission gardens were enlarged and a large fountain was installed.

In 1948, a 19-year restoration project which rebuilt much of the central quadrangle of the original mission neared its completion. The restored rooms were used as a Franciscan monastery. Almost all the labor was performed by Franciscan friars and novices.

In 1957, a new freeway on Highway 101 bypassed Mission San Miguel Arcángel. This led to a loss of about half in visits and the corresponding revenue. In 1958, Franciscans made thousands of adobe bricks prior to the construction of a residence hall and a long wall for the novitiate. In 1963, the Franciscans completed the final wing of the replication of the original mission.

In 1986, building analysis by Sanchez Architects, Inc. made re-commendations for projects to counteract observed drainage and settlement problems at Mission San Miguel Arcángel.

In 1996, a vibration investigation report was submitted by Edna Kimbro, an expert on mission structures. It recommended applying for a grant to finance various mitigation projects in order to assure the survival of the Munras frescoes, etc. In 1997, the rock and boulder bell tower (c. 1941) near the chapel was removed since it was considered unsafe. The bicentennial of the mission was observed on September 15.

In 2000, preliminary plans were under discussion for sale of the vineyard property and the construction of a new parish hall and possibly even a new parish church. Stabilization projects for the historical fabric were also considered important. A meeting of diocesan and Franciscan officials was held on 22 September to discuss these and other issues.

On December 22, 2003, the 6.6 magnitude San Simeon earthquake damaged the mission church structure so severely that it was closed to the public. The sacristy was especially impacted. Liturgical services were moved to a nearby social services center. In 2004, the museum and gift shop were reopened. Plans were made to reopen the front arcade of the mission. That same year, the Friends of the Mission Golf Tournament was founded and the event was instituted as an annual affair. $35,000 was raised the first year.

In August of 2005, a $300,000 rebuilding grant was included in the federal budget bill and was announced by the California Missions Foundation. However, no actual appropriation was included. Reopening of the arcade, cactus garden, and courtyard was scheduled for September 1, 2005.

In October of 2006, Mission San Miguel Arcángel was approved for designation as a national landmark, and the the Secretary of the Interior ratified the designation on January 13, 2007, making the mission eligible to receive funding from the Getty Foundation and other secular organizations. The official plaque was installed on June 15.

On August 26, 2006, Friends of Mission San Miguel and about 20 native Salinan Indians began making adobe replacement bricks to be used in the retrofit of the church structure. Dirt from an adjacent farm field proved to be ideal raw material, and 3000 new bricks were manufactured by 200 volunteers.

On September 9, 2006, an old tradition was revived at Chapel Hill, the private residence near Shandon of Judge and Mrs. William Clark where an outdoor concert encompassing a variety of musical traditions was given as a fundraising event for the mission restoration fund.

On July 22, 2007, Bishop Garcia presided over a groundbreaking ceremony for a new Mission Community Center building which would become a temporary church. In October of 2007, the Hearst Foundation of San Francisco contributed a grant of $500,000 to the California Missions Foundation toward restoration of the mission. It had contributed a total of $1.5 million so far. Total of funds raised from all sources was about $9 million at that point. Estimated total requirement was $14 to $15 million.

The newly-renovated mission church was dedicated with a solemn consecration by the Most Rev. Richard J. Garcia, 4th Bishop of Monterey in California, on September 29, 2009, the anniversary of which is celebrated each year in the mission church as a liturgical solemnity.

The parish celebrated the canonization of its founder, Saint Junípero Serra, on the evening of November 7, 2015, with Mass, followed by a reception.

Our Lady of Guadalupe

Bradley, Monterey County - 1943

In 1943, the Rev. Thaddeus Kreye, OFM, 17th pastor of the parish, requested permission of the Most Rev. Philip G. Scher, 2nd Bishop of Monterey-Fresno, to establish a mission station in Bradley. Permission was granted and regularly scheduled Masses began on December 1. In 1945, a building fund for the construction of a permanent chapel was initiated. In 1946, land for a chapel was donated by Mr. Michel Orradre. In 1948, the chapel was constructed at a cost of $3,000 and dedicated with a simple blessing by the Most Rev. Aloysius J. Willinger, Coadjutor Bishop and Apostolic Administrator of the Diocese of Monterey-Fresno, on December 12, the feast day of Our Lady of Guadalupe. In 1968, a porch roof was added to the Our Lady of Guadalupe Chapel.

Our Lady of Ransom

San Ardo, Monterey County - 1887

The parish's mission station of Our Lady of Ransom in San Ardo can trace its origins to 1887, when land for this purpose was donated to the Diocese of Monterey-Los Angeles. The original wooden mission station church was dedicated with a simple blessing on December 8 by the Rt. Rev. Francisco Mora y Borrell, 2nd Bishop of Monterey-Los Angeles.

In 1929, inspectors warned that the church structure in San Ardo was in imminent danger of collapse. The Most Rev. John B. MacGinley, 1st Bishop of Monterey-Fresno, gave permission for $600 worth of repairs.

In 1954, the Orradre family donated $40,000 for the construction of a new 88 by 34 foot mission station church and rectory. The actual cost was $73,000 and the Orradre family made additional donations. The Jame family contributed $20,000 for interior furnishings. The first Mass at the new mission station church was celebrated on May l, 1955.

Nativity of Our Lady

221 Daly Avenue, San Luis Obispo - San Luis Obispo County - www.NativitySLO.org

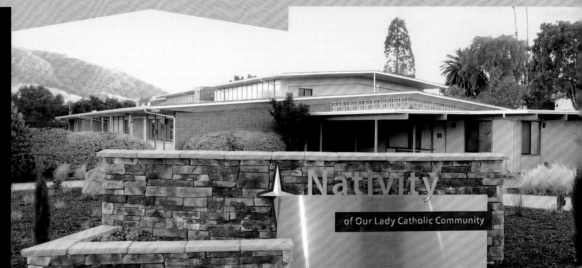

The parish of Nativity of Our Lady is named in honor of the **Nativity of the Blessed Virgin Mary** (*In Nativitate Beatæ Mariæ Virginis*). The source for the story of the birth of the Blessed Virgin Mary is the *Protoevangelium of James,* an apocryphal gospel written about A.D. 150. It gives the names of the Holy Virgin's parents, Joachim and Anne, as well as the tradition that the couple was childless until an angel appeared to Anne and told her that she would conceive.

The Nativity of the Blessed Virgin Mary is liturgically celebrated on September 8, exactly nine months after the solemnity of the Immaculate Conception. It is observed as a solemnity in the parish church.

The parish of the Nativity of Our Lady in the City of San Luis Obispo can trace its origins to 1956, when it began as a mission station of Old Mission San Luis Obispo. The Ferrini family donated land on Daly Street, in the northwest area of San Luis Obispo. A rectory and convent were constructed the following year. The Nativity of Our Lady was canonically established as a parish in its own right on September 15, 1964, by decree of the Most Rev. Aloysius J. Willinger, 3rd and last Bishop of Monterey-Fresno.

In 1966, the parish rectory was sold for $23,000 and an upstairs apartment in the multi-purpose structure was built to serve as the pastor's residence. The lower floor was converted into a more formal church and pews were added.

In 1970, the first parish council was established and a remodeling of the church interior began. In 1973, remodeling of church, rectory, and school continued. Two classrooms were converted into a social hall for the parish.

On the occasion of the 20th anniversary of the parish in 1984, new stained glass windows in the main entrance door of the church were blessed by the Most Rev. Thaddeus A. Shubsda, 2nd Bishop of Monterey in California.

In 1994, $6,000 of emergency electrical repairs became necessary. Original construction of parish plant did not conform to the building code. Also, a $47,000 addition to the parish office was constructed. Around 2003, the parish hall was renovated.

The parish church was solemnly dedicated or consecrated on November 21, 2014, by the Most Rev. Richard J. Garcia, 4th Bishop of Monterey in California.

Our Lady Help of Christians
(Valley Church)
2401 E. Lake Avenue, Watsonville - Santa Cruz County - ValleyCatholicChurch.org

Succession of Pastors

1.	Rev. Francis Mora	1856 – 1857
2.	Rev. Juan Comellar	7/1856 – 9/1856
3.	Rev. Benito Capdeville	1857 – 1859
4.	Rev. Appolinário Rousell	1859 – 1860
5.	Rev. Francis Mora	1860 – 1861
6.	Rev. Domingo Serrano	8/1861 – 9/1861
7.	Rev. Ángel Delfino Casanova	1861 – 1862
8.	Rev. Antonio Ubach	1862 – 1863
9.	Rev. Appolinário Rousell	1863 – 1874
10.	Rev. Francis Codiga, OFM	1874 – 1886
11.	Rev. Joseph Godiol, OSF	1886 – 1900
12.	Rev. Placidus Kreckler, OFM	1900 – 1901
13.	Rev. Theodore Arentz, OFM	1901 – 1902
14.	Rev. Antonio Payeras, OFM	1902 – 1903
15.	Rev. Gregory Knepper, OFM	1903 – 1912
16.	Rev. Florian Zettel, OFM	1912 – 1919
17.	Rev. Francis Burelbach	1919 – 1921
18.	Rev. Louis Galli, SDB	1921 – 1922
19.	Rev. Paschal Beccaria, SDB	1922 – 1924
20.	Rev. Frederick Barni, SDB	1924 – 1926
21.	Rev. Paschal Beccaria, SDB	1926 – 1928
22.	Rev. Matthew Cravero, SDB	1928 – 1930
23.	Rev. Frederick Barni, SDB	1930 – 1937
24.	Rev. Alfred Broccardo, SDB	1937 – 1938
25.	Rev. William Ryan, SDB	1938 – 1940
26.	Rev. Francis Parolin, SDB	1940 – 1941
27.	Rev. Joseph Galli, SDB	1941 – 1952
28.	Rev. Robert Ferguson, SDB	1952 – 1958
29.	Rev. Hamilcar Blanco, SDB	1958 – 1960
30.	Rev. James J. Kelly	1960 – 1968
31.	Rev. James Maguire	1968 – 1974
32.	Rev. Laurence O'Sullivan	1974 – 1995
33.	Rev. Manuel Bernardo Scares	1995 – 1999
34.	Rev. Harold Danielson, SDB	1999 – 2002
35.	Rev. Harold Rasmussen	2002 – 2006
36.	Rev. Albert Mengon, SDB	2006 – 2013
37.	Rev. Joseph M. Paradayil, SDB	2013 –

The parish of Our Lady, Help of Christians (Valley Church) in the City of Watsonville can trace its origins to May 9, 1854, when the first Mass in the Pajaro Valley was celebrated in a residence on Saint Mary's Farm by the Rev. Peter De Vos, SJ, a missionary from Santa Clara, under faculties granted by the Most Rev. Joseph Alemany, 1st Archbishop of San Francisco. Catholics in the 30 small farmhouses in the Watsonville area were customarily served from Mission San Juan Bautista.

On August 9, 1854, sites for a church and cemetery were chosen by Fr. De Vos on a 10-acre parcel donated to the Diocese of Monterey by William F. White and Eugene Kelly.

The first entry in baptismal register was for February 8, 1855. It was signed by Joseph S. Alemany, Bishop-elect of San Francisco and Administrator of Monterey. Under faculties from the Rt. Rev. Thaddeus Amat, 2nd Bishop of Monterey, the site and cornerstone for the first church were blessed by Fr. De Vos on November 25.

On May 25, 1856, the 36-foot-square-church was named in honor of the Most Holy and Immaculate Heart of Mary and dedicated with a simple blessing by Bishop Amat. It was a mission station of Holy Cross parish in Santa Cruz.

The church was later enlarged and on March 11, 1860, it was re-blessed. Our Lady Help of Christians was canonically established as a parish in its own right in 1861 by the Rt. Rev. Thaddeus Amat y Brusi, 2nd and last Bishop of Monterey. In January of 1874, Franciscans from the Santa Barbara Province were put in charge of the parish by Bishop Amat.

In 1901, a new Romanesque-style church was constructed at a cost of $20,000. The architect was Br. Leonard of St. Louis. The new church was dedicated with a simple blessing on July 27, 1902, by the Rt. Rev. George T. Montgomery, 3rd Bishop

The Blessed Virgin Mary is the titular patron of Valley Church under her title **Help of Christians** (Latin: *Auxilium Christianorum*; Spanish: *Auxiliadora*). This title was first used by Saint John Chrysostom († 407), but it was Saint John Bosco († 1888) who propagated devotion to the Blessed Virgin under this title.

"The title of 'Help of Christians', attributed to the august Mother of the Redeemer is not new in the Church of Christ, but in these latter times it has been proclaimed of the Blessed Virgin Mary for a special reason... we can truly say that Mary has been constituted by God as the Help of Christians and that in times of crisis she has shown herself to be the helper especially of those who suffer and fight for the faith...

"The Church has often experienced the powerful help of the Mother of God in times of trial and persecutions. Pope Pius VII established this feast when he returned to Rome on 24 May 1814 after a period of imprisonment and captivity. His safe release and return were attributed to the intercession of Mary, help of Christians" (St John Bosco: *The Liturgy of the Hours: For the Dioceses of Kenya*, 24 May).

The liturgical feast day of the Blessed Virgin Mary, Help of Christians, is May 24. Though it is not included on the General Roman Calendar, it is celebrated as a solemnity in the parish church.

of Monterey-Los Angeles. The original church was remodeled into study halls and classrooms. In 1919, the Franciscans relinquished their administration of the parish. The parish was entrusted to the Society of St. Francis de Sales or Salesians of Don Bosco in 1921.

On the night of February 6, 1927, the parish church and three surrounding buildings burned to the ground. [**Nota bene:** According to later accounts the fire occurred on January 6.]

On May 17, 1928, the cornerstone of the third and present parish church was laid and blessed by the Most Rev. John B. MacGinley, 1st Bishop of Monterey-Fresno. The general contractor was Jack Renfro and the architect was Charles Fantoni of San Francisco. Construction of the new parish church was completed in February of 1929. In 1930, the name of the parish was officially changed to Our Lady, Help of Christians.

In 1952, paving and furnace improvements at the church in the amount of $1850 were approved by the Most Rev. Aloysius J. Willinger, 3rd and last Bishop of Monterey-Fresno. Interior painting for $4,000 was approved in 1953.

In April of 1954, the church's altar was damaged by an earthquake. It was replaced at a cost of $4,000. On May 6, 1955, Bishop Willinger consecrated the new altar in observance of the centennial of the parish. The following day, he ordained new priests and sub-deacons for the Society of St. Francis de Sales or Salesians of Don Bosco and blessed a large painting of Our Lady, Help of Christians, for the sanctuary.

In 1965, plans were made to build a CCD Center. They were facilitated by a bequest for parish use of $12,000. The parish purchased a house and lot for $6,000 to use in the Release Time project. Work began on the center the following year, after $100,000 was donated by parishioners with an additional $10,000 pledged.

On October 17, 1989, the parish church was extensively damaged by the Loma Prieta earthquake. Masses were transferred to the Kennedy Center. In 1990, Ausonio Construction Co. repaired the earthquake damage at a cost of $42,600, partially paid by a grant of $10,000 from the diocese. Work on the tabernacle and altar remained to be done.

In 1995, the Charles Franks architectural firm was engaged by the parish Finance Committee to assist in planning for a remodeling of the church. Planning and interaction With Diocesan Design Consultant continued during the following year.

In 1999, the renovation of the parish church interior was completed. It included new sound system, carpeting, pews, stations, ambo, and altar. Proposed changes regarding the position of the tabernacle, etc., in accord with recent practice were not made at the insistence of parishioners.

In 1999, the parish was returned to the Salesian Fathers of the San Francisco Province. The agreement allowed the order to hold one annual collection for the benefit of its own seminaries. New Salesian pastor was appointed on April 12.

Our Lady of Mount Carmel

9 El Caminito, Carmel Valley Village - Monterey County - www.OurLadyCarmelValley.org

> Circa 1949. *Photo courtesy of the diocesan archives* > 1952. *Photo courtesy of the diocesan archives*

The parish of Our Lady of Mount Carmel in Carmel Valley Village can trace its origins to 1949, when it began as a mission station of the parish of Carmel Mission. The first Mass in area was celebrated in Barn Theater by clergy from the mission. In 1949, a three-acre site on *El Caminito* was purchased for a permanent church. An old stable or dairy barn on the property was converted using volunteer labor into a combination church and rectory under the direction of Harry Downie, curator of Carmel Mission. It could accommodate 110 worshippers. The first Mass was celebrated on Pentecost Sunday. In December of 1951, the first resident chaplain was appointed to the mission station. Our Lady of Mount Carmel was canonically established as a parish in its own right on March 11, 1953, by decree of the Most Rev. Aloysius J. Willinger, 3rd and last Bishop of Monterey-Fresno. A separate rectory was constructed and the whole parish property landscaped. The original rectory became the parish hall. In 1955, additional property was purchased for a parking lot.

In 1972, the parish church was enlarged and improved, which involved extending the original foundation. The parish hall received a new kitchen. The architect was Ron Cantrell of Sacramento and the contractor was Comstock Associates of Carmel. The renovation took several months to complete, during which time Sunday Masses were celebrated at the nondenominational Community Chapel. Work on the redwood structure was completed in mid-December. In 1973, the Community Chapel congregation was thanked for their hospitality with a special Mass and reception on July 1. The parish church was dedicated with a simple blessing by the Most Rev. Harry A. Clinch, 1st Bishop of Monterey in California, on December 1, 1973.

188

The Blessed Virgin Mary is the titular patron of the parish in Carmel Valley Village, under the title of **Our Lady of Mount Carmel** (Latin: *B.M.V. de Monte Carmelo*; Spanish: *Nuestra Señora del Carmen*). "Sacred Scripture celebrated the beauty of Carmel where the prophet Elijah defended the purity of Israel's faith in the living God. In the twelfth century, hermits withdrew to that mountain and later founded the Order devoted to the contemplative life under the patronage of Mary, the Holy Mother of God" (*The Liturgy of the Hours*, 16 July).

The liturgical feast of Our Lady of Mount Carmel is July 16, which is observed as a solemnity in the parish church.

Our Lady of Refuge

11140 Preston Street, Castroville - Monterey County - www.olorc.org

Construction of the wooden gothic-style church with its 82-foot spire was completed in 1875. An arson fire destroyed the parish church building in 1959.

Photo courtesy of the diocesan archives.

The Blessed Virgin Mary is the titular patron of the parish in Castroville, under the title of **Our Lady of Refuge** (Spanish: *Nuestra Señora del Refugio*). The title "Refuge of Sinners" (Latin: *Refugium Peccatorum*; Spanish: *Refugio de los Pecadores*) finds its origins with Saint Germanus of Constantinople († 733 or 740).

On January 4, 1843, the Rt. Rev. Francisco José Vicente Garcia Diego y Moreno, OFM († 1846), 1st Bishop of California, proclaimed Our Lady of Refuge patroness of the Californias: "We make known to you that we hereby name the great Mother of God in her most precious title, *del Refugio*, the principal patroness of our diocese... With so great a patroness and protectress, what can we not promise ourselves? What can be wanting and whom need we fear?" (Mission Santa Clara, *Libro de Patentes*).

Since 1982, the liturgical feast of Our Lady of Refuge is celebrated as an obligatory memorial on July 5 in all the dioceses of California. It is celebrated as a solemnity in the parish church.

The parish of Our Lady of Refuge in Castroville can trace its origins to 1865, when the parish of Immaculate Heart in Pajaro established a mission station on land that had been acquired from the Castro family. In 1869, a small church was constructed at McDougall and Preston Streets and Our Lady of Refuge was canonically established as a parish in its own right by the Rt. Rev. Thaddeus Amat y Brusi, 2nd Bishop of Monterey. The sacrament of Baptism was celebrated for the first time on May 23. Our Lady of Refuge is the oldest Catholic church in Monterey County that did not begin as a mission (cf. *Herald*, October 29, 1988, p. 21).

In 1873, the Castro family donated additional land for use as a parish cemetery. In 1874, the parish church was moved to its current site and the small church became the sacristy of the larger church. In 1875, new wooden gothic-style building with an 82-foot spire was completed and the cornerstone was laid on October 3.

The boundaries of the parish were defined by decree of the Most Rev. John B. MacGinley, 1st Bishop of Monterey-Fresno, on January 1, 1927. They were later modified by the Most Rev. Philip G. Scher, 2nd Bishop of Monterey-Fresno, on October 26, 1933.

In 1950, the Diamond Jubilee was celebrated and the parish church was renovated. A new parish rectory was built between 1953 and 1954. On December 12, 1959, an arson fire destroyed the parish church building. In 1962, a new brick church in "simplified modern mission" style was completed and the first Mass was celebrated on October 28.

In May of 1977, the Castroville Nutrition Center was set up in the parish hall. It provided a daily free lunch and various recreational activities for senior citizens. On June 23, 1978, groundbreaking for the expansion and renovation of the parish hall took place. Ausonio Construction projected completion for October 1. The parish hall was later renamed **Richards Hall**, in honor of Msgr. Vincent Richards.

In September and October of 1983, a parish census of 1,800 homes was conducted. 60 volunteers were involved in this project, which reconciled a considerable number of non-practicing Catholics.

On October of 1988, the parish celebrated the fiftieth anniversary of its annual ham dinner, the parish's main fundraiser (cf. *Herald*, 29 October 1988, p. 21).

Our Lady of Solitude

235 Main Street, Soledad - Monterey County

Mission Soledad

The parish of Our Lady of Solitude in the City of Soledad can trace its roots to October 9, 1791, when Fray Fermín de Lasuén († 1803), 3rd Father-President of the Alta California Mission System, founded the thirteenth California Mission named *La Misión de María Santísima, Nuestra Señora Dolorosísima de la Soledad*, Spanish for "The Mission of Mary Most Holy, Our Most Sorrowful Lady of Solitude," popularly known as Mission Soledad.

In 1797, the first thatch-roofed adobe mission church was completed. By 1800, the neophyte population was about 500. In 1802, an epidemic killed a large number of natives. In 1805, the mission church structure was enlarged. In 1808, work on a new more permanent mission church began.

> In 1826 the mission owned about thirty-six thousand head of cattle, and a greater number of horses and mares than any other mission in the country. So great was the reproduction of these animals that they were not only given away but also driven in bands into the bay of Monterey in order to preserve the pasturage for cattle. It had about seventy thousand sheep and three hundred yoke of tame oxen. In 1819 the major-domo of this mission gathered three thousand four hundred bushels of wheat from thirty-eight bushels sown. Its secularization has been followed by decay and ruin. The mission possessed a fine orchard of a thousand trees, but very few were left in 1849. There was also a vineyard about six miles from the mission in a gorge of the mountains.[1]

1 • ELLIOTT & MOORE, *History of Monterey County, California, With Illustrations* (1881); reprinted by Valley Publishers, 1979, p. 17.

In 1824 and in 1828, floods destroyed the mission church and replacement chapel and in 1831, the mission church building collapsed. In 1832, another disastrous flood occurred and a smaller chapel was constructed where the present replica stands.

Between 1834 and 1835, Mission *Nuestra Señora de la Soledad* was secularized, Fr. Vicente Sarria died at the altar, and the remaining Indians dispersed. In 1846, mission property consisting of 8,900 acres was sold for $800 to Feliciano Soberanes. In 1859, the mission ruins and 34.47 acres were restored to the Church, but all of the buildings were disintegrating. In 1874, the mission church structure itself collapsed.

Our Lady of Solitude Church

In 1894, the parish of Saint John the Baptist in King City established a mission station in honor of "Saint Mary" on land donated by Charles Romie and the Zabala family. In 1901, a fifth lot was purchased. Between 1911 and 1914, a wooden church in Soledad was acquired in a foreclosure. In 1914, Saint Mary in Soledad became a mission station of the parish of Saint Theodore in Gonzales, although they functioned more or less as dual parishes in the later years.

On October 26, 1933, Saint Mary in Soledad was renamed Our Lady of Solitude and canonically established as a parish in its own right by decree of the Most Rev. Philip George Scher, 2nd Bishop of Monterey-Fresno. In 1934, work on a new parish rectory began. It was completed in 1935 and blessed by Bishop Scher.

In 1939, fundraising for the construction of a new parish church began and in 1940, additional lots at Main and Monterey Streets were purchased. In 1942, the new parish church was completed at a cost of $15,000. The contractor

was Mr. Florindo Franscioni, an immigrant from Switzerland. The new parish church was dedicated with a simple blessing in December by the Most Rev. Philip G. Scher, 2nd Bishop of Monterey-Fresno. The parish hall was constructed between 1953 and 1954.

In 1968, a lot adjacent to the parish church facing Encinal Street was purchased for $4,000. In September of 1977, plans were announced for a building program to include new classrooms and enlarging the parish church. Cost of the classrooms was projected at $150,000. In 1982, a catechetical center was built and the church was remodeled with the addition of a portico.

In 1993, the Diocesan Building Commission granted permission for building a new catechetical center at 240 Encinal Street with seven classrooms, restrooms, director's office, and faculty lounge. Total projected cost was $441,000 and the contractor was Ausonio Construction, Inc. of Castroville. In February of 2004, a perpetual adoration chapel was established.

The renovated parish church was re-dedicated with a solemn consecration on April 17, 2007, by the Most Rev. Richard J. Garcia, 4th Bishop of Monterey in California, the anniversary of which is celebrated each year in the parish church as a liturgical solemnity. The baptismal font, statues, stations, reconciliation room, sacristy, floor, heating and air conditioning systems had all been improved.

The parish celebrated the canonization of Saint Junípero Serra on the afternoon of November 1, 2015, with a procession and prayer service with native peoples.

The Blessed Virgin Mary is the titular patron of the parish in Soledad under the title of **Our Lady of Solitude** (Spanish: *Nuestra Señora de la Soledad*). Devotion to Our Lady of Solitude is practiced in Spanish-speaking countries to commemorate the solitude of the Blessed Virgin on Holy Saturday.

The liturgical feast of Our Lady of Solitude is December 18. Though it is not included on the General Roman Calendar, it is celebrated as a solemnity in the parish church.

The old and new parish churches, c. 1950.
Photo courtesy of the diocesan archives.

In 1934, 60 years after the collapse of the mission church, a large wooden cross and flagpole were erected on the old mission grounds. In 1939, properly defined boundaries and access to the county road were established for the mission property. In 1954, the chapel (not the original larger church) was rebuilt under sponsorship of Native Daughters of the Golden West who provided a $30,000 grant. Work was performed under the supervision of Harry Downie. Only a few feet of the walls at the front corner of the original structure survived. The new chapel became a mission station of the parish of Our Lady of Solitude, three miles to the east. In 1958, the first annual fiesta was celebrated to raise funds for mission restoration.

Between 1961 and 1963, the west wing which originally included the padres' residence and granary was rebuilt. 18,000 adobe bricks were manufactured on site using rubble from the original structure. Contractor was Joseph F. Triano of San Carlos. The 144-ft. wing now houses a gift shop and museum of artifacts. Only 12½ acres of the original property now remain. Funds for restoration were raised partly by the Native Daughters and partly by an annual Mission Fiesta supported by the entire Soledad community.

In June of 1971, the first annual Soledad Mission Barbecue was held and in 1972, the first annual grape stomp was held in the fall to raise funds for the restoration of the mission. In the 1980s, extensive archeological studies were conducted with scientific excavations. In 1983, the original "*Las Animas*" bell was returned to the mission. It had been preserved for 143 years, first at Mission San Antonio de Padua and then at Mission San Carlos Borromeo de Carmelo.

In 2000, the restoration of another wing was planned; $250,000 was on hand. In 2001, the restoration and expansion of an olive tree grove were begun. Sales of olive oil were envisioned to benefit mission reconstruction. Cuttings were taken from Mission *Purisima Concepcion* in Lompoc. On November 12, 2005, the first harvest of the restored olive grove was celebrated. One goal is to supply the holy oils (Oil of the Sick, Oil of Catechumens, and Sacred Chrism) to all of the parishes in the diocese.

> One of the many Hannon / Smith statues of St. Junípero Serra. *Photo courtesy of John Glover, 2015.*

JOSÉ JOAQUÍN DE ARRILLAGA

KNOWN AFFECTIONATELY AS PAPÁ BY HIS SOLDIERS, COMPANIONS AND FRIENDS, HE SERVED TWICE AS GOVERNOR OF CALIFORNIA UNDER SPANISH RULE. UPON HIS DEATH IN 1814, HE WAS, AT HIS REQUEST, GARBED IN THE FRANCISCAN HABIT AND BURIED IN THE MISSION CHURCH

José Joaquín de Arrillaga († 1814), 7th (1792-1794) and 10th (1800-1814) Governor of Alta California, is the only Spanish governor to be buried in California destroyed the parish church building in 1959.
Photo courtesy of the diocesan archives.

Our Lady of Assumption

Succession of Pastors

1. Rev. Gilbert Meyer   1953 – 1967
2. Rev. Peter Guisto   1967 – 1973
3. Rev. Victor Farrell   1973 – 1974
4. Rev. Max Santamaria   1974 – 1986
5. Rev. Raul Cavajal   1987 – 1996
6. Rev. Antonio Sanchez
   administrator   1996 – 1997
   pastor   1997 – 2007
7. Rev. Walter Espinoza   2007 – 2011
8. Rev. Victor M. Prado   2011 –

The parish of Our Lady of the Assumption in Pajaro (Royal Oaks) can trace its origins to 1950, when it began as a mission station of the parish of Saint Patrick in Watsonville. Property was purchased on the Salinas Road at Bishop Road at a cost of $6,500 and plans for a church were drawn up by the architect Charles E. Butner. A church was constructed by T.H. Rosewall at a cost of $60,000. The mission station church was dedicated with a simple blessing on December 23, 1951, by the Most Rev. Aloysius J. Willinger, 3rd Bishop of Monterey-Fresno.

Our Lady of the Assumption was canonically established as a parish in its own right by decree of Bishop Willinger on September 15, 1953. Its "mother church" of Saint Patrick in Watsonville donated an initial working balance of $1,400. In 1954, a fundraising campaign with a goal of $6,000 began in order to construct a parish rectory. The pastor had been living in the sacristy until moving into the new parish rectory by 1957.

In December of 1956, land was donated for a catechetical center near the Springfield School. In 1957, the pastor received permission to celebrate additional Sunday Masses in the Aromas and Moss Landing areas, primarily for the benefit of Mexican agricultural workers. The bishop discouraged the idea of building a parish hall near the church, even though land for it would be donated by the Men's Catholic Aid Society.

In November of 1960, permission to build a parish hall and catechetical center was finally granted. However, plans for construction were postponed until suitable land and more funds could be found. Only $13,000 was on hand. By November of 1963, the new parish hall was in use and had been paid for. It had been constructed as an addition to the church structure.

In June of 1965, additional adjacent land (the Kwock property) was acquired for $15,000 to expand the parking area and allow for future additions to the parish church and hall. The parish parking lot was paved between October and November of 1967.

On January 3, 1973, the boundary lines of the parish were adjusted to conform to county lines so that the parish was entirely in Monterey County.

Between 1976 and 1980, the capacity of the parish church was increased from 220 to 420, and capacity of the parish hall was doubled. These projects cost about $150,000. Sunday Mass attendance at that time was about 2,500 faithful and 800 children attended the parish religious education program.

In March of 1995, the surrounding area was badly damaged by flooding of the Pajaro River. Large-scale relief efforts were provided by Catholic Charities and other organizations. In 1996, the parish

The parish of **Our Lady of the Assumption** (Spanish: *Nuestra Señora de la Asunción*) is named in honor of the dogma that the Blessed Virgin Mary, "preserved free from all stain of original sin, when the course of her earthly life was finished, was taken up body and soul into heavenly glory, and exalted by the Lord as Queen over all things, so that she might be the more fully conformed to her Son, the Lord of lords and conqueror of sin and death" (Second Vatican Council, *Lumen gentium* (1965), n. 59; cf. Pius XII, *Munificentissimus Deus* (1950), n. 44).

The Assumption of the Blessed Virgin Mary (Latin: *In Assumptione Beatæ Mariæ Virginis*; Spanish: *Asunción de María*) is celebrated liturgically as a solemnity on August 15 and it is a holy day of obligation.

Parishes

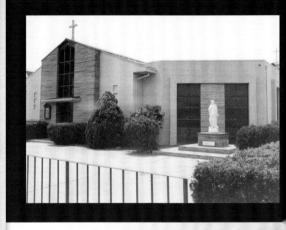

Circa 1951. *Photo courtesy of the diocesan archives.*

entered into an agreement with the Sisters of Charity of Saint Vincent de Paul to provide for a part-time Director of Religious Education. More flooding was experienced in 1998, which forced the closure of the parish church for a period of two weeks. Food vouchers were distributed to needy families in the area.

The parish church of Our Lady of the Assumption was re-dedicated with a solemn consecration on October 12, 2010, by the Most Rev. Richard J. Garcia, 4th Bishop of Monterey in California, the anniversary of which is celebrated each year in the basilica as a liturgical solemnity.

Our Lady, Star of the Sea

515 Frederick Street, Santa Cruz - Santa Cruz County - www.OurLadyStar.org

The parish of Our Lady, Star of the Sea, in the City of Santa Cruz was canonically established on September 20, 1947 by decree of the Most Rev. Aloysius J. Willinger, Auxiliary Bishop of Monterey-Fresno. The parish boundaries were taken in part from the parish of Holy Cross in Santa Cruz and the parish of Saint Joseph in Capitola. Three acres on Frederick Street at Effey in the Seabright area were purchased for $6,500. Although temporary use of a Quonset hut was contemplated, Mass was celebrated at the old Seabright Hotel, which was used as a temporary rectory, office, and church hall. The first Mass was celebrated in late September. Holy Cross parish in Santa Cruz contributed $10,000 as a start-up fund. The first parish census in November of 1947 counted 268 families and 1,380 individuals.

In 1948, an architect was hired to design a mission-style parish church with a tile roof. Six bids were received from contractors and a $58,000 offer from the Rosewall Co. was accepted. Complimentary cement was pledged from the Portland Co. and groundbreaking took place on November 3. In 1949, work was completed and the first Mass was celebrated on August 5. Debt to the diocese was $25,000. On February 12, 1950, the new parish church was dedicated with a simple blessing by the Most Rev. Aloysius J. Willinger, 3rd Bishop of Monterey-Fresno.

In October of 1951, the parish accepted a $3,500 loan from the parish of Saint Patrick in Watsonville, in order to construct a parish hall. In 1954, the parish received a bequest of $5,000 for the purpose of building a rectory.

In 1957, several lots near the parish church were purchased and plans were made for the expansion of the church site, including the addition of a school and a convent, with a resolution to the parking problems. The City of Santa Cruz granted a Use Permit on February 13, with many conditions. Bishop Willinger discouraged immediate action because of financial deficiencies and urged better coordination with nearby parishes on school matters. On June 6, 1957, a fire in the sanctuary of the church caused $575 worth of damage. In 1958, the parish acquired additional land through a donation from the Bryant family.

On January 2, 1969, children playing with matches set fire to the parish church and caused $16,300 worth of damage. As part of the $70,000 restoration project, seating for an additional 100 worshippers was added. The repaired parish church was solemnly re-dedicated on December 14.

In 1974, the parish school building was leased for 20 years to the Parks and Recreation Department of the City of Santa Cruz, in exchange for maintenance of the building, the adjoining park, and the parking lot.

In 1982, the first annual "Star of the Sea Festival" was held as a fundraising event. In 1986, a new heating system for the parish church was installed and the classrooms were re-roofed. A building was moved onto the campus and the parish rectory was renovated.

The Blessed Virgin Mary is the titular patron of the parish in Santa Cruz, under her title **Star of the Sea** (Latin: *Stella Maris*; Spanish: *Estrella de Mar*). The title emphasizes the Blessed Virgin's role as a sign of hope and as a guiding "star" for the faithful.

Saint Bernard of Clairvaux († 1153) teaches that "there is indeed a wonderful appropriateness in this comparison of her with a star, because as a star sends out its rays without harm to itself, so did the Virgin bring forth her Child without injury to her integrity. And as the ray does not diminish the brightness of the star, so neither did the Child born of her tarnish the beauty of Mary's virginity. She is therefore that glorious star, which, as the prophet said, arose out of Jacob, whose ray enlightens the whole earth, whose splendor shines out for all to see in heaven and reaches even unto hell..." (*Hom.* II *super* "*Missus est,*" 17).

Our Lady, Star of the Sea, is celebrated liturgically on September 27. Though it is not included in the General Roman Calendar, it is celebrated as a solemnity in the parish church.

Parish Mission Statement

*We are a faith-filled Catholic Community.
We come together to
celebrate God's presence in our lives
and to nurture one another.*

*As a welcoming community
we honor diversity.
We are committed to reach
beyond ourselves
into the greater community,
to bring to life the Word of God.*

In 1990, plans were made to utilize the former convent for pastoral needs, such as office space and meeting rooms. In 1993, a vacant property at 437 Frederick Street was acquired by bequest. In 1996, the parish received a (confidential) charitable remainder trust of approximately $1 million from Mr. and Mrs. Enrique Melendez, with the principal payable after their deaths.

In 1997, the parish's 50th anniversary was celebrated with a special Mass, procession, variety entertainment night, barbecue, and ecumenical evensong (Vespers). At this time the parish was about one-third Hispanic and included approximately 1,000 households.

In 2006, various parish activities were organized to assist in the improvement of **Star of the Sea Park** which was used by many in the surrounding community. A new play structure, raised planter boxes, and refurbishment of the playing fields were planned.

Resurrection

7600 Soquel Drive, Aptos - Santa Cruz County - www.Resurrection-Aptos.org

Circa 1964.
Photo courtesy of the diocesan archives.

Resurrection parish in Aptos can trace its origins to 1868, when Rafael de Jesus Castro († 1878) donated two acres of land at the corner of what is now Soquel Drive and State Park Drive for a Catholic cemetery where members of his family would be buried, as well as for the construction of a chapel. In 1870, American Indian remains that were on a commercial site were moved to the new Catholic cemetery.

Mass was celebrated in private homes until prominent citizens donated the funds required for a chapel to be built. In 1874, Adolph Claus J. Spreckels († 1908) deeded five acres to the Diocese of Monterey-Los Angeles, which would later become home to the current parish church, cemetery, and the parish hall.

The parish in Aptos is named in honor of the **Resurrection of Christ** (Latin: *Resurrectio Christi*; Spanish: *Resurrección de Jesús*), "the reanimation of the body in the tomb by the soul of Christ on the morning of the third day after His death. Christ's body, though it has entered a glorified existence, forever remains a true, material, physical human body, numerically identical with the body crucified on Calvary" (Donald Attwater, *A Catholic Dictionary* (1958), p. 429).

"Christ, 'the first-born of the dead' (*Col* 1:18), is the principle of our own resurrection, even now by the justification of our souls, and one day by the new life He will impart to our bodies" (*Catechism of the Catholic Church, Second Edition* (1997), n. 658).

In addition to the "solemnity of solemnities" that is Easter Sunday of the Resurrection of the Lord (*Dominica Paschæ in Resurrectione Domini*), the Resurrection of Christ is commemorated liturgically every Sunday.

Parish Mission Statement

Resurrection Catholic Community is dedicated to growing in Christ and to the challenges of loving service.

On November 17, 1874, the Rev. Joaquin Adam celebrated the first Mass in the incomplete 45-by-120-foot chapel. The chapel was completed and dedicated with a simple blessing in October of 1875. Masses were celebrated every first and third Sunday of the month (cf. *Aptos Times*, October 15, 2015). Both the cemetery and chapel were named in honor of Our Lady of Mount Carmel. In 1899, the chapel of Our Lady of Mount Carmel became a mission station of Holy Cross parish in Santa Cruz.

In 1903, Our Lady of Mount Carmel in Aptos was canonically established as a parish in its own right by the Rt. Rev. Thomas J. Conaty, 4th Bishop of Monterey-Los Angeles. Around the same time, property in Capitola was donated to the Diocese of Monterey-Los Angeles by the F.A. Hinh Company. In 1904, the parish was renamed in honor of Saint Joseph and relocated to Capitola. Around 1924, the original chapel in Aptos that was built in 1875 was sold and burials on the Castro property were extended to the entire site.

Between 1964 and 1965, the parish of Saint Joseph in Capitola established a mission station in Aptos, constructing a church named in honor of the Resurrection of the Lord. Resurrection in Aptos was canonically established as a parish in its own right on August 23, 1968, by decree of the Most Rev. Harry A. Clinch, 1st Bishop of Monterey in California.

Around 1991, the parish rectory at 133 Vista Mar Court was purchased. Fundraising efforts to construct a larger church were initiated. A goal of $1.7 million was set.

In 1997, the new parish church reserve fund contained $950,000 in cash and pledges. The project architect was Mr. William Bagnall and the liturgical consultant was Br. Joseph Aspell, SM. The intended site was across the street from the Rancho Del Mar shopping center. It was the front area of the cemetery on land the Castro family was said to have originally intended as a church site. This plan would have involved movement of approximately 70 to 109 previous burials to the rear area of the property. Strong opposition was immediately encountered. In 1998, a final design was worked on and plans were drawn up. A decision was made to locate the new parish church in such a way that no grave relocations would be required.

In January of 1999, the final fundraising drive for new parish church building began. In March, Santa Cruz County approved the plans. The contractor was Mr. George W. Davis. Final cost was estimated to be $1.5 million. In September, a grant of $100,000 was received from the Mary Stuart Rogers Foundation. Groundbreaking was scheduled for January 1999, but it was delayed until September. The new parish church was opened on March 8, 2002. The old parish church became the parish hall.

Resurrection Church was originally planned as a parish hall. Ground was broken on the new church in 2000 and in the spring of 2002, the new parish church was ready for use. The original church then became the parish hall and was named **Markey Community Center**, in honor of the Rev. Francis Markey, first pastor of the parish.

The parish church of the Resurrection was dedicated with a solemn consecration on March 8, 2002, the anniversary of which is celebrated each year in the parish church as a liturgical solemnity.

Original Church building, now Markey Community Center.

Sacred Heart

22 Stone Street, Salinas - Monterey County - www.shSalinas.org

Succession of Pastors		
1. Rev. Cajetan Sorretini		1877 – 1893
2. Rev. P. Stoters		1893 – 1902
3. Rev. Edward P. Griffith		1902 – 1906
4. Rev. Patrick Browne		1906 – 1918
5. Rev. John Coen		1918 – 1926
6. Rev. P. Gerald Gay		1926 – 1933
7. Very Rev. Patrick O'Connor		1933 – 1950
8. Rev. Msgr. Thomas J. Earley, V.G., P.A.		1950 – 1981
9. Rev. Msgr. Thomas J. Neary, V.G.		1981 – 1983
10. Rev. Jim Burdick		1983 – 1993
Very Rev. Matthew Pennington. V.F. *administrator*		1993 – 1994
11. Rev. Thomas J. Fransiscus, C.Ss.R.		1994 – 1995
Rev. Manuel Canal, *administrator*		1995 – 1995
12. Rev. Paul R. Valdez		1995 – 1999
13. Rev. Michael J. Miller		1999 – 2011
14. Rev. Ignacio Martinez		2011 –

The parish of Sacred Heart in the City of Salinas can trace its origins to 1874, when it began as a mission station of the parish of Our Lady of Refuge in Castroville. A two-parcel property located at Stone and Castroville (now Market) Streets was purchased for the construction of the mission station chapel for $2,400.

In 1876, Sacred Hearts of Jesus and Mary in Salinas was canonically established as a parish in its own right by the Rt. Rev. Thaddeus Amat y Brusi, 1st Bishop of Monterey-Los Angeles, with a small wooden church that had been erected before 1875 used for liturgical services. The name "Sacred Hearts of Jesus and Mary" would be forgotten over the years, so that now the parish is officially known simply as "Sacred Heart."

In 1877, the first resident pastor was appointed and Mr. George Graves donated land for a Catholic cemetery. In 1879, the cornerstone for a new brick church was laid by the Most Rev. Francisco Mora y Borrell, 3rd Bishop of Monterey-Los Angeles. The new parish church was finally completed in 1883 and dedicated with a simple blessing on April 3. It was an elaborate structure, with a $1,500 Italian marble altar.

On April 18, 1906, the parish church and most of its contents were destroyed by the San Francisco earthquake. Liturgical celebrations were temporarily held in the hall of the new school building. In 1908, a new parish church was constructed and dedicated with a simple blessing on May 31 by the Most Rev. Thomas J. Conaty, 5th Bishop of Monterey-Los Angeles. The new parish church was a wooden structure of colonial design and seated 725.

On Christmas Eve of 1926, a fire destroyed the parish church. Replacement costs were estimated at $55,000; $16,000 was covered by insurance. The boundaries of the parish were defined by decree of the Most Rev. John B. MacGinley, 1st Bishop of Monterey-Fresno, on January 1, 1927. That same year, the old rectory was moved from Stone & Market Streets to Maple Street.

On May 13, 1928, the new Roman-basilica-style church and parish rectory were blessed by the Most Rev. John B. MacGinley, 1st Bishop of Monterey-Fresno. Total costs were $90,000. The boundaries of the parish were modified by the Most Rev. Philip G. Scher, 2nd Bishop of Monterey-Fresno, on October 26, 1933.

A celebration of the renewal and renovation of the parish church and its organ took place in the afternoon of Sunday, November 22, 1981.[1] Various musical organizations participated in the ceremony. The parish hall was remodeled in 1989.

In August of 2003, groundbreaking took place for two new buildings at Stone & West Market Streets. A gymnasium and youth center, and a building for the Saint Vincent de Paul Society, were planned. The total cost of the project was estimated at $3.3 million.

1 • *The Observer*, November 18, 1981, vol. 13, no. 32, p. 4.

First parish church, circa 1906
Photo courtesy of the diocesan archives.

Third parish church, circa 1908
Photo courtesy of the diocesan archives.

Circa 1928. *Photo courtesy of the diocesan archives.*

Sacred Heart and Saint Benedict

680 College Street, Hollister - San Benito County - www.shsbparish.org

Sacred Heart Church - Fifth & College Street, Hollister

Circa 1938.
Photo courtesy of the diocesan archives.

The parish of Sacred Heart and Saint Benedict in the City of Hollister can trace its origins to 1873, when on February 25 of that year, James Hodges and William W. Hollister († 1886) donated a plot of land for a church that would be named in honor of the Most Sacred Heart of Jesus. Construction began soon thereafter and in December of 1877, the parish of Sacred Heart in Hollister was canonically established by the Rt. Rev. Thaddeus Amat y Brusi, 1st Bishop of Monterey-Los Angeles. The new parish consisted of 12 families and included mission stations at *Tres Piños* and New Idria. In 1878, construction of the parish rectory was completed. A four-acre burial ground two miles east of the church was purchased from James Jones for $360. In 1880, the interior of church was completed. Mass was celebrated at 10:30am and the evening prayer of Vespers was celebrated at 3:30pm on Sundays and holy days.[1]

In 1897, a transept was added to the parish church, thereby doubling the seating capacity. Stained glass windows and new pews were also installed. Frescoes were added in 1904. In 1921, the parish church was renovated and sidewalks were installed.

The boundaries of the parish were defined by decree of the Most Rev. John B. MacGinley, 1st Bishop of Monterey-Fresno, on January 1, 1927. They were later modified by the Most Rev. Philip G. Scher, 2nd Bishop of Monterey-Fresno, on December 2, 1935.

In 1939, the City of Hollister purchased parish lands for $20,000 to establish a public park. The Sacred Heart parish church and rectory were moved to its current present site at 5th and College Streets and subsequently renovated. The parish church was dedicated with a simple blessing by the Most Rev. Philip G. Scher, 2nd Bishop of Monterey-Fresno, on October 15. Most of parish debt was eliminated by using $12,500 surplus from the relocation project.

1 • ELLIOTT & MOORE, *History of Monterey County, California, With Illustrations* (1881); reprinted by Valley Publishers, 1979, p. 150.

T he parish of the Sacred Heart and Saint Benedict is named in honor of the Most Sacred Heart of Jesus and is under the titular patronage of Saint Benedict of Nursia.

The **Most Sacred Heart of Jesus** (Latin: *Sacratissimi Cordis Iesu*; Spanish: *Sagrado Corazón de Jesús*) is "a devotion to Jesus Christ consisting in the divine worship of His heart of flesh considered as united to His divinity and as the symbol of His love for us in dying for our redemption: particularly in reparation for human ingratitude for His goodness and mercy" (Donald Attwater, *A Catholic Dictionary* (1958), p. 442). The devotion to the Most Sacred Heart of Jesus is one of the most widely practiced and well-known Roman Catholic devotions, taking Christ Jesus' physical heart as the representation of His divine love for humanity.

The liturgical feast of the Most Sacred Heart of Jesus has been observed since 1856 and is on the Friday after the Second Sunday after Pentecost. The first Friday of every month is also especially dedicated to the Sacred Heart.

Parish Mission Statement

*Sacred Heart / Saint Benedict Parish,
a Catholic Community,
is an established, diverse,
faith-centered family, serving the spiritual
and temporal needs of all people
by proclaiming the Christian message
of God's love.*

Parishes

In April of 1969, a fundraising campaign was launched for debt reduction, cemetery repair, school support and new construction. In the first weeks, $200,000 was pledged. The parish consisted of 1,500 families at that time. In 1970, a new rectory was constructed.

On December 21, 1986, the **Sacred Heart Pastoral Center** was blessed; the building was previously a convent. In 1989, the parish church was temporarily closed due to damage sustained from the Loma Prieta earthquake on October 17. Mass was celebrated the parish hall.

205

Saint Benedict Church - 1200 Fairview Road, Hollister

For nearly five years, the parish of Sacred Heart in Hollister discerned "how best to address the impact of a burgeoning population in San Benito County on their existing house of worship" (*Observer*, no. 5, May 1998, p. 10). Sacred Heart parish church seats 340 and had been celebrating eight Sunday Masses each weekend, with the church usually "filled beyond capacity." The issue was first raised in 1993 by the parish pastoral council. By early 1994, a feasibility committee determined that a new and larger church building was required.

On April 1, 1996, a fundraising campaign began for a new parish church named in honor of Saint Benedict of Nursia, and a parish hall, to be constructed on a donated 14.7-acre site on Fairview Road. It was donated by Janet P. Roberts of Hollister. Total projected costs were to be $6 million. Initial fundraising goal was $3.5 million. Hyndman & Hyndman of Cardiff prepared the initial design for the project.

In 1997, the Use Permit application and the Master Plan were submitted to county authorities for the project and an additional 2.3 acres of adjacent property with a residence (1270 Fairview Road) were purchased for $325,000. The Master Plan called for a 14,000 square foot parish church seating 750, and an 11,000 square foot parish hall. Total project costs had risen to $7.4 million. Almost $5 million was in hand or already spent. A loan from the diocese was approximately $2 million.

Groundbreaking took place on May 10, 1998. Church construction costs were about $4 million and construction of the parish hall ($1.6 million) was postponed. The general contractor was Mr. Greg Opinski.

The parish of the Sacred Heart and Saint Benedict is named in honor of the Most Sacred Heart of Jesus and is under the titular patronage of Saint Benedict of Nursia.

Saint Benedict of Nursia (Latin: *Sanctus Benedictus de Nursia*; Italian: *San Benedetto da Norcia*; Spanish: *San Benito de Nursia*) "was born as Norcia, in Umbria, about the year 480. Educated at Rome, he began the eremitic life at Subiaco where he gathered disciples, and then departed for Monte Cassino. There he established the famous monastery and composed the Benedictine Rule. Because this rule was subsequently adopted throughout Europe, he received the title 'Patriarch of Western Monasticism'. He died on March 21, 547" (*The Liturgy of the Hours*, 11 July).

Saint Benedict of Nursia was declared co-patron of Europe, together with Saints Cyril and Methodius, in 1980 by Saint John Paul II. His feast day is observed on July 11 and is celebrated as a solemnity in the parish church. In the Extraordinary Form of the Roman Rite, St. Benedict is celebrated on March 21.

The new church was dedicated with a solemn consecration on October 31, 1999, by the Most Rev. Sylvester D. Ryan, 3rd Bishop of Monterey, the anniversary of which is celebrated each year in the parish church as a liturgical solemnity.

The church of Saint Benedict in Hollister was "not intended to be a fourth parish in the growing San Benito County region, replacing Sacred Heart and Immaculate Conception. It is anticipated that it will be the Sunday gathering place for the Hollister parish. The current parishes will retain their own identities. Should the diocese determine that another parish is warranted in the area, St. Benedict's will be ready to meet the need" (*Observer*, May 1998, no. 5, p. 10).

Saint Angela Merici

146 – 8th Street, Pacific Grove - Monterey County - www.StAngelaMericiPacificGrove.org

Succession of Pastors

1. Rev. Charles T. Kerfs	1928 – 1949
Rev. Joseph Balker *administrator*	1949 – 1950
2. Rev. Edward T. Harkins	1950 – 1955
3. Rev. Msgr. William Lane	1955 – 1974
4. Rev. Msgr. Joseph Stieger	1974 – 1986
5. Rev. Msgr. Philip F. Maxwell	1986 – 1990
6. Rev James J. Kelly	1990 – 1991
Rev. Thomas Fransiscus, C.Ss.R. *administrator*	1991 – 1992
7. Very Rev. Jerry McCormick, V.U.	1992 – 2008
8. Rev. Paul Murphy	2008 – 2013
9. Rev. Seamus O'Brien	2013 –

The sanctuary of the parish church. In September of 1993, a 24-foot color-splashed mural of the Good Shepherd was installed in a tall narrow niche just above the Blessed Sacrament Chapel. The icon was painted by Jean Maynard, a native of Zimbabwe and parishioner. The work was commissioned by the parish altar and rosary society.

Photo courtesy of John Glover, 2015.

The parish of Saint Angela Merici in the City of Pacific Grove was canonically established on May 30, 1928, by decree of the Most. Rev. John B. MacGinley, 1st Bishop of Monterey-Fresno. The parish boundaries include New Monterey and "the adjacent parts of the Del Monte properties." Sunday Mass was at first celebrated in the Theosophical Society Hall on Monterey Street and daily Masses were celebrated in the residence of the first pastor, Rev. Charles T. Kerfs, on 19th Street. In September, a house on Central Avenue was purchased as a residence for Fr. Kerfs, thereby becoming the parish rectory.

Parishioners raised $1,400 to purchase the adjoining lots from the Jacks family. The original parish church was designed by Swartz & Rylands of Fresno to hold 180 people. The exterior was patterned after village churches in Brittany, in the north-west of France, and the interior was heavily influenced by Miss Euphemia Charlton Fortune († 1969), a well-known local artist. The original parish church was dedicated with a simple blessing by Bishop MacGinley on the Second Sunday in Lent, February 24, 1929. That same year, 14 additional nearby lots were purchased for the future construction of a parish school. In 1931, the parish church's design was highlighted in the first issue of *Liturgical Arts* magazine.

In 1940, a Works Progress Administration (WPA) project provided sidewalks and curbing around the parish church and rectory. The sanctuary was also remodeled, and a new altar and tabernacle were donated by Miss E. Charlton Fortune († 1969). In 1944, the parish debt was paid off and a fundraising drive for a parish school began on December 3. Construction of which began on August 1, 1947.

By the 1950s, six Masses were celebrated every Sunday morning, making it apparent that a larger church was needed to accommodate the expanding local population. In 1954, an adjacent block of property was purchased: 8th to 9th and Lighthouse to High Streets. In March of 1955, a 3-year fundraising campaign for the new $300,000 parish church was initiated. Msgr. William Lane, the third pastor, broke ground on the new parish church on August 1, 1956. This new building, located on Lighthouse Avenue, was designed to seat 400 to 750 people.

On December 8, 1957, liturgical services were moved to the new parish church. Initially, the parish hall area in the basement was used. The original parish church building was converted into a gymnasium and library. On April 26, 1964, the new parish church was dedicated with a simple blessing by the Most Rev. Aloysius J. Willinger, 3rd and last Bishop of Monterey-Fresno.

In 1968, the new rectory on 9th Street and Lighthouse was dedicated with an open house on October 29. The original rectory on Central Avenue had earlier been converted into a convent. In 1971, the original rectory became a teenage activities center. Around 1974, an annual Saint Patrick's Day corned beef and cabbage dinner was instituted by the parish altar society.

In 1975, the parish church was renovated and the seating plan altered to place a new main altar at the center of one of the long walls with the pews fanning out in a semicircular pattern. The altar designed by Miss E. Charlton Fortune in 1928 became an altar of repose for the tabernacle.

S aint Angela Merici (Spanish: *Santa Ángela de Mérici*), virgin, "was born in 1470 in Desenzano in the territory of Lombardy (Italy). She took the habit of the Third Order of Saint Francis and called together girls whom she instructed in charitable works. In 1535, under the patronage of Saint Ursula, she founded at Brescia a congregation of women who instructed poor girls in the Christian life. Saint Angela died in 1540" (*The Liturgy of the Hours*, 27 January).

Her liturgical feast day is January 27; May 31 in the Extraordinary Form of the Roman Rite. It is celebrated as a solemnity in the parish church.

Parish Mission Statement

We, the family of St. Angela Merici, a welcoming community with a rich heritage, live out our baptismal call to become the Body of Christ through Eucharist, Evangelization and Stewardship.

The Most Rev. Harry A. Clinch, 1st Bishop of Monterey, solemnly re-dedicated the renovated parish church on November 23.

In 1978, a Golden Jubilee celebration of the parish was observed from May 31 through June 3. A commemorative booklet, an art exhibit, and various reunions were included in the activities. On March 9, 1980, a blessing of automobiles, bicycles, and motorcycles took place in the parish parking lot.

In 1994, a fundraising campaign for a new church renovation project began. In 1996, the parish church was again reconfigured and renovated. The side porch was enclosed, and a central baptismal font and new sound and lighting systems were installed. A new exterior facade at the front of the church was also built. The renovated parish church was re-dedicated with a solemn consecration by the Most Rev. Sylvester D. Ryan, 3rd Bishop of Monterey, on May 25, 1998, the anniversary of which is celebrated each year in the parish church as a liturgical solemnity.

> The first parish church and rectory, c. 1928. *Photo courtesy of the diocesan archives.*

> Circa 1948. *Photo courtesy of the diocesan archives.*

Saint Elizabeth Ann Seton

2050 Palisades Avenue, Los Osos – San Luis Obispo County – www.seasparishlo.org

1. Rev. Jim Frerkes — 1984 – 1993
   Rev. Michael T. Bell
   administrator — 1994
2. Rev. Paul R. Valdez — 1994 – 1995
3. Rev. Mark Stetz — 1995 – 2001
   Deacon David Leach
   administrator — 2001 – 2005
4. Rev. Edward Holterhoff — 2005 – 2006
5. Rev. Heibar Castañeda — 2004 – 2008
6. Rev. Lucas Pantoja — 2008 – 2014
   Rev. Joey R. Buena *administrator* — 2014 –

The parish of Saint Elizabeth Ann Seton in Los Osos can trace its origins to January 2, 1983, when local Catholics met with the Most Rev. Thaddeus A. Shubsda, 2nd Bishop of Monterey, at the parish hall of Saint Timothy in Morro Bay, to discuss the possibility of establishing a new parish in Los Osos. A diocesan survey had found that there were 500 Catholic families living in Los Osos. Beginning in October 1983, regularly scheduled "Masses of Accommodation" were celebrated for the local faithful at the Trinity United Methodist Church on Los Osos Valley Road.

On June 4, 1984, Mr. Patrick Willson gifted a one-acre parcel of land on Palisades Avenue to the Diocese of Monterey in California. Saint Elizabeth Ann Seton in Los Osos was canonically established as a parish in its own right on July 2, 1984, by decree of the Most Rev. Thaddeus A. Shubsda, 2nd Bishop of Monterey in California. This would be the forty-fifth parish in the diocese, and yet it did not yet have a parish church to call home. Sunday Mass was celebrated in the auditorium of the Sunnyside Elementary School. Daily Mass was celebrated and Confessions heard in the residence of a retired Josephite priest, the Rev. Carl Scheljens, SSJ.

> Bishop Shubsda shakes hands with Al Switzer, vice-president of Morro Palisades. John Curci, president of the firm, is in the center. *February 16, 1986.*

210

Saint Elizabeth Ann Seton (Latin: *Sancta Elizabeth Anna Seton*; Spanish: *Santa Isabel Ana Seton*), SC, titular patron of the parish, was born Elizabeth Ann Bayley in New York City on August 28, 1774 and raised in the Episcopal Church. She was received into the Catholic Church on March 14, 1805. She died at the age of 46 in Emmitsburg, Maryland, on January 4, 1821. She was beatified by Pope St. John XXIII in 1963 and canonized by Pope Bl. Paul VI in 1975, making her the first native-born citizen of the United States to be canonized.

Her liturgical feast is January 4. It is celebrated as a solemnity in the parish church.

Parish Mission Statement

We are a Christ-centered community joined together in honor of our deeply rooted Catholic traditions, celebrated through multicultural diversity, a commitment to family values and dedication to service. All are welcome.

On January 10, 1986, an adjacent parcel of land measuring two acres was donated by the Morro Shores Company, who also sold one acre. The deed was transferred at a groundbreaking ceremony on February 16, which was followed by Mass at Sunnyside School. The church was constructed at a cost of $78,000 and included two multipurpose rooms and a kitchen.

The parish church was dedicated with a simple blessing by Bishop Shubsda on January 4, 1987 (*The Observer*, vol. 18, no. 26, December 25, 1986 & January 1, 1987, p. 4). It was Bishop Shubsda who had suggested naming the forty-fifth parish of the diocese in honor of St. Elizabeth Ann Seton, as she could serve as a role model for a variety of vocations, having been a wife, a mother, a convert, and the founder of a religious community.

Saint Francis Xavier

1475 LaSalle Avenue, Seaside - Monterey County - www.StFXavier.org

The parish of Saint Francis Xavier in the City of Seaside can trace its origins to 1949, when it began as a mission station of the parish of San Carlos Borromeo in Monterey. Plans began as early as 1944, but it was not until May of 1949 when 10 lots in the Ord Terrace area of Seaside were purchased. Construction of the mission station church began in August of 1949 on what was then Pine Avenue (now LaSalle). Thomas Elston, Jr. of Carmel was the architect and the project was partly financed by the Catholic Church Extension Society (Catholic Extension) and the total cost was $20,000. The first Mass in the new church was celebrated on December 11, 1949.

> A new chapel was part of the latest renovations.
Photo courtesy of the parish.

Saint Francis Xavier was canonically established as a parish in its own right on April 16, 1950, by decree of the Most Rev. Aloysius J. Willinger, Coadjutor Bishop of Monterey-Fresno. [**Nota bene:** The decree was dated April 8, 1950]. The parish boundaries included almost all of the area of Fort Ord and part of present-day Marina and "was home to 30 families" (*The Herald*, August 26, 1989, p. 18). The parish church was dedicated with a simple blessing by Bishop Willinger on January 7, 1951.

In 1951, additional lots adjacent to the church were purchased for $1,240 and the Catholic Church Extension Society (Catholic Extension) donated $1,980 toward building a rectory. In 1952, Catholic Extension forwarded a gift of $500 for completing the rectory, which was constructed by a parishioner. In 1953, the Metz family donated two more lots in the Ord Terrace Tract.

In 1956, two lots on Del Monte Avenue (Hot Spring Tract) that were originally intended for the church were sold for $8,000 and in 1958, a large lot across Pine Avenue was added to the property for $3,000. In 1959, fundraising for the construction of a larger church began, with a parish school and a convent being envisioned as a second priority. A goal of $150,000 was set.

Photo courtesy of Agnieszka A. Klasa, 2016.

212

Saint Francis Xavier (Latin: *Sanctus Franciscus Xaverius*; Spanish: *San Francisco Javier*), the "Apostle to the Far East", is the titular patron of the parish church in the city of Seaside.

Born Francisco de Jasso y Azpilicueta at Xavier in the Kingdom of Navarre (Spain) in 1506, St Francis Xavier was a "priest of the Society of Jesus, confessor and Apostle of the Indies. He was renowned for his conversion of the heathen, his gifts and miracles, and he was filled with merits and good works when he fell asleep in the Lord. Pope [Saint] Pius X chose and appointed him the heavenly protector of the Society for the Propagation of the Faith and of the work for the same object. Pope Pius XI confirmed this and appointed him the special patron of all the Foreign Missions" (*The Roman Martyrology*, December 2).

Saint Francis Xavier died at the age of 46 on Shangchuan Island (China) on 3 December 1552. He was beatified by Pope Paul V in 1619 and canonized by Pope Gregory XV in 1622. By decree of Pope Alexander VII, his liturgical feast is kept on December 3. It is celebrated as a solemnity in the parish church.

Parish Mission Statement

St. Francis Xavier Parish is a diverse, loving community of faithful stewards dedicated to the Gospel of Jesus and His Church.

We are an all-embracing Christian Family that welcomes, nurtures, and serves all of God's people.

Relying on Prayer, Worship, Understanding, Forgiveness and Respect, we strive to continually Renew and Recommit ourselves to this Mission of Faith.

On December 5, 1960, construction of the new church, next door to the old, began with $80,000 on hand. It was designed by Nargis and Dardin of Fresno to seat 1,040 worshippers. Projected total cost was $165,000. The old church became a parish hall and the original rectory became parish offices. Construction of the new parish church was completed on August 21, 1961, and it was blessed soon after, making Saint Francis Xavier the largest Catholic church in the Diocese of Monterey in California.

In 1962, the parish boundaries were adjusted to include all of Fort Ord. In 1965, an additional lot, intended for a convent, was purchased for $13,500. The parish census of 1968 counted 1,296 families. In 1969, the parking area was improved under a $20,000 contract with Granite Construction Co.

In September 1970, the parish hired their first full-time, paid, lay director of religious education. In the summer of 1971, the annual International Festival (originally *Fiesta*) was inaugurated. There was a variety of international food booths, game booths, and various entertainments. Beginning in January 1977, three new classrooms for religious education were planned as part of an expansion project for the parish hall. On June 10, 1979, the Most Rev. Harry A. Clinch, 1st Bishop of Monterey, blessed the remodeled and enlarged parish hall.

In early 1981, a new Allen Digital Computer Organ was installed in the parish church and an inaugural concert was presented on February 1. That same year, the parish rectory was enlarged under a $12,444 contract with Ausonio Construction.

The parish church was re-dedicated with a solemn consecration by the Most Rev. Thaddeus A. Shubsda, 2nd Bishop of Monterey, on January 20, 1985, the anniversary of which is celebrated each year in the parish church as a liturgical solemnity.

On Sunday, August 27, 1989, the parish held its 18th annual International Festival, which welcomed the Most Rev. Tod D. Brown, 7th Bishop of Boise and pastor emeritus and former vicar general of the diocese.

On August 15, 1993, the administration of the parish was entrusted to the **Atonement Friars** of Garrison, New York, for a period of five years. In 1996, the interior of church was remodeled. In 1998, a large-scale and multi-lingual parish stewardship drive was conducted. A significant increase in contributions was reported; however, an operating deficit continued.

Beginning in the summer of 2010, the parish church underwent another renovation, inspired by the altar and ambo that had been designed and constructed especially for the Papal Mass at Laguna Seca in 1987. Through the stewardship of many parishioners, a "sanctuary wall" was constructed to resemble the altar and ambo. Renovation efforts continued for the next five years, consisting of tile floors, plastered walls, new paint both inside and out, new wood front doors, and new windows. Many in the parish have generously shared their gifts and talents to beautify the sacred space with murals and window panels depicting images of the saints. The renovated parish church was re-dedicated with a solemn consecration on the First Sunday of Advent, November 29, 2015, by the Most Rev. Richard J. Garcia, 4th Bishop of Monterey in California.

Saint John

120 Russell Avenue, Felton - Santa Cruz County - www.StJohnsCCh.com

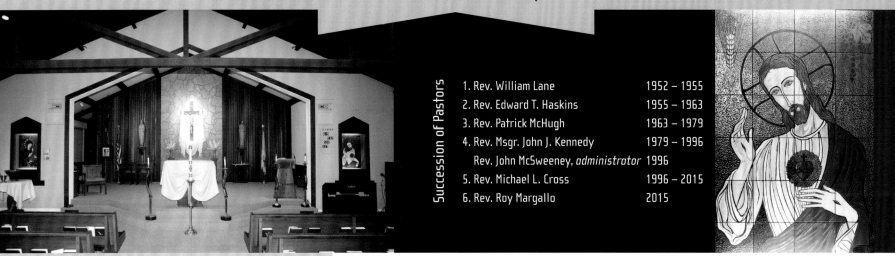

Succession of Pastors

1. Rev. William Lane	1952 – 1955
2. Rev. Edward T. Haskins	1955 – 1963
3. Rev. Patrick McHugh	1963 – 1979
4. Rev. Msgr. John J. Kennedy	1979 – 1996
Rev. John McSweeney, *administrator*	1996
5. Rev. Michael L. Cross	1996 – 2015
6. Rev. Roy Margallo	2015

As part of the 50th anniversary celebration in 2002, Cliff Short was commissioned to design a new altar, ambo, and tabernacle base, all in redwood. To better highlight the crucifix behind the altar, light-colored stonework was applied to the wall.

The parish of Saint John in Felton can trace its roots to 1929, when the Catholic faithful of the local area attended Mass in the local residence of the Rev. Patrick D. Hassett, former pastor of Saint Patrick in Watsonville (1897-1918) and of Sacred Heart in Hollister (1918-1924). During the summer months, Mass was celebrated at campgrounds by priests from Alma College in Los Gatos. Beginning in 1947, the Rev. John Nelson, 5th pastor of Saint Vincent de Paul in Davenport, celebrated Mass in the Felton Community Hall.

In August of 1951, land at Russell Avenue and Highway 9 was purchased for a church, with construction beginning in September. Local Catholics pledged the necessary funds, sought donated materials, and received a loan from the parish of Saint Patrick in Watsonville. Benefactors also included both Catholic and non-Catholic friends of the future parishioners.

In March of 1952, the Rev. William Lane arrived as chaplain of the community. That same year, a grant of $5,000 was received from the Catholic Church Extension Society (Catholic Extension) and plans for constructing a $50,000 church and rectory were approved. The architect was James B. Croker and the contractor was L.W. Roth.

St. John's
Catholic Church

SAT. VIGIL 4:00 P.M.
SUNDAY

WED. 7:00 P.M.
THUR.-FRI. 8:30 A.M.
HOLY DAYS 7:00 PM

Saint John the Apostle and Evangelist (Latin: *Sanctus Ioannes apostolus et evangelista*; Spanish: *San Juan el Apóstol y Evangelista*), was the son of Zebedee and Salome, and the brother of St. James the Greater. In the Gospels the two brothers are often called after their father 'the sons of Zebedee' and received from Christ the honorable title of Boanerges, i.e. 'sons of thunder' (*Mark* 3:17). Originally they were fishermen and fished with their father in the Lake of Genesareth.

Saint John authored five books of the New Testament: one gospel, three epistles, and the Apocalypse (Book of Revelation).

His liturgical feast day is December 27. It is celebrated as a solemnity in the parish church.

> The altar crucifix above the altar.

Parish Mission Station of
Saint Matthias
1970 - 1975

In November 1970, Saint Matthias Mission Station was established at a church building at Noche Buena and Kimball, on the border of Del Rey Oaks, which was owned by the Protestant Episcopal Church in the USA. Originally, the mission station was staffed by the Diocesan Director of Religious Education and the Superintendent of Schools. Later, a nearby house for the two resident priests, Rev. Tod D. Brown and Rev. Joe Watt, was purchased as their personal investment. In September 1973, the Saint Matthias Mission Station began the process of being merged back into the parish; liturgical services ceased in October 1975.

Both the church and the rectory were completed in 1953, and the first Mass was celebrated on Easter Sunday, April 5, 1953. The parish of Saint John in Felton was canonically established by the Most Rev. Aloysius J. Willinger, 3rd Bishop of Monterey-Fresno, on February 7, 1954, when the parish church was also dedicated with a simple blessing.

Around 1963, religious education classes and parish meetings were being held in the homes of parishioners. It became obvious that the parish needed more space. In 1969, land adjoining the parish was purchased and the parish hall was constructed. In 1970, additional adjacent land was purchased and plans for an addition to the parish church and parish hall were approved. In 1981, a new organ was purchased and the installer presented a workshop on its use in September.

In 1982, the San Lorenzo River overran its banks and caused devastation in the valley. The parish hall was turned over to the American Red Cross for use as a shelter. In 1989, the parish church suffered exterior damage from the Loma Prieta earthquake. Later that same year, Cliff Short, a local artist, was commissioned to create a 16-foot redwood cross etched with vines, 12 grape clusters, and an eagle—the traditional symbol of St. John the Evangelist, for the façade of the parish church.

Saint John the Baptist

504 N. Third Street, King City - Monterey County

The parish of Saint John the Baptist in King City can trace its roots to 1776, when Fray Pedro Font, OFM, celebrated the first Mass in the area. Over 100 years later, around 1885, one year after the founding of King City, the first liturgical services in King City were held at the Brunetti Hotel and later at the Vanderhurst Hall, for which priests commuted from Salinas.

The Brunetti Hotel, where the local Catholic community first gathered for Mass, c. 1885.

In 1891, Charles H. King († 1910), for whom King City was named, donated both land and funds for a church to be built and the parish of Saint John the Baptist was canonically established by the Rt. Rev. Francisco Mora y Borrell, 2nd Bishop of Monterey-Los Angeles. The original parish church was built without a rectory and the pastor residing at a local hotel.

In 1894, the pastor was transferred to the parish of Saint Theodore in Gonzales and San Lucas was added as a mission station. One Mass per month was celebrated at King City during this period. In 1900, the pastor was transferred to Saint John the Baptist in King City. Between 1902 and 1903, the parish church was refurbished, with a choir loft and an organ being added. In 1918, the parish rectory was constructed.

The original parish church, c. 1943

The boundaries of the parish were defined by decree of the Most Rev. John B. MacGinley, 1st Bishop of Monterey-Fresno, on January 1, 1927. They were later modified by the Most Rev. Philip G. Scher, 2nd Bishop of Monterey-Fresno, on October 26, 1933.

In 1944, fundraising for a new church building on a four acre site on North Third Street was initiated. In 1949, the new $50,000 church was constructed. The first Mass was celebrated on August 7. On May 6, 1951, the new church was dedicated with a simple blessing by the Most Rev. Aloysius J. Willinger, 3rd and last Bishop of Monterey-Fresno. The parish hall / auditorium and gymnasium were constructed in 1958.

In 1968, the administration of the parish was entrusted to the **Missionaries of Saint Charles Borromeo** and the seventeenth pastor, the Rev. Rino Spada, CS, was the first of three Scalabrini Fathers to serve as pastor. In 1973, the parish hall was renamed in honor of Msgr. Martin McHugh, the fourteenth pastor of the parish.

In 1976, the Diocesan Board of Education recommended improvements in the parish religious education program including hiring a professional director, more involvement by the clergy, regular visits to labor camps, reassessment of financial priorities, and the use of approved texts. On July 4, 1976, a plaque and bicentennial bells were blessed and rung for two minutes to commemorate national independence.

In 1992, the Scalabrini Fathers returned the administration of the parish to the diocese.

Parish Mission Station of
Saint Luke the Evangelist

Corner of Main and Rosa Streets,

San Lucas

Monterey County

In 1894, the parish of Saint Theodore in Gonzales established a mission station in San Lucas, later becoming a mission station of the parish of Saint John in King City.

In 1903, the site for a chapel was donated by the Trescony family. The chapel was constructed the following year using redwood lumber. In 1981, a restroom was added.

Saint Joseph

The parish of Saint Joseph in Capitola can trace its origins to 1903, when priests from the parish of Holy Cross in Santa Cruz celebrated the sacraments for the Catholic faithful of the area. In 1904, the parish of Saint Joseph was canonically established by the Rt. Rev. Thomas J. Conaty, 4th Bishop of Monterey-Los Angeles. Frederick A. Hihn († 1913), a German immigrant and a dominant figure in the commercial, political, and social life of Santa Cruz County, donated land for a church at the southwest corner of Bay and Capitola Avenues. Construction began on 15 June and the first Mass in the original church was celebrated on 18 December. The parish church was dedicated with a simple blessing by Bishop Conaty on July 23, 1911.

In 1912, an adjoining lot was purchased and the parish rectory was constructed, followed by the parish hall in 1915. In 1924, the parish church was reconditioned and the property was landscaped. In 1925, the parish hall was renovated and in 1927, additional land was purchased.

In 1965, the original parish church was found to be structurally unsafe and land for a new church on Monterey Street was purchased. In 1970, planning for the construction of a new parish church began. The capital fund drive was initiated and Thomas R. Richmond was hired as the architect and the contractor was the Reese Construction Co. The ground breaking for the new parish church and catechetical center at Monterey Avenue took place on May 14, 1972. The last Mass said at the original parish church was celebrated on March 19, 1973, the Solemnity of Saint Joseph, Spouse of the Blessed Virgin Mary. Construction was completed in 1973 and the first Mass in the new parish church was celebrated on June 23. Four stained glass windows from the

> Circa 1924. *Photo courtesy of the diocesan archives.*

original church were utilized. A wood statue of Our Lady of Mount Carmel, which had been brought from Spain in 1876 for use at the mission station chapel of Our Lady of Mount Carmel (now Resurrection parish) in Aptos, was used in the new parish church. The bell at the front of the property was also brought to the new site from the original site. The new parish church was dedicated with a simple blessing by the Most Rev. Harry A. Clinch, 1st Bishop of Monterey in California on February 24, 1974. [1]

On June 3, 1979, the Diamond Jubilee of the parish was celebrated with a solemn Mass and festive dinner. In 1996, renovation and redecoration of the church were undertaken. A Blessed Sacrament chapel was added, and new carpeting, refurbished pews, new altar, and sound system were included. Perpetual adoration was established in December of 1999.

1 • The Observer, February 20, 1974, vol. 5, no. 45, pp. 1, 11, and 16.

Saint Joseph

360 Park Avenue, Cayucos - San Luis Obispo County - www.StJosephCayucos.org

The parish of Saint Joseph in Cayucos can trace its origins to 1873, when Swiss-Italian dairy farmers moved into the area. Clergy from Old Mission San Luis Obispo's mission station of Santa Rosa in Cambria provided the sacraments. In 1900, a small church was constructed at Ocean Avenue and E Street for $1,200. The first Mass was celebrated on July 15. A priest from Mission San Luis Obispo celebrated Mass each third Sunday of the month.

On January 26, 1904, the Board of Consultors of the Diocese of Monterey-Los Angeles voted to separate the Cayucos, Cambria, and San Simeon area from the parish boundaries of Old Mission San Luis Obispo, at the request of its pastor. On June 9, 1905, Bishop Conaty sent for the Rev. Joseph Warner of San Diego, in order to appoint him as pastor of the new parish. The first entry in the Saint Joseph in Cayucos sacrament register was dated June 18, 1905. Between 1905 and 1906, the parish rectory for the resident pastor was constructed with a barn and stable.

In 1910, the interior of the church was improved. In 1911, the Saint Joseph in Cayucos became a mission station of the parish of Old Mission San Luis Obispo. Mass was celebrated on the first and third Sundays at Saint Joseph in Cayucos, on the second and fourth Sundays at Santa Rosa in Cambria, and on the fifth Sunday in San Simeon.

In 1920, a resident priest was installed again at Cayucos, but the parish was unable to provide adequate support and in 1921, the pastor relocated his residence to Cambria. The boundaries of the parish were defined by decree of the Most Rev. John B. MacGinley, 1st Bishop of Monterey-Fresno, on January 1, 1927. Both the parish church and rectory were renovated in 1943.

Saint Joseph (Latin: *Sanctus Ioseph*; Spanish: *San José*) is the titular patron of the parish churches located in Capitola, Cayucos, Nipomo and Spreckels.

St. Joseph is the spouse of the Blessed Virgin Mary and the foster father of Jesus Christ. In 1870, Pope Blessed Pius IX, "yielding to the desires and prayers of the whole Catholic world", declared him Patron of the Universal Church. He is also the unofficial patron of a happy death. In 1962, Pope St. John XXIII added the name of St. Joseph to the Roman Canon (Eucharistic Prayer I). Pope Benedict XVI approved the adding of his name to the three other Eucharistic Prayers, and this decision was officially promulgated by Pope Francis in 2013.

His liturgical feast day (solemnity) is March 19. In 1955, Pope Venerable Pius XII established the optional memorial of Saint Joseph the Worker on May 1.

Parish Mission Statement

St. Joseph's Parish is a welcoming, caring, and accepting faith community, nourished by the Word and Eucharist, celebrating the presence of Jesus Christ in the Sacraments, and inspired by the Holy Spirit to share the Word of God, reaching out through prayer, love, and service.

On September 15, 1961, Saint Joseph in Cayucos was canonically established as a parish in its own right by the Most Rev. Aloysius J. Willinger, 3rd and last Bishop of Monterey-Fresno. [1]

In 1965, the construction of a new, concrete block and redwood church on Park Avenue near Highway One took place. The first Mass in the new church was celebrated on October 3. In early October of 1970, the old Saint Joseph's church was destroyed by fire. In 1996, both the parish church and rectory were once again renovated.

1 • *Central California Register*, September 22, 1961, vol. 37, no. 39, p. 1

Saint Joseph

298 S. Thompson, Nipomo – San Luis Obispo County – http://StJoNipomo.org

Succession of Pastors		
1. Rev. Silvano Girolami	1968 – 1977
2. Rev. Msgr. James Marron	1977 – 1987
3. Rev. James R. Cadera	1987 – 1993
4. Rev. James J. Frerkes	1993 – 2001
5. Very Rev. James Henry, V.F.	2001 – 2007
6. Rev. Ron Green	2007 – 2010
7. Rev. Ignacio Martinez	2010
8. Rev. Alberto Cabrera	2010 –

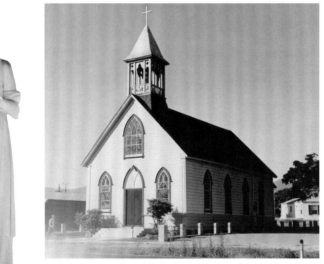

The original mission station church, circa 1951.
Photo courtesy of the diocesan archives.

The parish of Saint Joseph in Nipomo can trace its origins to around 1900, when it began as a mission station of the parish of Saint Patrick in Arroyo Grande. The original mission station church was constructed in 1902 from redwood imported from Oregon at the corner of North Thompson Road and Tefft Street.

In 1967, a 10-acre site for the construction of a new church was purchased on South Thompson Road. Saint Joseph in Nipomo was canonically established as a parish in its own right on April 4, 1968, by the Most Rev. Msgr. Harry A. Clinch, 1st Bishop of Monterey in California, making it the southern-most parish in the new diocese.

Between 1968 and 1969, fundraising for a new parish church, rectory, and hall was conducted. The goal was $60,000 and $76,000 was realized. The new site was a short distance from the original church. Groundbreaking occurred on March 9, 1969.

In July of 1970, construction of the new 52-by-92 foot slump stone block church was completed. It was a hybrid mission style and contemporary building with a tile roof and was blessed on November 1 by Bishop Clinch. The general contractor was M.J. Hermreck, who utilized many hours of volunteer labor. Stained glass windows were relocated from the original church which was renovated to become a catechetical center. A nearby lot with a house was purchased to be the parish rectory. The original parish church that had been constructed in 1902, later becoming the parish catechetical center, was eventually sold to an evangelical protestant community to become Calvary Chapel Nipomo.

Parish Mission Statement

*Worship, Respect, Love & Honor God
with Our Best.
Love our neighbor as ourselves.*

SAN YSIDRO Y SANTA MARIA

Saint Joseph

Succession of Pastors

1. Rev. Daniel C. Cronin	1969 – 1974
2. Rev. Msgr. James Marron	1974 – 1977
3. Rev. Silvano Girolami	1977 – 1983
4. Rev. Larry Betrozoff	1983 – 1985
5. Rev. Victor Farrell	1985 – 1994
Rev. Marvin J. Steffes, C.FF.S.	
administrator	1994 – 1995
6. Rev. James Nisbet	1995 – 2011
7. Rev. Roy Shelly, SDB, V.U.	2011 –

The parish of Saint Joseph in Spreckels can trace its origins to 1897 or 1898, when a small church named in honor of Saint Joseph was constructed in the Alisal (East Salinas). The faithful were from Chicago and had relocated to the Salinas Valley. Calling themselves the Saint Joseph Colony, they dispersed a few years later. The church and the land it was on came into the possession of the parish of Sacred Heart in Salinas.

Around 1910 or 1911, the old Saint Joseph colony's church was moved to the southeast corner of First and Llano in the company town of Spreckels on land donated by the Spreckels Sugar Company. In 1911, this mission station of the parish of Sacred Heart in Salinas was dedicated with a simple blessing by the Rt. Rev. Thomas J. Conaty, 4th Bishop of Monterey-Los Angeles.

The altar society was founded in 1936, which was the first step in becoming an independent parish. In 1963, seven lots were purchased and a new church with seating for 350 was constructed and dedicated with a simple blessing by the Most Rev. Aloysius J. Willinger, 3rd and last Bishop of Monterey-Fresno, on March 31. [1] A catechetical center with four classrooms was also constructed.

Saint Joseph in Spreckels was canonically established as a parish in its own right by decree of the Most Rev. Harry A. Clinch, 1st Bishop of Monterey in California, on June 6, 1969. In 1970, plans for a rectory were approved and the current parish office on Railroad Avenue was soon constructed. The parish hall was constructed between 1977 and 1983. In 1996, plans were made to expand the parish hall and to alter parking arrangements to include 80 extra spaces.

1 • *Central California Register*, April 5, 1963, vol. 39, no. 14, p. 10.

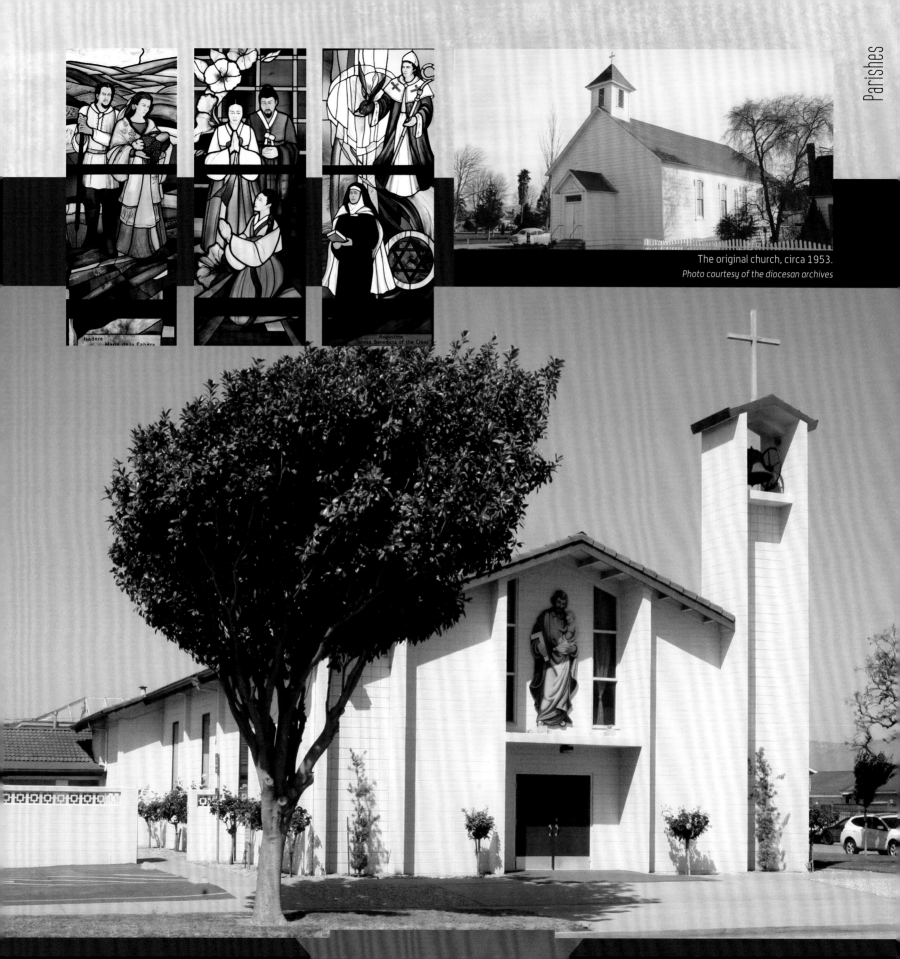

The original church, circa 1953.
Photo courtesy of the diocesan archives

Isadore
Maria de la Cabeza

Augustine
Teresa Benedicta of the Cross

Saint Jude

303 Hillcrest Avenue, Marina - Monterey County

First Masses celebrated on Reindollar Avenue, c. 1963. *Photo courtesy of the diocesan archives*

Circa 1968. *Photo courtesy of the diocesan archives*

The parish of Saint Jude in the City of Marina can trace its origins to 1963, when the parish of Saint Francis Xavier in Seaside established the mission station of Blessed John Neuman in Marina, which served approximately 300 Catholic families. The first Mass was celebrated on Easter Sunday in the back garden of a private home. Masses were later celebrated at the local Grange Hall and then in the garage of the mission station's resident chaplain, the Rev. Jeremiah G. O'Sullivan. The decision was eventually made to locate a new parish on Hillcrest Avenue property that had been donated by Janikula family in 1956.

In 1964, the Most Rev. Aloysius J. Willinger, 3rd and last Bishop of Monterey-Fresno, was determined to relocate the old mission station church in Seaside to Marina and to forestall new construction, but that idea withered away. The Catholic Church Extension Society (Catholic Extension) pledged a grant of $10,000 for building a new parish church and hall to be dedicated to Saint Jude. Other offers of assistance were also received. Mr. Sid Bergman of Los Angeles pledged the balance of construction costs.

In January of 1965, construction of the new church began. It was designed by Patrick J. Quinn and Dennis J. Shanager. In 1965, the annual "Monterey Peninsula Championship of Ireland" Golf Tournament was inaugurated at Del Monte Course. Proceeds were designated for the Saint Jude building fund. In July of 1966, the construction of a church-hall-rectory of noteworthy contemporary design was completed. Saint Jude in Marina was canonically established as a parish in its own right on July 25, 1966, by decree of the Most Rev. Aloysius J. Willinger, 3rd and last Bishop of Monterey-Fresno,

Saint Jude the Apostle (Latin: *Sanctus Iudas Thaddaeus*; Spanish: *San Judas Tadeo*) is the titular patron of the parish and shrine.

Also known as Thaddeus, St. Jude "was the apostle who asked the Lord at the Last Supper why He had manifested Himself only to His disciples and not the whole world (cf. *Jn* 14:22)" (*The Liturgy of the Hours*, 28 October). St. Jude preached the Gospel in Mesopotamia and was later martyred with Saint Simon the Apostle in Persia (cf. *The Roman Martyrology*, October 28).

His liturgical feast is October 28, which is shared with Saint Simon. It is celebrated as a solemnity in the parish church.

and dedicated with a simple blessing on October 30. The parish was also officially designated as a diocesan shrine, which is "a church or other sacred place which, with the approval of the local Ordinary, is by reason of special devotion frequented by the faithful as pilgrims".[1]

The parish rectory was constructed in 1968, and in 1969, the National Liturgical Conference gave an Award of Merit for the design of the parish church, considered to represent "modern Scandinavian" architecture.

In October of 1983, it was announced that monthly Masses in Korean would be celebrated at the parish church. In 1983, the Diocesan Building and Finance Committee approved plans for a new 4,700 square-foot multi-purpose building.

In 1988, the Silver Anniversary of the parish was celebrated, at which time the parish was serving as a host church for the Polish Catholic community and the Korean Catholic community. In 1988, the new parish hall was constructed at a cost of $230,000.

1 • *Code of Canon Law* (1983), can. 1230

227

Saint Mary of the Nativity

424 Towt Street, Salinas - Monterey County - www.StMarySalinas.org

The parish of Saint Mary of the Nativity in the City of Salinas can trace its origins to 1947 as a mission station of the parish of Sacred Heart in Salinas. There were about 800 local Catholic residents and 700 Mexican farm workers who lived at Camp McCallum. The first local Mass was celebrated on June 22 at the Old Barn on Williams Road. A 10-acre tract of land at Alma and Towt Streets in the Alisal district of Salinas was purchased for $16,500 for the construction of a church.

Saint Mary of the Nativity was canonically established as a parish in its own right by decree of the Most Rev. Aloysius J. Willinger, Coadjutor Bishop of Monterey-Fresno, on September 20, 1947. The name of the parish was intended to perpetuate the name of the *Rancho La Natividad*.

The boundaries of the new parish included the county hospital, the juvenile hall, and the prison farm. The new parish church was constructed at a cost of $15,500. Al Juncker was the contractor and Charles E. Butner was the architect. The first Mass was celebrated on October 5. The parish church dedicated with a simple blessing by Bishop Willinger on December 14. The parish rectory was constructed in 1948.

In 1960, a fundraising drive for a new parish church was completed, raising $164,000. On March 3, 1963, the groundbreaking for the new parish church took place. The contractor was Ekelin and Small of Salinas and the architect was Nargis and Darden of Fresno. On May 17, 1964, the first Mass in the new parish church was celebrated. The original parish church was remodeled to become the parish hall. The new parish church was dedicated with a simple blessing by the Most Rev. Msgr. Harry A. Clinch, 1st Bishop of Monterey in California, on March 17, 1968. 900 families were enrolled in the parish at the time.

In November of 1981, the groundbreaking for a new parish hall took place. Fundraising had begun in 1979. Kuska and Fox were the architects and the Summit Construction Co. was to be the builder. The new parish hall was blessed on February 13, 1983 by the Most Rev. Thaddeus A. Shubsda, 2nd Bishop of Monterey in California. It was named **Buckley Hall** in honor of the parish's first pastor.

Saint Michael

13005 Pine Street, Boulder Creek - Santa Cruz County - www.St-MichaelsChurch.org

Succession of Pastors

1.	Rev. Thomas J. O'Brian	1921 – 1924
2.	Rev. Patrick M. O'Flynn	1926 – 1928
3.	Rev. Alex R. Munro	1929 – 1942
4.	Rev. Harold S. Goodwin	1942 – 1951
5.	Rt. Rev. Michael J. Slack	1951 – 1963
6.	Rev. (Msgr.) Eamon MacMahon	1963 – 1973
7.	Rev. James Kelly	1973 – 1987
8.	Rev. Martin McDonald	1987 – 1999
9.	Rev. Paul R. Valdez	1999 – 2005
10.	Rev. Robert Murrin	2005 –

The original parish church, circa 1921.

Photo courtesy of the diocesan archives.

The parish of Saint Michael in Boulder Creek can trace its origins to the 1890s, when the Rev. Michael A. McKey, SJ († 1916), would travel by train from the Santa Clara / San Jose area to Boulder Creek and celebrate the sacraments in the private homes of the Catholic faithful that lived in the area. Mass was later celebrated in Odd Fellows Hall and in Old Fire Hall. The 1898 edition of *The Official Catholic Directory* listed the community of Saint Michael in Boulder Creek as a mission station of Saint Mary of the Immaculate Conception in Los Gatos, itself a mission station of Saint Claire in Santa Clara in what was then the Archdiocese of San Francisco.

The property where the parish church is today was originally owned by local businessman, Santa Cruz County Supervisor, and California State Senator Samuel H. Rambo (*b.* 1843). In December of 1897, two adjacent property lots were donated by another local prominent businessman and Episcopalian, Henry L. Middleton (cf. *The Mountain Echo*, December 25, 1897).

In May of 1899, it was decided that the new church in Boulder Creek would be named in honor of Saint Michael the Archangel. Construction commenced in November of 1899, using 30,000 board feet of lumber. The architectural style was gothic and the total cost was around $2,500 (cf. *The Mountain Echo*, November 18, 1899). The new church was dedicated with a simple blessing by the Most Rev. Patrick W. Riordan († 1914), 2nd Archbishop of San Francisco, on October 14, 1901. In 1904, H.L. Middleton donated an altar to the new church. At Easter in 1906, two new statues from Germany were donated to the parish. There was a fundraising campaign to purchase a church bell; it was dedicated later in the year.

230

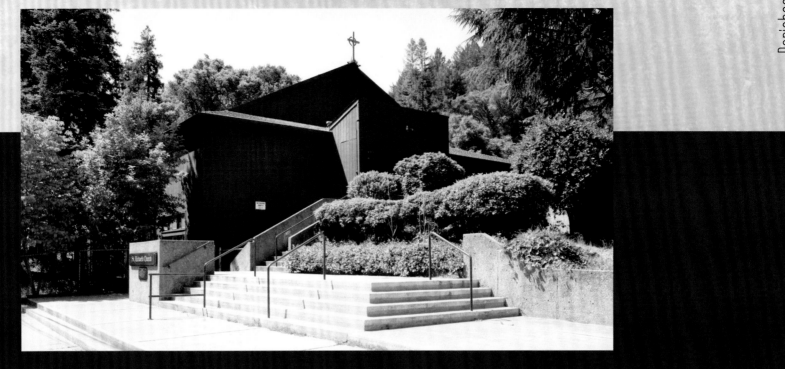

In 1905, Saint Michael in Boulder Creek became a mission station of the parish of Saint Joseph in San Jose in what was then the Archdiocese of San Francisco. In 1909, a house was purchased to serve as the parish rectory. In 1913, Saint Michael in Boulder Creek became a mission station of the parish of Saint Claire in Santa Clara, where all sacramental records prior to 1910 are said to be on file.

Saint Michael in Boulder Creek was canonically established as a parish in its own right in 1921 by the Most Rev. Edward J. Hanna († 1944), 3rd Archbishop of San Francisco. In 1922, the Diocese of Monterey-Los Angeles was split into the new Diocese of Los Angeles-San Diego and the new Diocese of Monterey-Fresno. As a consequence of the boundary change, the parish of Saint Michael was transferred to the Diocese of Monterey-Fresno. Between 1924 and 1925, Saint Michael temporarily became a mission station of the parish of Holy Cross in Santa Cruz.

By 1950, the parishioners doubled, requiring a new parish church and rectory to be constructed. In 1954, the original church was torn down and the second parish church was constructed. In 1968, the groundbreaking for a new (third) permanent church with a seating capacity of 500 took place. Construction of the new brick and redwood church began in December and was completed in 1969, at a cost of about $200,000. It was dedicated with a simple blessing by the Most Rev. Msgr. Harry A. Clinch, 1st Bishop of Monterey in California, on September 28. The previous (second) parish church became a meeting hall and classroom space. [**Nota bene:** Another account states that an entirely new hall and rectory were constructed.]

Saint Patrick

501 Fair Oaks Avenue, Arroyo Grande - San Luis Obispo County - www.StPatsAg.org

Saint Patrick in Arroyo Grande can trace its origins to 1884, when property was acquired in Arroyo Grande for the construction of a church. In 1886, the first church building was constructed on Branch Street and an independent parish was canonically established by the Rt. Rev. Francisco Mora y Borrell, 2nd Bishop of Monterey-Los Angeles. It was the second parish to ever be established in San Luis Obispo County [*Nota bene:* Old Mission San Luis Obispo was the first]. In 1890, the wooden church was destroyed by fire and rebuilt shortly thereafter.

The boundaries of the parish were defined by decree of the Most Rev. John B. MacGinley, 1st Bishop of Monterey-Fresno, on January 1, 1927.

In 1944, extensive improvements were made (stained glass, roofing, heating). In 1957, the parish hall was built. In April of 1968, the original parish church on Branch Street was condemned as unsafe and the last Mass there was celebrated on April 14. Property for a new parish church on Fair Oaks Avenue was purchased. The parish hall was moved from Branch Street to serve as a temporary church. In 1969, the windows were removed from the old church and refurbished for use in a new structure for which fundraising was in progress. New site was next to the parish school on Highway One.

In 1970, plans were drawn up for the new multi-purpose building. The new site consisted of 9.6-acres on Fair Oaks Avenue and Valley Road. In 1972, a new 2,500-square foot rectory and a parish church and hall were constructed.

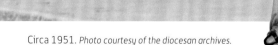

Circa 1951. *Photo courtesy of the diocesan archives.*

232

Parish Mission Station of
Saint Francis of Assisi

1711 Beach Street, Oceano
San Luis Obispo County

Circa 1950. *Photo courtesy of the diocesan archives.*

John R. Ross of San Luis Obispo was the architect. Seating capacity of the parish church was 600 and the assembly room held 300. In 1974, fundraising was in progress for a new parish church in a separate structure. $70,000 was pledged the first year.

In 1979, a regular 9am Sunday Mass in Spanish was inaugurated at the beginning of the year. That same year, a set of Stations of the Cross in mosaic was completed in September by Peter Ladochy, MFA, of Cayucos. These stations included the optional "fifteenth station" depicting the Resurrection of the Lord.

The new parish church was dedicated with a simple blessing by the Most Rev. Harry A. Clinch, 1st Bishop of Monterey in California, on March 2, 1980. It contained the stained glass windows from the original church and various original works by contemporary artists. The building was a contemporary interpretation of the mission style. The architect was Ross & Levin of San Luis Obispo and the general contractor was Hubble Construction of Santa Maria.

In 1950, the Saint Francis of Assisi mission station in Oceano was established. An abandoned Episcopal church in Arroyo Grande was purchased and relocated to Oceano. In 1973, a Spanish-speaking priest was appointed specifically to serve the faithful at Saint Francis of Assisi in Oceano. Three Masses in Spanish were offered each Sunday and fundraising soon began to provide an adjacent rectory.

Saint Patrick

721 Main Street, Watsonville - Santa Cruz County - www.SPatricks.org

The original church, c. 1942.
Photo courtesy of the diocesan archives.

The second and current church, undated.
Photo courtesy of the diocesan archives.

The parish of Saint Patrick in the City of Watsonville can trace its origins to 1860 or 1861, when it began as a mission station of the parish of the Most Holy and Immaculate Heart of Mary (Valley Church) in Watsonville (later renamed Our Lady, Help of Christians). Land was purchased on Main Street. Pending the construction of a church, Mass was celebrated in the old Maher Hall.

On July 3, 1864, the Rt. Rev. Thaddeus Amat y Brusi, 2nd and last Bishop of Monterey, laid the cornerstone of the original church. The original church, built in the Romanesque style, measured 48 by 110 feet in size and consisted of redwood lumber and a brick foundation. In 1865, the church bell was salvaged from Mission San Antonio de Padua in Jolon. In 1866, a property on Pajaro Street was added at a cost of $1,163.50.

234

In 1868, the same year that Watsonville was incorporated by the California legislature, Saint Patrick in Watsonville became a mission station of the newly-established parish of Our Lady of Refuge in Castroville. On October 11, 1869, Saint Patrick in Watsonville was canonically established as a parish in its own right and the sacrament of Baptism was celebrated for the first time. On May 14, 1871, Bishop Amat celebrated the sacrament of Confirmation for 33 candidates for the first time at the parish.

In 1874, the interior construction and fittings of the parish church were finally completed. On May 9, 1875, the parish church was solemnly dedicated by the Rt. Rev. Francisco Mora y Borrell, Coadjutor Bishop of Monterey-Los Angeles, in the presence of Bishop Amat, now the first bishop of Monterey-Los Angeles. In 1882, an addition to the church lot was purchased for $150. In 1897, fundraising for a new, larger, redbrick parish church was initiated. Around 1898, additional adjacent property was purchased.

On September 10, 1901, the contract for the construction of the new parish church was awarded to W.E. Greene. Architect was W. H. Weeks. Contract price was $35,220. At a cost of $875 the old church had been moved to the rear of the lot to make room for the new structure.

In 1902, work on the 68 by 130 foot cruciform, English gothic style structure proceeded as rapidly as possible. It was made of brick with cream terra cotta trim. Foundations were of heavy concrete. Green slate from Vermont was used as the roof. The spire was 132 ft. high with a copper trim. The auditorium was designed to seat 600 on a sloping floor. Art glass was installed in the three largest and various other windows.

On January 11, 1903, the solemn dedication of new parish church was celebrated by the Rt. Rev. George T. Montgomery, 3rd Bishop of Monterey-Los Angeles. The original parish church became the parish hall.

In April of 1906, the parish church's spire and gables were damaged as a result of the San Francisco Earthquake. Approximately $3,000 worth of repairs was required. The rectory repairs amounted to $2,370. In 1908, Main Street in front of the parish church was paved.

In 1920, repairs on the parish hall (the original church) were made for about $5,000. In 1924, a $12,000 organ, built in New York, was installed. In 1925, the parish cemetery was cleaned and renovated. A $5,000 organ was purchased for the parish hall and repairs costing $1,800 were required. The exterior was also altered to make it look less like a church.

In January of 1927, work began on the new parish house. The priests had been forced to move out of the old rectory due to its decrepitude. Fundraising for the project was threatened by a drive sponsored by the Jesuits to restore Mission Santa Clara. At the request of Bishop MacGinley, the Jesuits called off fundraising in Watsonville. Work on the house, garage, and sidewalks was completed in July, and the new parish rectory was blessed by Bishop MacGinley on August 3. Total cost was $25,540. In August of 1927, all of the parish debt was eliminated.

In 1935, alterations in the sanctuary were made at a cost of approximately $2,300. The interior of the parish church was repainted and redecorated at a cost of $1,875. In 1936, the **Catholic Welfare Association of the Pajaro Valley** was organized to provide services to the youth and poor on an inter-parish basis. It became one of the more important Community Chest recipients. In 1937, in connection with the parish's youth program (CYO), showers, tennis courts and handball courts were constructed behind the parish hall. In February of 1937, the Bishop ceded a small triangle of church property to the City of Watsonville in return for construction of new sidewalk, curbs and gutters on the revised Main Street frontage. In 1939, as a gift from the Zills family, the old wooden altar was replaced with a new marble one, and a Lourdes shrine was constructed.

In 1940, the parish rectory was renovated at a cost of approximately $1,000. Roads in the cemetery were re-paved at the cost of $317. In June of 1941, the Division of Highways condemned part of the church property to provide for improving the state highway. Compensation of $4,000 was offered. The Diocese considered this inadequate. However, it was eventually accepted. In 1942, the military population at Camp McQuade in Watsonville was increased to 10,000. This necessitated additional Sunday Masses at the parish. In 1943, the parish of Saint Patrick participated in a fundraising effort to pay off the $20,000 debt of the Valley Church parish. In all, the parish raised $10,000 for Valley Church. In 1944, 3,800 lbs. of clothing was collected by the Catholic Action committee to assist the liberated people of Europe.

On October 14, 1949, a fire of unknown origin caused $1,450 worth of damage to the altar rail and carpeting in the church. In 1951, a new furnace and heating system for the church was installed. In 1954, the interior of the parish church was redecorated by the Hackett Co. of Chicago and Los Angeles. In 1955, the exterior of the parish church was refurbished at a cost of approximately $4,300. In 1958, a new Italian marble altar was erected in the parish church at a cost of $15,000 to $20,000. In 1966, a new suspended acoustical tile ceiling was installed in the parish church. The centennial of the parish was celebrated in 1969, and a parish history was undertaken by Miss Roberta Norton of Watsonville. [Nota bene: This written history has also been dated to 1963.]

In March of 1975, a new Wilkes custom-built pipe organ was installed at a cost of $27,000. After another arson fire on September 26, 1978, the parish church's interior was renovated. The sacristy and small chapel had been destroyed. In the restoration the dropped acoustical tile ceiling was removed and the original ceiling was replicated. New sacristy rooms were added. Exterior repairs to the steeple were made.

In 1979, a new parish hall on Brennan Street was constructed. On March 9, 1980, the new parish hall / school gymnasium was officially blessed. In 1982, a handicapped access via a ramp was added to the parish church.

On October 17, 1989, the parish church was severely damaged by the Loma Prieta earthquake. The celebration of Mass was transferred to the parish hall and other sites. The parish concentrated at first on providing relief to those made homeless by the disaster. A half million dollars of emergency aid was provided. The steeple atop the tower had to be removed for the safety of everyone in the vicinity. After many meetings an initial decision was made to restore and expand the gothic-style church rather than to replace it with a modern building. G.W. Davis, Inc. was selected as general contractor. After much analysis it had become necessary to remove all of the original brick structure and to build a seismically safe replica in its place.

In March of 1994, exterior work was completed on rebuilding the church and a symbolic cornerstone was installed on Saint Patrick's Day. After much analysis it had become necessary to remove all of the original brick structure and to build a seismically safe replica in its place. Total cost was about $3.8 million. Stained glass windows, various interior furnishings, and doors from the old church were reused. The first Mass in the new parish church was celebrated on May 26. The renovated parish church was dedicated with a solemn consecration on October 17, 1994, the fifth anniversary of the earthquake, by the Most Rev. Sylvester D. Ryan, 3rd Bishop of Monterey in California, the anniversary of which is celebrated each year in the parish church as a liturgical solemnity.

Saint Paul the Apostle

800 Bello Street, Pismo Beach – San Luis Obispo County – www.StPaulsPismoBeach.com

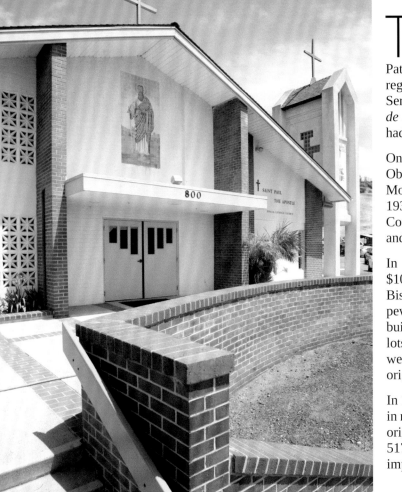

The first parish church, c. 1942.
Photo courtesy of the diocesan archives.

The parish of Saint Paul the Apostle in the City of Pismo Beach can trace its origins to 1925, when it began as a mission station of the parish of Saint Patrick in Arroyo Grande. Sunday Mass was celebrated regularly at the Truelove Theatre. In 1772, Saint Junípero Serra had baptized three native children at the *Rancheria de Pismo* while he was on his way to Monterey. In 1924, the McNamara family had donated land for the eventual construction of a church.

On September 1, 1929, the Pismo Beach area of the Old Mission San Luis Obispo parish was canonically established as a parish in its own right by the Most Rev. John B. MacGinley, 1st Bishop of Monterey-Fresno. On August 14, 1930, the Conventual Franciscan Friars (OMC / OFM Conv.) of the Our Lady of Consolation Province based in Louisville, Kentucky, organized the new parish and have administered it ever since.

In 1930, a church and rectory were constructed on Pismo Street at a cost of $10,000. The church seated 160, and was dedicated with a simple blessing by Bishop MacGinley on March 9. In 1933, stained glass windows and additional pews were added to the church. Some furnishings, such as the altar railings, were built by the first pastor, the Rev. Mathias Schneiders, OMC. In 1942, additional lots were purchased for future expansion. In 1959, the original church and rectory were moved to land on Bello Street provided by the State of California. The original site was taken by eminent domain to make room for U.S. Highway 101.

In 1966, a new church building of brick and stucco, seating 480, was constructed in modified mission style. The cost was $70,000. Stained glass windows from the original church were preserved. The old church was converted into a parish hall. 517 names were on the parish roster at this time. Between 1971 and 1978, major improvements to the parish campus were made.

238

Saint Paul the Apostle (Latin: *Sanctus Paulus Apostolus*; Spanish: *San Pablo el Apóstol*) is the titular patron of the parish in Pismo Beach. Born Saul of Tarsus around A.D. 5, St. Paul was at first a great persecutor of the infant Church. In the second year after the Ascension of the Lord, he was miraculously converted while on his way to Damascus and chosen to form part of the College of Apostles by Christ Himself.

An ardent preacher of the Gospel, St. Paul was a great missionary, earning him the title "Apostle of the Gentiles." Saint Paul authored 13 books of the New Testament.

St. Paul was martyred by beheading around A.D. 65 in the *Tre Fontane* along the *Via Ostiensis* (Italian: *via Ostiense*) and buried nearby. The tomb of St. Paul is believed to be below a marble tombstone in the crypt of the Papal Basilica of Saint Paul outside the Walls (Latin: *Basilica Sancti Pauli extra mœnia*).

Saint Paul the Apostle has several liturgical feasts. The following are in the General Roman Calendar: January 25 (The Conversion of St. Paul the Apostle), June 29 (The Solemnity of Sts. Peter and Paul, Apostles), and November 18 (The Dedication of the Basilicas of Saints Peter and Paul, Apostles). St. Paul is also commemorated in the Extraordinary Form of the Roman Rite on June 30.

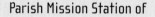

> In 2006, a new four-piece silver monstrance (ostensorium) was blessed by the Most Rev. Sylvester D. Ryan, 3rd Bishop of Monterey in California, on the Solemnity of Corpus Christi. It was produced by artistic silver artisans in Spain and was intended to foster a revival of adoration of the Most Holy Eucharist among the faithful.

Between 1973 and 1974, the Most Rev. Harry A. Clinch, 3rd Bishop of Monterey in California, notified the Conventual Franciscans that he had decided to transfer pastoral responsibilities to the secular clergy of the diocese. The Franciscan Province reminded Bishop Clinch that Bishop MacGinley had entrusted the administration of the parish to their order *in perpetuum*. The matter was referred to the Congregation for the Clergy (Latin: *Congregatio pro Clericis*) in Rome, who decided in favor of the Conventual Franciscans.

On September 27, 1998, an early evening fire caused extensive damage to the interior of the parish church. A candle was blamed for the accidental blaze that occurred shortly after the Sunday evening Mass. Statues were blackened, pews were burnt, and wall coverings were destroyed. The exterior of the church was not damaged, but the interior was a total loss. The congregation of 500 to 600 worshiped in the parish hall until the interior was refurbished. Mass was once again celebrated inside the parish church on October 16, 1999. [1]

The parish church was dedicated with a solemn consecration by the Most Rev. Sylvester D. Ryan, 3rd Bishop of Monterey, on April 9, 2000, the anniversary of which is celebrated each year in the parish church as a liturgical solemnity.

In 2004, the parish celebrated the 75th anniversary of the arrival of the "Black Franciscans" in Pismo Beach. By 2007, the parish had become known as a site offering daily confession before and after Mass and regular sessions every Saturday afternoon. The presence of two retired Conventual Franciscan Friars, along with the regular ministers, made this situation possible. Many Catholics from neighboring parishes, as well as tourist visitors, were taking the opportunity to perform regular traditional penitential practices.

1 • *Observer*, November 1998, vol. 30, no. 10, p. 1

Parish Mission Station of

Saint Peter

Avila Beach
San Luis Obispo County

1953 – 1970

Mention of the parish mission of Saint Peter in Avila Beach first appears in the 1950 edition of *The Official Catholic Directory*. According to letters dated August 10 and 12 of 1954, the chapel was constructed on land not owned by the parish and cost $2,000, which was paid by the parishioners.

The chapel of Saint Peter was blessed in 1953, and Mass was celebrated there on the Sundays from Memorial Day to Labor Day. Mention of the parish mission of Saint Peter in Avila Beach last appears in the 1970 edition of *The Official Catholic Directory*.

The original parish church, c. 1926. *Photo courtesy of the diocesan archives.*

Saint Rose of Lima

820 Creston Road, Paso Robles – San Luis Obispo County – www.SaintRoseChurch.org

Succession of Pastors

1. Rev. Leo J. Foin	1922 – 1930	8. Rev. Msgr. James Marron	1969 – 1974
2. Rev. Leo J. Beacon	1930 – 1939	9. Rev. Douglas F. Keating	1974 – 1991
3. Rev. Patrick Leddy	1939 – 1940	10. Rev. James P. Henry	1991 – 1996
4. Rt. Rev. Michael Sullivan	1940 – 1954	11. Rev. Derek Hughes	1997 – 2004
5. Rev. Timothy Cummins	1954 – 1956	12. Rev. Michael Volk	2004 – 2007
6. Rev. Patrick E. Flood	1956 – 1960	13. Rev. Wayne Dawson	2007 – 2011
7. Rev. Brendan McGuinness	1960 – 1969	14. Rev. Roberto Vera	2011 –

The parish of Saint Rose of Lima in the City of *El Paso de Robles,* Spanish for "The Pass of the Oaks," can trace his origins to 1892, when it began as a mission station of the parish of Mission San Miguel. The first baptism was recorded that year and Mass was celebrated on Saturdays. In 1890, three years after the city was founded, the Blackburn family donated land at 15th and Park Streets to the Diocese of Monterey-Los Angeles for the construction of a chapel. The chapel was constructed using logs that were hauled by horses from San Luis Obispo.

In 1916, Ignace J. Paderewski († 1941) purchased a ranch west of town and attended Mass at Saint Rose of Lima whenever he visited there, until 1939. Paderewski was a world-famous pianist, composer, politician, and promoter for Polish independence, serving as the prime minister and foreign minister of Poland, representing his country at the Paris Peace Conference in 1919.

Saint Rose of Lima was established as a canonical parish in its own right on November 11, 1921, by the Rt. Rev. John J. Cantwell, 5th and last Bishop of Monterey-Los Angeles. The first resident pastor took up his duties the following year. In 1922, eight acres in northwest Paso Robles were purchased for a cemetery. Also five lots for a new parish church and residence were purchased on Vine Street. In June of 1925, a new rectory was built. In 1926, the existing parish church was relocated to the new site at 14th and Vine Streets. It was remodeled and additions were made.

In 1938, stained glass windows were added to the parish church. In 1947, an 11-acre property at Creston Road and Trigo Lane for a parish school and larger parish church was acquired. In 1948, the total Catholic population of Paso Robles was estimated to be 1,750.

The first Mass in the new parish church was celebrated on April 15, 1965. The new church on Creston Road seated 500 on the main floor and 80 in the choir loft. The project included a new parish rectory with a separate office complex.

In 1968, an electronically tolled bell in the parish church's 50-foot tower was installed in memory of Robert Fryer, the first Paso Robles man killed in the Vietnam War (1955-1975).

In 1978, the original parish church building on Vine Street was sold and became a restaurant. In 1981, the parish center building on Creston Road was completed. In June of 1982, Mass in Spanish began to be regularly celebrated at 5pm each Sunday. In 1991, the number of parishioners was estimated at 1,300.

The 75th anniversary of the parish was commemorated on November 16, 1997, with a Mass concelebrated by the Most Rev. Sylvester D. Ryan, 3rd Bishop of Monterey in California, followed by a reception in the parish hall.

In 2015, the Saint Rose Gregorian Youth Choir was established in an effort to rediscover the musical tradition of the Church.

Photo courtesy of Josh McNair,
CaliforniaThroughMyLens.com.

Parish Mission Statement

*St. Rose of Lima is a Eucharistic,
Christ-centered, Spirit-filled,
Roman Catholic community
committed to living a sacramental life
of prayer, service and stewardship.*

Parish Mission Station
Saint Junípero Serra

McMillan Canyon Road,
Shandon
2015

Saint Rose of Lima (Latin: *Sancta Rosa Limensis*; Spanish: *Santa Rosa de Lima*) is the titular patroness of the parishes in Paso Robles and in Cambria. Born Isabel Flores y de Oliva at Lima in Peru, then a viceroyalty of the Spanish Empire, on April 20, 1586, she joined the Third Order of St. Dominic (Lay Dominicans) at the age of 20.

Saint Rose of Lima died at Lima in Peru in 1617 at the age of 31. She was beatified in 1667 or 1668 by Pope Clement IX and canonized in 1671 by Pope Clement X. She was the first person born in the Americas to be canonized.

Her liturgical feast is August 23; August 30 in some Latin American countries and in the Extraordinary Form of the Roman Rite. It is celebrated as a solemnity in the parish church.

This mission-style chapel was originally constructed in 1993 by the late William P. Clark Jr. († 2013), a California rancher, judge, and public servant who served under President Ronald Reagan as Deputy Secretary of State (1981-1982), U.S. National Security Advisor (1982-1983), and Secretary of the Interior (1983-1985). Judge Clark was called "the most important and influential person" in the administration by Reagan biographer Edmund Morris.

Judge Clark, who suffered from Parkinson's disease, once said, "God gave Parkinson's to such saints as John Paul II and my father, and now he has gotten around to the sinners, such as myself".[1] Chapel Hill, as it was originally called by the late judge, is located on a steep hill that is covered in grape bushes on the Clark family ranch in Shandon, just off of Highway 46, east of Paso Robles.

In October of 2015, the chapel was dedicated with a simple blessing by the Most Rev. Richard J. Garcia, 4th Bishop of Monterey in California, and renamed in honor of Saint Junípero Serra. Though on private land, the chapel is now open to the public and administered as a mission station of the parish.

1 • *Paso Robles Daily News*, August 13, 2013

The original parish church.
*Photo courtesy of
the diocesan archives.*

Saint Theodore

125 Center Street, Gonzales - Monterey County

The parish of Saint Theodore in the City of Gonzales can trace its origins to 1884, when the Gonzales family donated three lots for a future parish church. The celebration of the sacraments had been provided for the local Catholic community from the parish of Sacred Heart in Hollister and then from the parish of Sacred Heart in Salinas. In 1889, construction was officially underway and final construction payments were made in 1892.

Saint Theodore in Gonzales was canonically established as a parish in 1893 by the Rt. Rev. George T. Montgomery, 3rd Bishop of Monterey-Los Angeles. The Rev. Patrick Brady, the first pastor, resided in a hotel in Gonzales.

In 1911, the parish of Saint Theodore became a mission station of the new parish of Saint John the Baptist in King City. In 1914, Saint Theodore once again became a parish in its own right. The parish church was renovated and electrified through the donations of the local Swiss Catholic population. A lot with a house was purchased to serve as the parish rectory. This was later sold in 1922 and a new rectory constructed.

Saint Theodore of Amasea (Latin: *Sanctus Theodorus Tiro*; Spanish: *San Teodoro de Amasea*) is the titular patron of the parish in Gonzales.

Born in the East (Syria or Armenia are mentioned by some writers), Saint Theodore "enlisted in the army and was sent with his cohort to winter quarters in Pontus. When the edict against the Christians was issued by the emperors, he was brought before the Court at Amasea and asked to offer sacrifice to the gods. Theodore, however, denied their existence and made a noble profession of his belief in the Divinity of Jesus Christ. The judges, pretending pity for his youth, gave him time for reflection. This he employed in burning the Temple of Cybele. He was again taken prisoner, and after many cruel torments was burned at the stake (AD 306)... In the twelfth century his body was transferred to Brindisi, and he is there honored as patron; his head is enshrined at Gaeta" (Francis Mershman, *The Catholic Encyclopedia* (1912), vol. 14).

His liturgical feast is November 9. Though it is not included on the General Roman Calendar, it is celebrated as a solemnity in the parish church.

Parish Mission Station of

Capilla de Guadalupe

Scott and Grant Streets, Chualar

Monterey County

1969

During the 1920s, the parish of Saint Theodore in Gonzales and Our Lady of Solitude in Soledad functioned essentially as a dual parish until 1933. The boundaries of the parish were defined by decree of the Most Rev. John B. MacGinley, 1st Bishop of Monterey-Fresno, on January 1, 1927. The boundaries of the parish were later modified by the Most Rev. Philip G. Scher, 2nd Bishop of Monterey-Fresno, on October 26, 1933, when Our Lady of Solitude was canonically established as a parish in its own right.

In 1939, fundraising for the construction of a new parish church began. In 1948, the new $50,000 mission-style, 400-seat parish church was constructed. Designed by Charles E. Butner, the new parish church was dedicated with a simple blessing by the Most Rev. Aloysius J. Willinger, 3rd and last Bishop of Monterey-Fresno, on December 12. The original parish church was moved to the east end of the property and remodeled to serve as the parish hall.

In 1959, a $125,000 fundraising drive for a tile roof, campanile (bell tower), new parish hall, rectory, and convent was launched. The parish church, hall, and rectory were completed within that year. The 150-year old bell in the campanile was to be managed electronically. The boundaries of the parish were rebounded by decree of Bishop Willinger on June 20, 1962.

In 1993, the parish centennial was marked on July 17 with a special Mass celebrated by the Most Rev. Sylvester D. Ryan, 3rd Bishop of Monterey in California, which was followed by a reception in the parish hall.

On November 9, 2005, the renovation of the parish church was celebrated. New paint, flooring, lighting, pews, baptismal font, altar, ambo, and chair were installed. Bishop Ryan blessed the new altar.

In 1969, *Capilla de Guadalupe* (Guadalupe Chapel) was established in Chualar as a parish mission station. The small chapel was also used for religious education classes staffed by the **Our Lady of Victory Missionary Sisters** (Victory Noll Sisters).

Saint Timothy

Succession of Pastors

1. Rev. James Sweeney   1954 – 1974
2. Rev. Cornelius Sweeney 1974 – 1998
3. Rev. Edward J. Holterhoff 1998 –

The parish of Saint Timothy in the City of Morro Bay can trace its origins to 1948, when the first Sunday Masses in the area were celebrated in American Veterans Hall as a convenience to local Catholics, which was estimated to number 50 families. In 1949, the parish of Saint Joseph in Cayucos established a mission station in Morro Bay under the titular patronage of Saint Peter, utilizing a Quonset hut from a former local naval base. The celebration of the sacraments was provided by Conventual Franciscans from the parish of Saint Paul the Apostle in Pismo Beach. The mission station's name was later changed from Saint Peter to honor of the Most Sacred Heart of Jesus.

In 1950, the Herrera sisters of the historic Quintana family donated nearly three acres for a new church in Morro Bay. (The gift was later enlarged.) In 1950, the Catholic Church Extension Society donated $3,800 toward the construction of a church to be named in honor of Saint Timothy. On November 18, 1951, the first Mass in the new building was celebrated. Total cost was around $16,000.

Saint Timothy in Morro Bay was canonically established as a parish in its own right on April 13, 1954, by decree of the Most Rev. Aloysius J. Willinger, 3rd and last Bishop of Monterey-Fresno.

In 1957, Miss Lorena Herrera donated an additional 5 acres of adjacent property. In 1959, fundraising began for the construction of a larger parish church. Construction of the new parish church facing Kennedy Way was completed in August of 1964, and the original parish church became the new parish hall and classrooms.

In August of 1976, an advisory board was formed to formulate plans to satisfy future needs in the parish community. On January 17, 1981, the parish hosted the San Luis Obispo Religious Education "Mini-Institute." In 1983, the area of Los Osos was detached from the parish and the parish hall and kitchen were refurbished.

In March of 2005, the groundbreaking took place for a major remodeling of the entrance area of the parish church and for other projects. The parish church was dedicated with a solemn consecration by the Most Rev. Richard J. Garcia, 4th Bishop of Monterey in California, on September 15, 2012, the anniversary of which is celebrated each year in the parish church as a liturgical solemnity.

Saint Timothy (Latin: *Sanctus Timotheus*; Spanish: *San Timoteo*), is the titular patron of the parish in Morro Bay. Along with Saint Titus, Saint Timothy was one of the most beloved and trusted disciples of Saint Paul the Apostle, accompanying him in many of his journeys. St. Timothy is mentioned in the Acts of the Apostles (16:1, 17:14-15, 18:5, 19:22, 20:4), in Saint Paul's letter to the Romans (16:21), in first Corinthians (4:17), second Corinthians (1:1, 19), in the letters to the Philippians (1:1, 2:19) and the Colossians (1:1), in first Thessalonians (1:1, 3:2-6) and second Thessalonians (1:1), in first Timothy (1:2-18, 6:20) and in second Timothy (1:2), and in the letters to Philemon (1:1) as well as the letter to the Hebrews (13:23). According to the old *Roman Martyrology*, St. Timothy died first Bishop of Ephesus.

His liturgical feast is January 26 in the Ordinary Form of the Roman Rite, January 24 in the Extraordinary Form, and January 22 in the Eastern churches. It is celebrated as a solemnity in the parish church.

The original parish church, c. 1951.
Photo courtesy of the diocesan archives.

Saint Vincent de Paul

123 Marine View Avenue, Davenport – Santa Cruz County

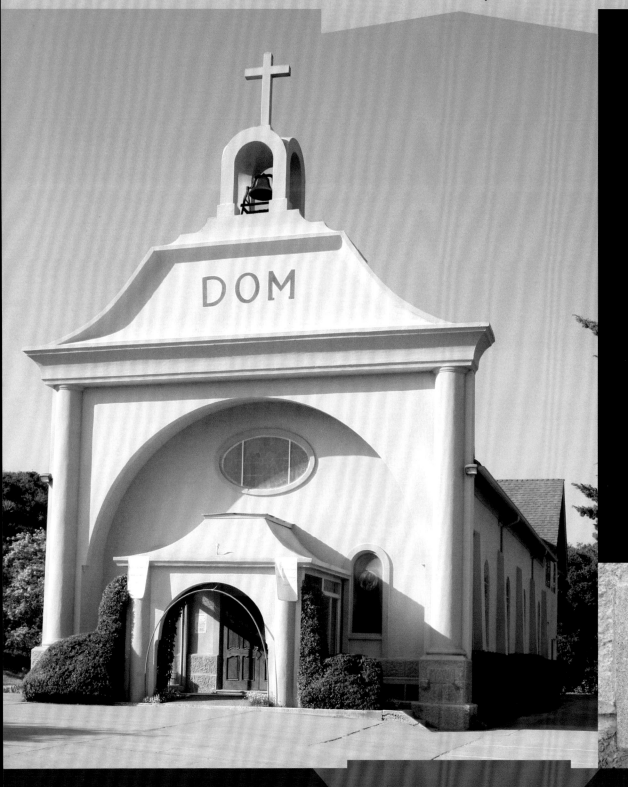

Succession of Pastors

1.	Rev. Patrick Leddy	1935 – 1940
2.	Rev. Patrick M. O'Flynn	1940 – 1946
	Rev. Marzio Gaioni, OSJ *administrator*	1946 – 1946
3.	Rev. Roger L. McCann	1946 – 1947
4.	Rev. John Nelson	1947 – 1952
5.	Rev. William Lane	1952 – 1955
6.	Rev. Marzio Gaioni	1955 – 1961
7.	Rev. Paul Pavese, OSJ	1961 – 1964
8.	Rev. Lupe Sanchez	1964 – 1967
9.	Rev. James Catalano, OSJ	1967 – 1970
0.	Rev. Matthew Peraino, OSJ	1970 – 1980
11.	Rev. Bronius Kaunas, OSJ	1980 – 1989
12.	Rev. Siro del Degan, OSJ	1989 – 1992
13.	Rev. James Catalano, OSJ	1992 – 1994
14.	Rev. Siro del Degan, OSJ	1995*
15.	Rev. Philip Massetti	1995 – 2003
16.	Rev. Brian Crawford	2003 – ????
17.	Rev. James Catalano, OSJ	2008 – 2013
18.	Rev. Jackson Pinhero, OSJ	2013 –

Saint Vincent de Paul (Latin: *Sanctus Vincentius a Paulo*; Spanish: *San Vicente de Paúl*), the titular patron of the parish in Davenport, was born in Gascony in the Kingdom of France in 1581. "After completing his studies, he was ordained a priest and went to Paris where he served in a parish. He founded the Congregation of the Mission (Vincentians) to supervise the formation of priests and to give support to the poor. With the help of Saint Louise de Marillac, he also founded the Congregation of the Daughters of Charity" (*The Liturgy of the Hours*, 27 September).

Saint Vincent de Paul died in Paris the age of 79 in Paris in 1660. He was beatified by Pope Benedict XIII in 1729 and canonized by Pope Clement XII in 1737.

His liturgical feast day is September 27 in the Ordinary Form of the Roman Rite and July 19 in the Extraordinary Form. It is celebrated as a solemnity in the parish church.

The parish of Saint Vincent de Paul in Davenport can trace its origins to 1915, when the parish of Holy Cross in Santa Cruz established a mission station on land donated by the Coast Dairy and Land Co. Building materials were donated by the Santa Cruz Portland Cement Co. and volunteer labor was used in construction. The name of the mission station church was inspired by nearby San Vicente Creek. The church was dedicated with a simple blessing in May of 1915.

On December 2, 1935, Saint Vincent de Paul in Davenport was canonically established as a parish in its own right by decree of the Most Rev. Philip G. Scher, 2nd Bishop of Monterey-Fresno. In 1947, the parish church building was again renovated and the grounds paved. Two nearby lots were donated for a rectory, but it was never built. In 1948, the pastor moved to the parish of Saint John in Felton, from where he continued to serve the parish in Davenport.

In 1955, a resident pastor was restored to the parish of Saint Vincent de Paul in Davenport. In 1961, the resident pastor was withdrawn and all subsequent pastors were Oblates of St. Joseph from the Shrine of Saint Joseph in Santa Cruz.

In 1987, repair and renovation of the structure were accomplished. In the early fall of 2005, the first annual Wine Tasting and Auction was inaugurated. In May of 2015, the parish celebrated its 100th anniversary.

Saint William

6410 Santa Lucia Road, Atascadero - San Luis Obispo County - www.StWilliams.org

Succession of Pastors

1. Rt. Rev. A.C. Stuhlmann   1948 – 1962
2. Rev. D. Declan Murphy   1962 – 1971
3. Rev. Henry D. Freiermuth   1971 – 1980
4. Rev. Joseph R. Hercek   1980 – 2006
5. Rev. George Batchelder   2006 – 2014
6. Rev. Edwin Limpiado   2014 –

The parish of Saint William in the City of Atascadero can trace its origins to 1943, when it began as a mission station of the parish of Holy Angels (later re-named Saint Margaret of Cortona) in Santa Margarita. Masses were first celebrated in a rented hall at Moran Junior College, moving to the *La Moda* Theater later that summer. Fundraising for the construction of a church soon began, with future parishioners offering free materials and labor.

In 1945, a one-acre lot on Santa Lucia Avenue was purchased for $250. Plans were made to build the church in the same pattern as Saint Paul the Apostle in Pismo Beach. Construction by the Louis A. Mack Co. began in June but it was suspended due to the wartime scarcity of building materials. The parish rectory was later built on those foundations.

In 1947, the Most Rev. Aloysius J. Willinger, Coadjutor Bishop and Apostolic Administrator of the Diocese of Monterey-Fresno, secured $4,875 from the Catholic Church Extension Society (Catholic Extension) for the construction of the parish church. Catholic Extension requested that the new parish church be named in honor of Saint William of Vercelli († 1142).

Saint William in Atascadero was canonically established as a parish in its own right in 1948 by the Most Rev. Philip G. Scher, 2nd Bishop of Monterey-Fresno. In June, Bishop Willinger requested that the parish church be built on a different site and three adjacent lots were subsequently purchased for $2,000.

248

Saint William of Vercelli (Latin: *Sanctus Gulielmus*; Spanish: *San Guillermo de Vercelli*), also known as St. William of Monte Vergine, is the titular patron of the parish in Atascadero.

Born in 1085, St. William was the son of noble parents, both of whom died when he was still a child. At the age of 15, he made up his mind to renounce the world and lead a life of penance. He went on the *Camino de Santiago* (English: Way of Saint James; Latin: *Peregrinatio Compostellana*) to venerate the relics of St. James the Greater in the Cathedral of Santiago de Compostela in Spain. After this pilgrimage, St. William constructed a hut on Monte Vergine, wishing to become a hermit and live in solitude, but it was not long before many people flocked to him to put themselves under his guidance. Soon a monastery was built and by 1119, the Congregation of Monte Vergine was founded. St. William he died on June 25, 1142 (cf. *The Catholic Encyclopedia* (1912), vol. 15).

His liturgical feast is June 25. Though it is not included on the General Roman Calendar, it is celebrated as a solemnity in the parish church.

Parish Mission Statement

Saint William, pray for us, that we might have our sight restored—that we might see with the eyes of our hearts and souls God's presence in and around us. Teach us to nourish our spiritual journeys with prayer so that we too might be instruments of God's light and love to others. In the spirit of Saint Benedict, help us to be people of hospitality who let our work become prayer. Let us find God in each other.

In March of 1949, an army chapel at Camp San Luis Obispo was purchased for $1,190 and moved by the Nichols & Peterson Co. to Atascadero. The first Mass in this original parish church was celebrated on July 17, 1949, with 175 persons in attendance. That same year, M.D. Hodges constructed the parish rectory at a cost of $10,882. In February of 1950, the rectory was blessed by Bishop Willinger and on April 9, Easter Sunday, the new parish church was dedicated with a simple blessing by the Rt. Rev. Msgr. Michael Sullivan, Vicar General of the Diocese of Monterey-Fresno and 4th pastor of the parish of Saint Rose of Lima. In 1953, the parish altar society was established.

In 1962, a building fund for a larger parish church was established. In September of 1968, ground breaking took place and construction began. The new $170,000 parish church with a seating capacity was over 500 was designed by Ralph McCarty & Associates of Paso Robles and was constructed by the Mandella Construction Co. The new parish church was blessed in June of 1969 and the original parish church became the parish hall. The new parish church was dedicated with a simple blessing by the Most Rev. Harry A. Clinch, 1st Bishop of Monterey in California, on December 7.

In October of 1972, a parish council was formed. On August 26, 1973, the parish's Silver Anniversary was commemorated with a Solemn Mass followed by a barbecue at Lake Atascadero Park.

In 1977, the parish religious education program was re-invigorated under the direction of the Diocesan Board of Education. It involved certification of catechists, the addition of students to the youth ministry committee, and more adult catechesis.

San Augustín

257 Glenwood Drive, Scotts Valley - Santa Cruz County - www.SanAgustinCC.com

The parish of San Agustín in the City of Scotts Valley can trace its origins to 1969, when property for a new parish was purchased on Glenwood Drive and an organizing pastor was appointed in May, with the first Mass being celebrated outdoors on June 8. A house on the property was remodeled to become the parish rectory. Masses were celebrated at the Scotts Valley School and then in an enlarged garage on the parish grounds. In September of 1969, the ground breaking for the new multipurpose building took place.

The parish was canonically established on December 1, 1969 by decree of the Most Rev. Harry A. Clinch, 1st Bishop of Monterey in California. The boundaries of the new parish included territory taken from the parishes of Saint John in Felton and Saint Joseph in Capitola. Christ Child chapel on Summit Road became the mission station of the new parish.

In January of 1970, the contract for a multi-use parish center was awarded and construction was completed by September. General contractor was Joseph B. Fratessa and the designer was Joseph Kiktavi of Scotts Valley. It was dedicated with a simple blessing by Bishop Clinch on October 25. In 1971, a large wooden cross outside the front of the church was dedicated and the first annual parish barbecue was held. In 1972, the "Bell of *San Agustín*" was dedicated in honor of the parish's first pastor. It had been salvaged from a train wreck in New Mexico in 1932.

By the tenth anniversary of the parish in 1979, its debt had been reduced from $300,000 to $100,000. A larger draining culvert and many improvements to the interior of the parish church and meeting rooms and classrooms had also been made. In 1998, approval was granted by the diocese for the construction of handicapped restroom facilities.

In 2005, the parish church was renovated and a new sound system, ambo, baptismal font, ambry for holy oil, and Stations of the Cross were installed. The renovated parish church was dedicated with a simple blessing by the Most Rev. Sylvester D. Ryan, 3rd Bishop of Monterey in California, on October 19, 2005.

250

San Agustín

Saint Augustine of Hippo (Latin: *Sanctus Augustinus Hipponensis*; Spanish: *San Agustín de Hipona*), Bishop and Father of the Church, is the titular patron of the parish in Scotts Valley.

Born at Tagaste, in Africa, in 354, St. Augustine "was unsettled and restlessly searched for the truth until he was converted to the Christian faith at Milan and baptized by Saint Ambrose. Returning to his homeland, he embraced an ascetic life and subsequently was elected bishop of Hippo. For thirty-four years he guided his flock, instructing it with sermons and many writings. He fought bravely against the errors of his time and explained the faith carefully and cogently through his writings. He died in 430" (*The Liturgy of the Hours*, 28 August).

His liturgical feast day is August 28 (June 15 in Eastern Christianity and November 4 in the Assyrian Church of the East). It is celebrated as a solemnity in the parish church.

Parish Mission Statement

We, Catholic Community of San Agustín in the Diocese of Monterey, united by our baptism and through the Gospels, seek to deepen our union with Jesus and grow as a faith community.

We seek to enrich our heritage of care and concern for all, especially for those in need, by being instruments of God's love and healing to the world around us. We foster a strong community atmosphere where individuals can share the Christian life with one another. We encourage our entire Church community to reach out to others as members of the body of Christ.

Guided by the Holy Spirit and united in prayer, we pledge ourselves to pursue this mission by active participation in the liturgical, educational and social ministries of the Church.

We recognize that to be effective, these ministries require spiritual, physical and financial resources, and we accept our responsibility as Christian stewards to provide them.

Santa Margarita de Cortona

22515 H. Street, Santa Margarita - San Luis Obispo County

The parish of Santa Margarita de Cortona in the Town of Santa Margarita can trace its origins to 1769, when the Santa Margarita Valley was visited and named by Fray Juan Crespi († 1782) in honor of Saint Margaret of Cortona. Fray Crespi noted the large number of friendly natives and the richness of the surrounding land. In 1787, the *Asistencia de la Misión de San Luis, Obispo de Tolosa* (Sub-Mission to the Mission San Luis Obispo de Tolosa) was founded by Fray Francisco Jose de Arroita († c. 1821). Its rich pastures were used both for livestock and growing crops, especially wheat. It was also considered to be safe from attack from the sea.

In 1808, the main building was constructed. It included living quarters, an extensive granary, and a chapel where Mass was celebrated monthly for the neophytes. All sacramental records were entered in the registers of Mission San Luis Obispo, approximately 14 miles away.

In 1830, the walls of the building were damaged but not overturned by an earthquake. In 1835, Mission San Luis Obispo and its *asistencia* of Santa Margarita were secularized by the Mexican government. In 1841, Joaquín Tomas Estrada († 1893) received a grant of 17,734 acres of former mission property which included the *asistencia* buildings. By this time the natives had been dispersed and the *rancho* was described as a "ghost ranch." The Estrada grant was later validated by the U.S. Land Commission.

In the 1860s, the chapel and living quarters fell into ruins after the roof tiles were removed. In 1861, Rancho Santa Margarita was purchased for $45,000 by Martin Murphy Jr. († 1884), a wealthy landowner from Santa Clara. It became a stagecoach stop for north-south traffic.

252

Saint Margaret of Cortona (Latin: *Sancta Margarita de Cortona*; Spanish: *Santa Margarita de Cortona*) is the titular patroness of the parish of Santa Margarita de Cortona in Santa Margarita. St. Margaret was born in Tuscany in 1247. In 1277, she joined the Third Order of Saint Francis, choosing to live in poverty, pursuing a life of prayer and penance at Cortona in Tuscany, Italy. There she established a hospital for the sick, homeless, and impoverished. To secure nurses for the hospital, she instituted a congregation of Tertiary Sisters, known as *le poverelle* (Italian for "the little poor ones"). St. Margaret died in Cortona on February 22, 1297. She was canonized in 1728 by Pope Benedict XIII. Her liturgical feast day is February 22. Though it is not included on the General Roman Calendar, it is celebrated as a solemnity in the parish church.

Parish Mission Station of

Saint James

Carissa Plains

1969 – 2013

Mention of the parish mission of Saint James at the Farm Bureau Building in Carrisa Plains, about 60 miles from Santa Margarita, first appears in the 1969 edition of *The Official Catholic Directory*. Bishop Clinch celebrated the sacrament of Confirmation there on February 5, 1975. In 1994, the mission station requested assistance from the Catholic Church Extension Society in providing the sacraments in the area on a regular basis. The mission station was closed in 2013.

In the 1870's, the town of Santa Margarita grew up primarily to serve the railroad workers attracted to the area when the Pacific Coast line was constructed. Sunday Mass was celebrated in private residences by priests first from Mission San Miguel and then from Mission San Luis Obispo. Sometime later, a temporary wooden church above the town was used.

In 1904, the interior walls of the original *asistencia* building were dynamited and rearranged to serve as a hay barn, which soon caught on fire. Afterwards only the charred stone walls remained. Later corrugated iron walls were added above the stone foundations. On October 29, 1906, a remodeled wooden schoolhouse and hall on H. Street was dedicated as a church by the Rt. Rev. Thomas J. Conaty, 4th Bishop of Monterey-Los Angeles. It served as a mission station of the parish of Old Mission San Luis Obispo. In 1908, the inner-wall partitions in the original stone structure on the *rancho* were removed.

Between 1933 and 1935, a new church was built on the H. Street site using locally raised funds and a $1,250 grant from the Catholic Church Extension Society (Catholic Extension). A condition of the grant was that the patronage be changed to Holy Angels. Lumber from the old church was re-utilized. In 1933, the Rev. John Coen was appointed first resident pastor.

Holy Angels in Santa Margarita was canonically established as a parish on June 29, 1934, by decree of the Most Rev. Philip G. Scher, 2nd Bishop of Monterey-Fresno. Construction proceeded during that year. The parish church was dedicated with a simple blessing on April 28, 1935.

In 1938, the parish rectory was constructed, and it was enlarged in 1940. In 1940, an annual *fiesta* was inaugurated for fundraising.

In 1943, the parish established the mission station of Saint William in Atascadero. In 1948, Saint William in Atascadero became a parish in its own right and Holy Angels in Santa Margarita became its mission station. In 1949, the pastor officially relocated his residence to Atascadero. Between 1951 and 1952, the parish church and rectory were renovated.

Holy Angels in Santa Margarita was again canonically established as a parish in its own right on September 29, 1961, by decree of the Most Rev. Aloysius J. Willinger, 3rd and last Bishop of Monterey-Fresno. On December 7, 1997, at the request of the parishioners, patronage of the parish church was restored to Saint Margaret of Cortona by the Most Rev. Sylvester D. Ryan, 3rd Bishop of Monterey in California.

Santa Rosa

Succession of Pastors

1. Rev. Msgr. Thomas Morgan	1961 – 1965
2. Rev. Laurence McHugh	1965 – 1974
3. Rev. James Sweeney	1974 – 1992
4. Rev. Larry Kambitsch	1992 – 1994
5. Rev. Derek Hughes	1995 – 1997
administrator	1994 – 1995
Rev. Larry Betrozoff	
administrator	1997
6. Rev. Dennis Gilbert	1997 – 2006
7. Rev. Emil Robu	2006 – 2009
8. Rev. Mark Stetz	2009 –

The parish of Santa Rosa in Cambria can trace its origins to 1869, when Mass was celebrated for the first time in what was then known as Santa Rosa or Roseville. In the early 1870s, the **Old Santa Rosa Chapel** was constructed on land donated by the Phelan family. The chapel was a mission station of the parish of Mission San Luis Obispo from 1869 to 1878, and of Mission San Miguel from 1878 to 1885. It was once again a mission station of the parish of Mission San Luis Obispo from 1885 until 1905, when it became a mission station of the newly-established parish of Saint Joseph in Cayucos. In 1921, the pastor relocated his residence from Cayucos to Cambria.

Santa Rosa in Cambria was canonically established as a parish in its own right on September 15, 1961, by decree of the Most Rev. Aloysius J. Willinger, 3rd and last Bishop of Monterey-Fresno. In December of 1961, the fundraising for the construction of a new parish church and rectory began. The new site was to be on land donated by the Fiscalini family. The Catholic Church Extension Society donated $10,000 towards the $100,000 goal, with the condition that the parish be named in honor of Saint Anne.

In 1962, construction by Mandella Co. began. An agreement between the Diocese of Monterey-Fresno and the Catholic Church Extension Society was reached whereby the parish community would remain named in honor of Saint Rose of Lima while the parish church building would be dedicated to Saint Anne. The parish church was dedicated with a simple blessing on July 26, 1963, the feast of Saint Anne. The parish rectory was completed in 1968.

In 2006, native crafts from *La Purisima* Mission were demonstrated during the "Old Mission Days" annual parish Fiesta, August 12 and 19-20. Stories from the Chumash culture were told by docents from the Morro Bay Museum. A solemn procession from the Old Chapel through town to the present church was held. Presentations on the history of the parish and various liturgical events were also part of the event.

Parish Mission Statement

As children of God, the parishioners of Santa Rosa Church welcome all to praise our Creator and grow closer to Jesus our Savior. In celebrating the Eucharist, a sacrament of love and thanksgiving, we express our gratitude for the world around us by serving others, neighbors and strangers, young and old, alike. We ask the Holy Spirit to lead us in the paths of truth and goodness.

The original chapel, now known as the Old Santa Rosa Chapel.
Photo courtesy of the Cambria Historical Society.

The current parish church, circa 1969.
Photo courtesy of the diocesan archives.

Old Santa Rosa Chapel

2353 Main Street, Cambria

San Luis Obispo County

After the final Mass was celebrated in the original 1870 parish church on May 26, 1963, both the chapel and cemetery fell into a state of neglect and disrepair.

On April 19, 1970, the Old Santa Rosa Chapel, was designated as a historical landmark by the Native Daughters of the Golden West, a non-profit organization for women born in California founded in 1886. In 1978, Cambria natives Marina Curti and Clementine Newman formed the Santa Rosa Chapel Committee and spearheaded the restoration efforts for seven years. The renovation project included locating original furnishings in a Fresno warehouse. The restored chapel was rented for weddings and local community activities.

In 1982, the Old Santa Rosa Chapel, one of the oldest churches in San Luis Obispo County, was listed on the National Register of Historic Places. A committee that included non-Catholics was placed in charge of the chapel and cemetery. Both the parish and the committee shared all income and expenses, thus safeguarding Church ownership of both the chapel and cemetery. The chapel was rededicated for community use on September 16, 1984. In 1993, a resident caretaker for the chapel and cemetery was hired as an employee of the diocese.

www.SantaRosaChapel.com

The Extraordinary Form of the Roman Rite

in the Diocese of Monterey in California

On July 7, 2007, Pope Benedict XVI promulgated the Apostolic Letter *Summorum Pontificum*, Latin for "Of the Supreme Pontiffs," decreeing that "any Catholic priest of the Latin rite… may use either the Roman Missal published in 1962 by [Saint] Pope John XXIII or the Roman Missal promulgated in 1970 by [Blessed] Pope Paul VI."[1]

Pope Benedict XVI added that the "Roman Missal promulgated by Pope [Blessed] Paul VI is the ordinary expression of the *lex orandi* (rule of prayer) of the Catholic Church of the Latin rite. The Roman Missal promulgated by Saint Pius V and revised by [Saint] John XXIII is nonetheless to be considered an extraordinary expression of the same *lex orandi* of the Church and duly honoured for its venerable and ancient usage. These two expressions of the Church's *lex orandi* will in no way lead to a division in the Church's *lex credendi* (rule of faith); for they are two usages of the one Roman rite."[2]

The Roman Rite thus currently consists of two equal forms, one *ordinary* and the other *extraordinary*. The Extraordinary Form of the Roman Rite utilizes the liturgical books that were in use in 1962, i.e., prior to the liturgical reforms that followed the Second Vatican Council. Mass celebrated according to the 1962 edition of the *Missale Romanum* (Roman Missal) is also referred to as the "Traditional Latin Mass," the "Tridentine Mass," the "Mass of Saint Pius V," the *"usus antiquior"* (older use) or *"forma antiquior"* (older form). The term "Latin Mass" is inaccurate and should be avoided, as the Mass of Blessed Paul VI (ordinary form) can and should be celebrated in the Latin language, and with Gregorian chant.[3]

In September of 2007, the Most Rev. Richard J. Garcia, 4th Bishop of Monterey, announced his intention to make Mass in the Extraordinary Form of the Roman Rite available in three separate locations in the diocese: in the northern area, central area, and southern area. Bishop Garcia stressed the need for the location "to be liturgically appropriate" and for "the assistance of Priests who can celebrate the Mass as our Holy Father has required, with the ability and heartfelt desire to celebrate the 1962 Latin Mass. Also it is necessary to offer this Mass at a time

of day that is convenient for the people and Priests but without infringing on the already busy Sunday schedule of Masses in many of our Parishes."[4]

Mass celebrated in the Extraordinary Form of the Roman Rite by the Rev. Peter Carota († 2016) of the Diocese of Stockton at Carmel Mission Basilica, Pentecost Sunday 2013. Fr. Carota was instrumental in the opening of the **Saint Francis Catholic Kitchen** on Beach Street in Santa Cruz on May 12, 1982.

---

1 • BENEDICT XVI, Apostolic Letter *Summorum Pontificum*, article 2.

2 • IBID., article 1.

3 • Cf. SECOND VATICAN COUNCIL, Constitution on the Sacred Liturgy *Sacrosanctum concilium*, nn. 36.1 and 54.

4 • MOST REV. RICHARD J. GARCIA, *Pastoral Letter*, September 2007.

The parish of **Saint Paul the Apostle** in Pismo Beach (San Luis Obispo County) began hosting Sunday celebrations of the Mass in November of 2007 for the southern part of the diocese. The Rev. Michael Bell celebrated the Mass there until his death in February of 2015. Since June of 2015, Dom Christopher Andrews, OSB, of Our Lady of Clear Creek Abbey in Oklahoma, has been celebrating the chaplain of the Traditional Latin Mass Community of St. Junípero Serra on California's Central Coast (southern part of the diocese).

In 2008, the Rev. Nicholas A. Milich of the Diocese of Yakima (Washington) was appointed the chaplain of the Traditional Latin Mass Community of the Monterey Bay (northern part of the diocese). Mass in the Extraordinary Form was first celebrated at **Mission San Juan Bautista** on Sunday, June 29, 2008, the solemnity of Saints Peter and Paul. The celebration of Mass in the Extraordinary Form of the Roman Rite continued every Sunday afternoon thereafter until July 3, 2011, when the community moved to the **Shrine of Saint Joseph** in Santa Cruz. On June 17, 2012, the community moved to the **Queen of Heaven Mausoleum Chapel** in Salinas. On May 22, 2016, the parish of **Sacred Heart and Saint Benedict** began hosting Mass in the Extraordinary Form at Sacred Heart church in Hollister.

Bishop Garcia celebrated the sacrament of Confirmation according to the 1961 edition of the *Pontificale Romanum* (Roman Pontifical) for the youth of the community at Mission San Juan Bautista on October 31, 2010, and again on November 6, 2012. Bishop Garcia celebrated the sacrament a third time for the community in the **Blessed Sacrament Chapel** of Carmel Mission Basilica on November 18, 2014.

On October 25, 2009, the feast of Christ the King, Mission San Juan Bautista hosted a Solemn High Mass.
The Rev. James Fryar, FSSP, was the celebrant, with the Rev. Nicholas Milich serving as deacon and the Rev. Marc R. Dauphine serving as subdeacon.
Photos courtesy of Juan Mendoza.

The Rev. Nicholas Milich celebrating Mass in the Extraordinary Form of the Roman Rite at Mission San Juan Bautista. While celebrating Mass "*ad orientem*" or "facing east" is optional in the Ordinary Form of the Roman Rite, it is the norm in the Extraordinary Form. Often referred to as having his "back to the people," the celebrant is actually leading the people in prayer.

Photo courtesy of Juan Mendoza.

The Most Rev. Richard J. Garcia, 4th Bishop of Monterey in California, celebrating the Sacrament of Confirmation according to the 1961 *Pontificale Romanum*.

Photo courtesy of Juan Mendoza.

At a Solemn High Mass, the subdeacon chants the Epistle reading in Latin.

Photo courtesy of Juan Mendoza.

Both forms celebrate our participation in sacrificial death and glorious Resurrection of Jesus Christ: in the ordinary form or post-Vatican II, we do so by means of our English (vernacular) language and communal prayer, while in the extraordinary or pre-Vatican II form, participation also includes listening to the prayers in Latin and joining our hearts to the words and actions.

–MOST REV. RICHARD GARCIA,
Pastoral Letter, September 2007

www.MontereyLatinMass.org

www.MontereyBayArea-TLM.blogspot.com

Saint Anne

Byzantine Catholic Church

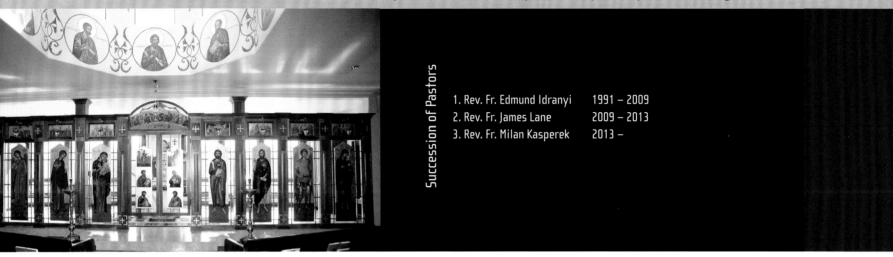

Succession of Pastors

1. Rev. Fr. Edmund Idranyi   1991 – 2009
2. Rev. Fr. James Lane   2009 – 2013
3. Rev. Fr. Milan Kasperek   2013 –

Geographically located within the physical boundaries of the Roman Catholic Diocese of Monterey in California is the Byzantine Catholic parish of Saint Anne in the City of San Luis Obispo. The Byzantine parish of St. Anne falls under the canonical jurisdiction of the Byzantine Catholic Eparchy of Phoenix, formally known as the Holy Protection of Mary Byzantine Catholic Eparchy of Phoenix (Latin: *Eparchia Sanctæ Mariæ a Patrocinio in urbe Phoenicensi*). The Byzantine Eparchy of Phoenix, which consists of 19 parishes and one mission, is a suffragan eparchy of the Byzantine Catholic Archeparchy of Pittsburgh (Latin: *Archieparchia Pittsburgensis Ritus Byzantini*), serving Byzantine Catholics living in the western United States. [***Nota bene:*** In the Eastern churches, archeparchy and eparchy correspond to an archdiocese and diocese in the Western church.]

Catholics of the Byzantine Rite, or Rite of Constantinople, "are those who use that rite and are subject to their own canon law... They are found in their countries of origin, USA, Canada, and elsewhere. They keep their rite and its customs in varying degrees of purity and in five languages, and are organized under bishops of the rite. All preserve the ancient customs of leavened altar-bread, communion under both kinds, the ordination of married men to the priesthood, baptism by immersion, etc."[1]

The Byzantine parish of Saint Anne in San Luis Obispo can trace its origins to the early 1950s when the Petrick, Kubek, and Beresky families settled in the area. The Rev. Fr. Anthony Kubek and the Rev. Fr. Eugene Beresky celebrated the Divine Liturgy (Mass) in their own private chapels for family and others for many years. After the death of the Rev. Frs. Kubek and Beresky, the small Byzantine Catholic community was ministered to by visiting priests from what was then the Exarchate of Pittsburgh. After the Second World War (1939-1945), Eastern Catholics began emigrating west from the East Coast of the United States.

By the mid-1980s, former parishioners of the Proto-Cathedral of Saint Mary in Sherman Oaks, Saint Nicholas Byzantine Catholic Church in Fontana, and the Church of the Annunciation in Anaheim who had relocated to the Central Coast of California requested a priest from the Eparchy of Van Nuys to serve their spiritual needs. In 1986, the Most Rev. Thomas Dolinay († 1993), 2nd Metropolitan Archbishop of the Byzantine Catholic Metropolitan Church of Pittsburgh, sent his secretary, the Rev. Fr. Edmund M. Idranyi, to ascertain the feasibility of beginning a new mission on the Central Coast of California. The City of San Luis Obispo was chosen as the ideal location, given its central location within the region.

With the blessing of the Most Rev. Thaddeus Shubsda, 2nd Bishop of Monterey in California, and the Rev. James Nisbet, 46th pastor of Old Mission San Luis Obispo, the new Santa Maria Byzantine

1 • Donald Attwater, *A Catholic Dictionary* (1958), p. 64.

Saint Anne (Latin: *Sancta Anna*; Spanish: *Santa Ana*; Greek: *Αγία Άννα*), the traditional name of the mother of the Blessed Virgin Mary and grandmother of our Lord Jesus Christ, is the titular patroness of the Byzantine Catholic parish in San Luis Obispo. The veneration of Saint Anne first began in the Eastern Church in the fourth century. She was not venerated in the Western Church before the thirteenth century "except, perhaps, in the south of France."

Saint Anne is celebrated liturgically on July 26 in the Western Church, which she now shares with Saint Joachim in the Ordinary Form of the Roman Rite. Her feast had been introduced in England by Pope Urban VI in 1378, "from which time it spread all over the Western Church. It was extended to the universal Latin Church in 1584." In the Eastern Church, her feast day is July 25, "which may be the day of the dedication of her first church at Constantinople or the anniversary of the arrival of her supposed relics in Constantinople (710)" (November 20 in the Coptic Church) (cf. FREDERICK HOLWECK, *The Catholic Encyclopedia* (1907), vol. 1).

Catholic Mission in San Luis Obispo was granted use of the Old Mission's former convent chapel (now the Oratory of the Immaculate Heart of Mary) for the celebration of the Divine Liturgy on Sundays. The first Divine Liturgy was celebrated on Sunday, June 26, 1986, with about 25 Eastern Catholic faithful in attendance. Fr. Idranyi was appointed to care for the new mission community while continuing his duties at the eparchy's chancery office in the Northridge neighborhood of Los Angeles.

The Byzantine Catholic community was canonically established as a parish in its own right on January 17, 1989, by Bishop Dolinay. In 1991, the Most Rev. George Kuzma, 2nd Bishop of Van Nuys, granted his permission for the parish of Saint Anne to purchase the former Disciples of Christ church that had been located at 222 East Foothill Boulevard.

While the newly-acquired church was renovated, the parish community utilized the chapel of the local Catholic Newman Center, generously offered by the **Christian Brothers**. The first Divine Liturgy celebrated in the new parish church was celebrated on Christmas Day 1991. The Church was blessed on January 6, 1992, the feast of the Epiphany of the Lord (Theophany), by Bishop Kuzma.

In the spring of 2009, the Rev. Fr. Edmund Idranyi retired as first pastor of the parish and the Rev. Fr. James Lane, former parochial vicar of Saint Stephen's Pro-Cathedral in Phoenix, Arizona, was appointed as the new pastor. In August of 2013, Fr. Lane was transferred to Saint George Byzantine Church in Olympia, Washington, and the Rev. Fr. Milan Kasperek was appointed as the new pastor. Fr. Milan is Saint Anne's first married priest, which is common for Eastern Catholic priests outside of the United States.

Parish Family Trees

Many of the parishes in the Diocese of Monterey in California had their beginnings as mission stations of a mother parish church. These charts attempt to illustrate the "familial" relationship between all of the parishes of the diocese. Past and present parish mission stations are also included.

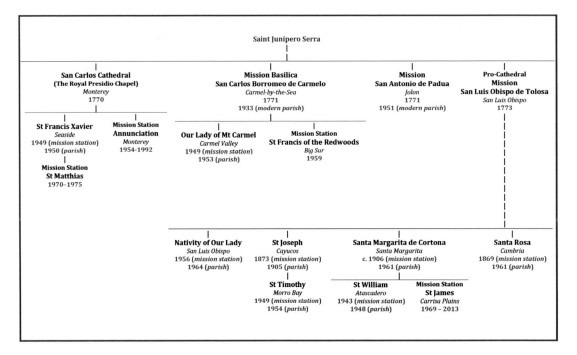

Saint Junípero Serra

San Carlos Cathedral
(The Royal Presidio Chapel)
Monterey
1770

St Francis Xavier
Seaside
1949 (*mission station*)
1950 (*parish*)

Mission Station
Annunciation
Monterey
1954-1992

Mission Station
St Matthias
1970–1975

Mission Basilica
San Carlos Borromeo de Carmelo
Carmel-by-the-Sea
1771
1933 (*modern parish*)

Our Lady of Mt Carmel
Carmel Valley
1949 (*mission station*)
1953 (*parish*)

Mission Station
St Francis of the Redwoods
Big Sur
1959

Mission
San Antonio de Padua
Jolon
1771
1951 (*modern parish*)

Pro-Cathedral
Mission
San Luis Obispo de Tolosa
San Luis Obispo
1773

Nativity of Our Lady
San Luis Obispo
1956 (*mission station*)
1964 (*parish*)

St Joseph
Cayucos
1873 (*mission station*)
1905 (*parish*)

St Timothy
Morro Bay
1949 (*mission station*)
1954 (*parish*)

Santa Margarita de Cortona
Santa Margarita
c. 1906 (*mission station*)
1961 (*parish*)

St William
Atascadero
1943 (*mission station*)
1948 (*parish*)

Mission Station
St James
Carrisa Plains
1969 – 2013

Santa Rosa
Cambria
1869 (*mission station*)
1961 (*parish*)

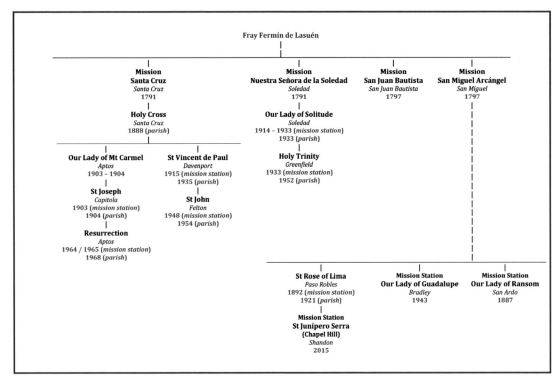

Fray Fermín de Lasuén

Mission
Santa Cruz
Santa Cruz
1791

Holy Cross
Santa Cruz
1888 (*parish*)

Our Lady of Mt Carmel
Aptos
1903 – 1904

St Joseph
Capitola
1903 (*mission station*)
1904 (*parish*)

Resurrection
Aptos
1964 / 1965 (*mission station*)
1968 (*parish*)

St Vincent de Paul
Davenport
1915 (*mission station*)
1935 (*parish*)

St John
Felton
1948 (*mission station*)
1954 (*parish*)

Mission
Nuestra Señora de la Soledad
Soledad
1791

Our Lady of Solitude
Soledad
1914 – 1933 (*mission station*)
1933 (*parish*)

Holy Trinity
Greenfield
1933 (*mission station*)
1952 (*parish*)

Mission
San Juan Bautista
San Juan Bautista
1797

Mission
San Miguel Arcángel
San Miguel
1797

St Rose of Lima
Paso Robles
1892 (*mission station*)
1921 (*parish*)

Mission Station
St Junípero Serra
(Chapel Hill)
Shandon
2015

Mission Station
Our Lady of Guadalupe
Bradley
1943

Mission Station
Our Lady of Ransom
San Ardo
1887

262

Fray José Manuel de Martiarena & Fray Pedro Adriano Martinez
|
Mission San Juan Bautista
San Juan Bautista
1797

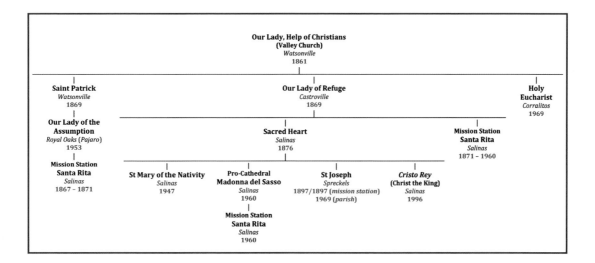

Our Lady, Help of Christians
(Valley Church)
Watsonville
1861

Saint Patrick
Watsonville
1869

Our Lady of Refuge
Castroville
1869

Holy Eucharist
Corralitos
1969

Our Lady of the Assumption
Royal Oaks (Pajaro)
1953

Sacred Heart
Salinas
1876

Mission Station Santa Rita
Salinas
1871 – 1960

Mission Station Santa Rita
Salinas
1867 – 1871

St Mary of the Nativity
Salinas
1947

Pro-Cathedral Madonna del Sasso
Salinas
1960

St Joseph
Spreckels
1897/1897 (*mission station*)
1969 (*parish*)

Cristo Rey
(Christ the King)
Salinas
1996

Mission Station Santa Rita
Salinas
1960

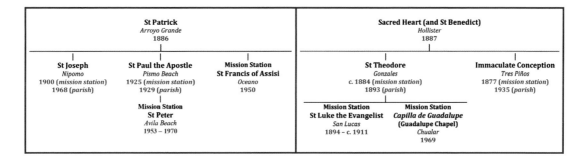

St Patrick
Arroyo Grande
1886

St Joseph
Nipomo
1900 (*mission station*)
1968 (*parish*)

St Paul the Apostle
Pismo Beach
1925 (*mission station*)
1929 (*parish*)

Mission Station St Francis of Assisi
Oceano
1950

Mission Station St Peter
Avila Beach
1953 – 1970

Sacred Heart (and St Benedict)
Hollister
1887

St Theodore
Gonzales
c. 1884 (*mission station*)
1893 (*parish*)

Immaculate Conception
Tres Piños
1877 (*mission station*)
1935 (*parish*)

Mission Station St Luke the Evangelist
San Lucas
1894 – c. 1911

Mission Station *Capilla de Guadalupe*
(Guadalupe Chapel)
Chualar
1969

St John the Baptist
King City
1891

Our Lady of Solitude
Soledad
1894 – 1914 (*mission station*)
1933 (*parish*)

Mission Station St Luke the Evangelist
San Lucas
c. 1911

Holy Trinity
Greenfield
1933 (*mission station*)
1952 (*parish*)

St Joseph
Capitola
1904

Christ Child
Los Gatos
1964 – 1969 (*mission station*)
1983 (*parish*)

Archdiocese of San Francisco
St Claire
Santa Clara

Mission Station St Mary of the Immaculate Conception
Los Gatos

St Michael
Boulder Creek
c. 1898 (*mission station*)
1921 (*parish*)

Christ Child
Los Gatos
1969 (*mission station*)
1983 (*parish*)

San Agustín
Scotts Valley
1969

Christ Child
Los Gatos
1969 – 1983 (*mission station*)
1983 (*parish*)

St Angela Merici
Pacific Grove
1928

Our Lady, Star of the Sea
Santa Cruz
1947

St Elizabeth Ann Seton
Los Osos
1984

Index of Parishes according to City

Recommended Reading

Art from the Carmel Mission by Gail Sheridan and Mary Pat McCormick, 2011

Fray Junípero Serra by Mark Brunelle, 1984

Junípero Serra: California, Indians, and the Transformation of a Missionary by Rose Marie Beebe and Robert M. Senkewicz, 2015

Junípero Serra: A Pictorial Biography by Martin J. Morgado, 1991